Mobile App Development with Ionic 2

Cross-Platform Apps with Ionic, Angular, and Cordova

Chris Griffith

Beijing · Boston · Farnham · Sebastopol · Tokyo

Mobile App Development with Ionic 2

by Chris Griffith

Copyright © 2017 Christopher Griffith. All rights reserved.

Printed in the United States of America.

Published by O'Reilly Media, Inc., 1005 Gravenstein Highway North, Sebastopol, CA 95472.

O'Reilly books may be purchased for educational, business, or sales promotional use. Online editions are also available for most titles (*http://oreilly.com/safari*). For more information, contact our corporate/institutional sales department: 800-998-9938 or *corporate@oreilly.com*.

Editor: Meg Foley	**Indexer:** WordCo Indexing Services
Production Editor: Melanie Yarbrough	**Interior Designer:** David Futato
Copyeditor: Amanda Kersey	**Cover Designer:** Karen Montgomery
Proofreader: Eliahu Sussman	**Illustrator:** Rebecca Demarest

April 2017:   First Edition

Revision History for the First Edition

2017-04-07: First Edition

See *http://oreilly.com/catalog/errata.csp?isbn=9781491937716* for release details.

978-1-491-93778-5

[LSI]

Table of Contents

Foreword

In 2013, our small team was then one year into working on drag-and-drop developer tools for the two most popular mobile and desktop web frameworks at the time: jQuery Mobile and Bootstrap. We saw the rapid rise of reusable components and frameworks for web development, and we were working hard to make it easier to use them through better and more inclusive tooling.

Around this time, the iPhone 5 came out, followed shortly by iOS 7, with dramatically faster web performance and new web APIs that unlocked previously inaccessible performance and features for mobile browser apps. We wondered: could a web framework be built that took advantage of this new performance to provide a native-like UI kit for web developers to build native-quality apps with standard browser technologies? A "Bootstrap for mobile," if you will?

Coincidently, Angular 1 was seeing incredible adoption in the broader web development space and seemed to provide a perfect answer for reusable JavaScript and HTML components for the web. We decided to try our hand at building a mobile-first web UI framework, using the fast-growing Angular 1 framework to make it interactive and distributable.

The first release of Ionic, at the end of 2013, was met with excitement from web developers, and the project quickly accumulated stars on GitHub and installs on NPM. Over the next year and a half, the project saw over one million apps built by startups, dev shops, and enterprise users alike.

Then in 2015, JavaScript seemingly evolved overnight. Suddenly, ES5, the JavaScript we all knew from the web 2.0 era, was old news. In its place was ES6, the next generation of JavaScript complete with major new features for object-oriented development, sharing and loading modules, easier syntax, and a whole lot more. The JavaScript world was turned upside down as browser runtimes and developers alike struggled to keep up with the rapid transition to ES6.

Transpilers were built to translate the new JavaScript syntax into the ES5 syntax that browsers could understand. Developers experimented to figure out the best way to distribute their JavaScript libraries as reusable modules. New build tools were created, thrown out, and created again to build and distribute disparate JavaScript modules. New projects like TypeScript and Flow took off in an attempt to reduce errors and standardize the syntax of modern JavaScript. Experimental features from ES7 and beyond made their way into transpilers and, much to the chagrin of conservative JavaScript developers, into production code bases before being deprecated and removed from the standards track. In short, it was chaos.

Framework authors from the pre-ES6 era were suddenly faced with the daunting task of throwing out custom abstractions in exchange for standardized ones now available in ES6 and beyond. Of those frameworks, few had developed such momentum with custom abstractions as Angular 1. For Angular, the question was clear: how do all these framework-specific things like scope, controllers, directives, and the like translate to the world of standardized JavaScript classes, web components, and beyond?

With the rare evolution of JavaScript, the Angular team saw an opportunity to take the lessons learned from building one of the first major JavaScript frameworks and apply them to a framework that would adapt and scale with the future of both web and mobile development. It didn't hurt that the majority of Angular 1 concepts mapped very naturally to ES6 concepts. In fact, in many cases, they felt much more natural in ES6.

When we heard about Angular 2, we knew immediately that it was our own opportunity to take the lessons learned from Ionic 1 and the over one million apps that had been built at the time to build our own framework for the future.

The Ionic team broke ground on Ionic 2 in spring of 2015. After almost a year and a half of development, mistakes made, novel solutions discovered, and a whole lot of experimentation, we are excited to finally roll out a major, production-ready release of Ionic 2.

At a high level, Ionic 2 is similar to Ionic 1. Components are used by writing custom HTML tags that Ionic turns into powerful mobile components. Actions are bound to callbacks in a class that acts as a controller for a given page in the app. The project is built and tested using the same command-line tool. The look, feel, and theming are similar, drawing on the classic Ionic look from the original release.

What's different is what goes under the hood. In this case, Ionic 2 was rewritten from the ground up using TypeScript and Angular 2. All of the Ionic code is typed, which has dramatically reduced bugs and type issues in our own code. It has also led to wonderful new features, such as inline documentation and easy refactoring, for developers using tools like Atom and Visual Studio Code. Also, the code is more object-oriented, which just makes more sense for a UI framework. That architecture wasn't as natural in Angular 1.

Angular 2 was rebuilt with the goal of running wonderfully on mobile by reducing overhead and streamlining core operations such as change detection. Thus, Ionic 2 apps run faster and can handle more complexity than Ionic 1 apps.

The goal of Ionic has always been to be the easiest way to build awesome mobile apps, period. We wouldn't have embarked on a costly and risky rewrite of the framework if we didn't truly believe we could make Ionic easier to use and more powerful at the same time. We believe that TypeScript makes Ionic code easier to write and to understand. We believe that Angular 2 is easier to use than Angular 1 and requires far less domain-specific language and understanding. We believe that Ionic 2 projects are cleaner and more organized and that using components is more straightforward.

In addition to the technologies underneath, Ionic 2 has some major new features. Today, Ionic 2 will adapt the look and feel of your app to match the platform underneath, with much-expanded support for Material Design and easier theming. Our navigation system makes it possible to build the kinds of flexible and parallel navigations native apps do uniquely well, but which don't have a natural analog in the browser. We've added a plethora of features, components, and a ton of native APIs.

Additionally, the mobile world saw a dramatic shift in 2016. Suddenly, the mobile web is back in vogue as progressive web apps have come onto the scene in a major way. With Google pushing a new world where apps run right in the browser with no install required and provide a great experience regardless of bandwidth and connectivity, mobile developers are faced with the daunting prospect of adding mobile web as a part of their mobile strategy.

Developers using Ionic 2 can now target the mobile web with practically zero code changes. Ionic apps work both as a native app on iOS and Android and as a progressive web app on the mobile web. Write once, run everywhere!

We've put our heart and soul into Ionic 2, and we're excited to finally be able to recommend Ionic 2 for production-ready mobile apps. We hope that you find it just as performant and flexible as we do and that it makes building mobile apps and mobile websites easier than you ever thought possible. After nearly three million apps built on Ionic, we've learned a thing or two about how to build a quality app framework, and we've taken every lesson learned and put them all into Ionic 2.

And if you like Ionic 2, we hope you take a look at some of the supporting tools we've built to give Ionic developers an edge up, including our rapid testing tool Ionic View, our fast prototyping and rapid app development tool Ionic Creator, and our suite of tightly integrated backend services with Ionic Cloud. Ionic is becoming a one-stop shop for everything mobile.

From all of us on the Ionic Team, please enjoy Ionic 2, and we hope to see you on the forum (*https://forum.ionicframework.com*)!

— Max Lynch
Cofounder/CEO, Ionic

Preface

My introduction to the world of mobile development happened back in 2007. I was being interviewed by the user experience team at Qualcomm to join as their UX engineer while Steve Jobs was announcing the first iPhone. Several of my interviews turned into an analysis of Apple's announcement. A day like that will leave a lasting impression upon one's professional career. Over the next decade, I have had a chance to explore a wide range of solutions for mobile development. Always, my underlying goal with any solution was to make sure it allowed for rapid development, enabling my group to quickly test and validate new ideas and concepts.

For many of the early mobile prototypes I worked on, the user interfaces were highly customized. Rarely was there a need to simulate a device's native component library. Occasionally, when native components were required, I could recreate them in the solution I was using at the time. Eventually, more and more of the prototypes were less customized, and more default in their design. I needed to find a solution that offered a rich component suite, because I was not interested in developing and maintaining a custom component library just for myself.

I explored using libraries like Ratchet and TopCoat on some projects. The "Intro to Mobile Development" course I taught at the University of California San Diego Extension program was based on jQuery Mobile (and PhoneGap Build). However, none of those solutions gave me the rich component library I needed to build my prototypes.

I don't recall when I discovered the Ionic Framework, but I do recall seeing that it was built atop Apache Cordova and AngularJS. I had just finished recording two video courses on PhoneGap Build and Apache Cordova but knew very little about AngularJS. As a rule, I had tended to shy away from large frameworks due to the nature of prototype development. Not long after, I saw another component library that leveraged the same base technology stack. Thus, I made the commitment to begin learning AngularJS and the Ionic Framework. I quickly saw the power that these two frameworks offered and was sold on them as my solution.

I began learning as much as I could about Ionic, even releasing my first commercial mobile app, *Hiking Guide: Sedona* using Ionic 1. Then Ionic 2 was announced in October 2015. This release was no mere update, but rather a quantum leap forward. So the journey began again: learning the new Angular syntax, working with first ES6, then TypeScript—even switching my default editor to one made by Microsoft! All this while Ionic 2 grew and matured.

Writing this book has been a long but fun process. Each release of Ionic has forced me to carefully review the changelog and see how it affected the chapters that were written and those left to write. This, in turn, has made me understand the framework at a deeper level. I hope this book will serve as a guide along your journey as you learn how to build hybrid mobile applications with Ionic.

Chris Griffith, San Diego, January 2017

Who Should Read This Book

This book is for anyone who is looking to get started with the Ionic Framework. It is expected that you are comfortable with JavaScript, HTML, and CSS. We will cover some key concepts of TypeScript, ES6, Angular 2, and Apache Cordova, but you may want to have resources available on those topics as well. We will take it step by step, so relax and get ready to learn how to build hybrid mobile apps with Ionic, Angular, and Cordova.

Navigating This Book

This book walks you sequentially through each part of the Ionic Framework. It is roughly organized as follows:

- Chapter 1, *Hybrid Mobile Apps*, is an introduction to the concept of hybrid mobile applications.
- Chapter 2, *Setting Up Our Development Environment*, covers what is needed to build Ionic applications.
- Chapter 3, *Understanding the Ionic Command-Line Interface*, digs into the CLI's functions.
- Chapter 4, *Just Enough Angular and TypeScript*, introduces the basic concepts of Angular and TypeScript.
- Chapter 5, *Apache Cordova Basics*, covers the foundations of Apache Cordova and how it is used as part of the Ionic Framework.
- Chapter 6, *Understanding Ionic*, provides an overview of what makes up an Ionic page.
- Chapter 7, *Building Our Ionic2Do App*, goes over creating a Firebase-enabled to-do application.

- Chapter 8, *Building a Tab-Based App*, uses the tab template to create a national park explorer application with Google Map integration.
- Chapter 9, *Building a Weather Application*, builds a side-menu–style application using the Forecast.io weather API and Google's GeoCode API.
- Chapter 10, *Debugging and Testing Your Ionic Application*, covers some common techniques to resolving issues that can arise during development.
- Chapter 11, *Deploying Your Application*, walks you through the steps needed to submit your application to the app stores.
- Chapter 12, *Exploring the Ionic Cloud*, explores the additional services offered by the Ionic platform.
- Chapter 13, *Progressive Web Apps*, explores how to use Ionic as a starter for your PWAs.
- Chapter 14, *Conclusion*, goes over some additional Ionic components and outlines additional resources.
- Appendix A, *Migrating Ionic 1 to Ionic 2*, touches on the key changes between the releases.
- Appendix B, *Understanding the Config.xml File*, covers the various attributes that configure our application's build process.
- Appendix C, *Ionic Component Library*, lists each of the available Ionic components and outlines their general use.

The entire code repository is hosted on GitHub, so if you don't want to type in the code examples from this book, or if you want to ensure that you are looking at the latest and greatest code examples, do visit the repository and grab its contents.

If you have done Ionic 1 development, then you might just want to skim Chapters 1 through 3. If you have experience with TypeScript and Angular 2, then feel free to skip Chapter 4. For those who have used Apache Cordova or PhoneGap, you can bypass Chapter 5.

Online Resources

The following resources are a great starting point for any Ionic developer and should be always available at your fingertips:

- The Official Ionic API documentation (*http://ionicframework.com/docs/*)
- The Official Angular 2 documentation (*https://angular.io/docs/ts/latest/*)
- The Official Apache Cordova documentation (*https://cordova.apache.org/docs/en/latest/*)
- The Ionic Worldwide Slack Channel (*http://ionicworldwide.herokuapp.com/*)

Conventions Used in This Book

The following typographical conventions are used in this book:

Italic
> Indicates new terms, URLs, email addresses, filenames, and file extensions.

`Constant width`
> Used for program listings, as well as within paragraphs to refer to program elements such as variable or function names, databases, data types, environment variables, statements, and keywords.

`Constant width bold`
> Shows commands or other text that should be typed literally by the user.

`Constant width italic`
> Shows text that should be replaced with user-supplied values or by values determined by context.

This element signifies a tip or suggestion.

This element signifies a general note.

This element indicates a warning or caution.

Using Code Examples

If you see the ↵ at the end of a code line, this indicates the line actually continues on the next line.

O'Reilly Safari

 *Safari* (formerly Safari Books Online) is a membership-based training and reference platform for enterprise, government, educators, and individuals.

Members have access to thousands of books, training videos, Learning Paths, interactive tutorials, and curated playlists from over 250 publishers, including O'Reilly Media, Harvard Business Review, Prentice Hall Professional, Addison-Wesley Professional, Microsoft Press, Sams, Que, Peachpit Press, Adobe, Focal Press, Cisco Press, John Wiley & Sons, Syngress, Morgan Kaufmann, IBM Redbooks, Packt, Adobe Press, FT Press, Apress, Manning, New Riders, McGraw-Hill, Jones & Bartlett, and Course Technology, among others.

For more information, please visit *http://oreilly.com/safari*.

Acknowledgments

First, I must thank the entire team at Ionic for all their hard work in creating this incredible framework. Foremost to Max Lynch and Ben Sperry for having that wild idea and the passion to grow Ionic into what it has become today. I can't wait to see what the future holds. Also to various members of the Ionic family: Adam Bradley, Mike Hartington, Brandy Carney, Dan Bucholtz, Tim Lancina, Alex Muramoto, Matt Kremer, Justin Willis, and Katie Ginder-Vogel, thank you for taking the time answer my questions, read early drafts of chapters, and offer guidance along the way. It has been a pleasure working with you. To the rest of the Ionic team, my thanks as well.

My deepest thanks to my two technical reviewers of this book: Ray Camden and Leif Wells. Your suggestions and thoughtfulness made this book better. I was truly honored when both of you took the time to carefully read through my first book.

At O'Reilly, a special thank you to Meg Foley, my kind and patient editor. This book took much longer than we planned as the technology kept evolving. And to my agent, Margot Hutchison at Waterside Productions, for introducing me to Meg.

To my friends, thank you for all the words of encouragement throughout this whole process. Now we can talk about important things like craft beer or rocket launches the next time we see each other.

Finally, to my wife Anita and my twins, Ben and Shira, thank you for giving me the time and support to retreat to my computer and work on this book. I know it was a sacrifice for you as well. I never thought I would ever attempt something like this, but you helped me believe I could.

CHAPTER 1

Hybrid Mobile Apps

Mobile application development is becoming one of the most important skills that a developer can possess. Over the past decade, we have seen an explosion of mobile devices—phones, tablets, and now wearables—that have given rise to a whole ecosystem of mobile applications. We are now living in an age of mobile apps. But learning how to create them is still a challenge. Typically, a developer will need to learn and master each platform's specific development language: Objective-C or Swift if you are creating iOS-based applications, or Java if you are creating Android-based applications. Wouldn't it be nice if there were a solution that allowed for one shared language that we could use across multiple platforms? There is: by leveraging the shared language of the web and some incredible frameworks, developers can now develop their applications in one code base and deploy it to a wide range of mobile platforms. This is known as a hybrid mobile application, because it blends the native capabilities of the mobile device with the ability to develop using web technologies.

What exactly is a hybrid mobile application? Unlike traditional native mobile apps that are built using the device's native development language. Hybrid apps are are built with web technologies (HTML, CSS, and JavaScript) instead. In fact, you probably have more than one hybrid app installed on your mobile device right now.

The Ionic Framework is one of the most popular hybrid mobile application frameworks in use today. The framework has over 26,000 stars on GitHub and has been forked over 5,700 times. With the release of the next major version of the framework, it is poised to continue its growth as the go-to solution for hybrid mobile developers.

This book presents the foundations required to build Ionic 2 applications by guiding you through the process of creating three separate applications. Each of these applications will give you insight into the various components available in the Ionic Framework, as well as an understanding of the Ionic ecosystem. Before we get into creating our first application, we need to make sure we have a good understanding of the various foundations that Ionic is built upon, as well as some of the tooling we will be using throughout this book.

What Is the Ionic Framework?

So what exactly is the Ionic Framework? Simply put, it is a user interface framework built with HTML, CSS, and JavaScript for use with hybrid mobile application development. Beyond just the user interface components, the Ionic Framework has expanded to include a robust command-line interface (CLI) and a suite of additional services such as Ionic View and Ionic Creator. We will explore each of these throughout the book.

Ionic is really a combination of several technologies that work together to make building mobile applications faster and easier. The top layer of this stack is the Ionic Framework itself, providing the user interface layer of the application. Just beneath that is Angular (formally known as AngularJS), an incredibly powerful web application framework. These frameworks then sit on top of Apache Cordova, which allows for the web application to utilize the device's native capabilities and become a native application.

The combination of these technologies enables Ionic to deliver a robust platform for creating hybrid applications. Each of these technologies will be explored further in this book.

What's New in Ionic 2?

To say that Ionic 2 is a major upgrade is almost an understatement. Not only did the Ionic Framework itself evolve significantly, but one of its underlying technologies, Angular, did as well. Although some things might look the same on the surface, under the hood, there are radical changes. Ionic 2 is almost a new framework. If you are familiar with Ionic 1, much of the component syntax will appear similar, but the code that brings them to life will be new.

Ionic (The Third Version)

In March 2017, Ionic announced version 3 of the framework. This new version is more like a traditional upgrade, and not the radical change that occurred from Ionic 1 to Ionic 2. They also announced that going forward, the framework will just be referred to as Ionic without the version number. For clarity, in this book, we will still refer to the framework as Ionic 2 to distinguish it from Ionic 1.

The following are some of the major improvements to the framework:

Overhauled navigation
> Completely control the navigation experience of your app without being tied to the URL bar. Navigate to any page inside of any view, including modals, side menus, and other view containers, while maintaining full deep-linking capability.

Native support
> There is now more native functionality directly into Ionic, making it easy to take advantage of the full power of the device without hunting down external plugins and code.

Powerful theming
> With the new theming system, it's easy to instantly match your brand colors and design.

Material Design
> Full Material Design support for Android apps.

Windows Universal apps
> Support for developing applications that will run on the Windows Universal platform.

> But with these improvements to Ionic comes the added effort of learning the new version of Angular, as well as learning TypeScript. We will touch on these requirements in a later chapter.

Comparing Mobile Solutions

When needing to deliver your application to a mobile platform, there are three primary solutions that are available, each with its own strengths and weaknesses. They can be grouped into native mobile applications, mobile web applications, and hybrid mobile applications. We'll look at each solution in a bit more detail to understand the overall mobile application landscape.

Native Mobile Applications

Typically, native code is the solution most developers think of when they need to create a mobile application. To build a native application, developers need to write in the default language for each targeted mobile platform, which is Objective-C or Swift for iOS devices, Java for Android, and C# or XAML for Windows Universal.

This type of development comes with several strong advantages over the other options. First, the development tools are tightly integrated into the device platform. Developers are able to work in IDEs that are configured to create mobile applications for that platform: Xcode for iOS, and Android Studio for Android. Second, since development is done in the native framework, all the native APIs and features are available to the developer without the need of additional bridge solutions. The third advantage is the performance of the application will be as good as possible. Since the application is running natively, there are no intermediate layers of code that can affect performance.

The primary disadvantage of native mobile application development centers around development language issues. Since quite often you will want to release your application for both iOS and Android (and possibly Windows), you will need to have proficiency in all the different languages and APIs. None of the client-side code can be reused, and it therefore must be rewritten. In addition, there is the technical burden of maintaining multiple code bases.

Mobile Web Applications

When the iPhone was first announced, there were no third-party applications—or even an App Store, for that matter. In fact, the initial vision was that third-party applications were only to be available as mobile web applications and not as native applications. While this is certainly not the case today, creating a mobile web app is still an option. These apps are loaded via the device's mobile web browser. Although the line between a mobile website and mobile app can become blurred, this option is really just about creating your application using web technologies and delivering it through the device's browser.

One of the advantages of this solution is that we can have a much wider reach with our application. Beyond iOS and Android, additional mobile platforms become available. Depending on the market that you are targeting, this may be a critical factor. Since you have direct access to your web server, the application approval process that can be tricky or slow at times for native apps is not an issue. Updating your application to add a new feature or resolve a bug is as simple as uploading new content to the server.

However, the fact that these applications run inside the native browser brings along a set of limitations. First, the browser does not have access to the full capabilities of the device. For example, there is no ability for the browser to access the contact list on the device. Second is the discoverability of the application. Users are used to going to their device's app store and finding the app. Going to the browser and inputting a URL is not common behavior.

Hybrid Mobile Applications

A hybrid application is a native mobile application that uses a chromeless web browser (often called a WebView) to run the web application. This solution uses a native application wrapper that interacts between the native device and the WebView. Hybrid apps have a number of advantages. Like mobile web applications, the majority of the code can be deployed to multiple platforms. By developing in a common language, maintaining the code base is easier, and if you are a web developer there is no need to learn a completely new programming language. Unlike mobile web applications, we have full access to the device's features, usually through some form of a plugin system.

However, this solution does have some real disadvantages. Since the application is still just a web app, it is limited by the performance and capabilities of the browser on the device. The performance can vary widely. Older devices often had very poor performing mobile browsers, meaning the app's performance was less than ideal. Although this solution is a native application, communication between the WebView and the device's native features is done via plugins. This introduces another dependency in your project and no guarantee that the API will be available through this method. Finally, the other native user interface components are not available within the WebView. Your application's entire UI/UX will be completely written by you.

The Ionic Framework takes the hybrid app approach. The team at Ionic has taken great care in recreating web-based UI components that look and feel like their native counterparts. With the framework leveraging Cordova and its plugin library, the lack of access to the device's capabilities is solved.

Understanding the Ionic Stack

Now that we have a general understanding of the types of mobile application development, let's look a bit deeper into how the Ionic Framework works. Ionic applications are built as part of three layers of technology: Ionic, Angular, and Cordova.

Ionic Framework

The Ionic Framework was first launched in November 2013, and its popularity has quickly grown and continues to increase. Ionic is provided under the MIT license and is available at the Ionic Framework website (*http://ionicframework.com*).

The primary feature of the Ionic Framework is to provide the user interface components that are not available to web-based application development. For example, a tab bar is a common UI component found in many mobile applications. But this component does not exist as a native HTML element. The Ionic Framework extends the HTML library to create one. These components are built with a combination of HTML, CSS, and JavaScript, and each behaves and looks like the native controls it is recreating.

Ionic also has a CLI tool that makes creating, building, and deploying Ionic applications much easier. We will be making extensive use of it throughout this book.

The Ionic platform also extends to several add-on services. These include an online GUI builder to visually lay out the interface of your Ionic applications and packaging and updating solutions. Although these Ionic services all have free developer access to test and develop with, any production use will require a monthly charge.

The main focus of the Ionic Framework is in the user interface layer and its integration with both Angular and Cordova to provide native-like experiences.

Angular

The next part of the Ionic stack is Angular (formally known as AngularJS), an open source project primarily supported by Google. Since its release in 2009, Angular has become one of the more popular web application frameworks. The goal of Angular is to provide an MVW (model-view-whatever) framework to build complex, single-page web applications. The Ionic team decided to leverage the power that this framework offers, so they built upon. For example, Ionic's custom UI components are just Angular components. Angular is licensed under the MIT license and is available at the Angular website (*https://angular.io*).

With the release of Angular 2, the framework has changed massively. This change did cause some discord within the Angular community, but many of the concerns about the new aspects of the framework have been addressed. We will explore Angular 2 in more detail in Chapter 4.

Cordova

The final element of the Ionic stack is Apache Cordova. Cordova was originally developed by Nitobi Software in 2009 as an open-source solution to build native applications using web technologies via an embedded WebView. In 2011, when Adobe Systems bought Nitobi—and along with it the PhoneGap name—the project had to be renamed. Although the project was always open source, the name was not. The open source version was eventually named Cordova (after the street where the Nitobi offices were located). As Brian Leroux, one of the founders of PhoneGap, put it: "PhoneGap is powered by Cordova. Think: Webkit to Safari." Adobe continues to be a major contributor to Cordova (along with several other major software companies) and it is licensed under the Apache 2.0 license.

Cordova provides the interface between the WebView and the device's native layer. The library provides a framework to bridge the gap between the two technology stacks (hence the original name of PhoneGap). Much of the functionality is handled through a system of plugin modules, which allows the core library to be smaller. Beyond working on the two primary mobile platforms, Cordova is used on a much wider range of mobile platforms, such as Windows Phone, Blackberry, and FireOS. For a full list, see *https://cordova.apache.org*.

Beyond the library, Cordova as has its own command-line tool to assist in scaffolding, building, and deploying your mobile applications. The Ionic CLI is built atop the Cordova CLI, and we will be making use of it throughout this book.

Prerequisites for Ionic Application Development

In order to develop Ionic applications, you will need to have some additional technical skills that are not covered in this book. While you do not need to be an expert in these skills, you will need a general knowledge in order understand the concepts of Ionic development:

Understanding HTML, CSS, and JavaScript

Since Ionic applications are built using HTML, CSS, and JavaScript, you should have a fundamental understanding of how these technologies combine to build web applications. We will be using HTML to create the foundational structure of our applications. Our CSS will provide the visual styling for our applications. Finally, JavaScript will provide the logic and flow for the applications.

While we will work a modest amount with JavaScript, you will need to be familiar with its syntax and concepts like variable scoping, asynchronous calls, and events.

Understanding Angular 2

Beyond understanding basic HTML, CSS, and JavaScript, you will need some understanding of building web applications. In this book, we will be writing our applications with JavaScript, specifically Angular 2. This means we will be developing in ES6 and writing the code in TypeScript. For many, this is probably something that is new to you. We will cover the basics in Chapter 4 to get you up and running.

Access to a mobile device

It goes without saying, you are going to need an actual mobile device to install and test your applications on. In fact, you will probably need at least one device for each platform you plan to develop for. While both the iOS and Android SDKs provide emulators/simulators that allow you to see what your app looks like and functions, they are no substitute for testing on a real device.

Summary

Hopefully now you have a better understanding of the difference between the types of mobile application solutions and how the Ionic stack is composed. In addition, you should have a clearer picture of the elements needed for Ionic development.

In the next chapter, we will demonstrate how to set up your computer to develop Ionic applications.

CHAPTER 2

Setting Up Our Development Environment

One of the initial challenges in developing with the Ionic Framework is the installation and setup of the several tools that Ionic requires. In this chapter, we will walk you through the process of installing all the necessary components and configurations for developing Ionic applications. The installation process can be broken down into to two main parts: the base Ionic installation, and the platform-specific SDK installations. The base installation will cover just the tools that you need to generate your first Ionic application and preview it in your browser. If you want to dive right in and start developing with Ionic, then this is all you will need to do. The second portion of the installation is about setting up your native development environment(s). Even though we are building our apps with web technologies, we will still need to have the native development environments installed on our computers. This will give us access to the emulators, as well as the ability to deploy and test the applications on our devices, and eventually submit them to the app stores.

Throughout this book, we will be using the command line to use the Ionic CLI. On macOS, we will be using the Terminal application. We recommend adding either a shortcut on the desktop or adding it to your Dock. If you are developing on a PC, I personally recommend using Git Bash (which can be installed when we install Git) instead of the default command prompt. Its command syntax is the same as in macOS, so following along with the code samples should be easier.

Installing the Ionic Framework

This section we will get the essential Ionic development environment set up, then generate our first Ionic application and preview it in our browser. You may be wondering why we want to preview our application in a browser. Remember, we are writing our application with web technologies, so it makes sense to target a browser as our first "platform." We can leverage browser debugging tools and iterate through our development more quickly. My personal development cycle is to try to stay away from testing on a mobile device until I need to.

There are four components we need to install; in the following table, you can see the software we need to get started along with their corresponding URLs.

Tool	URL
Node.js	nodejs.org
Git	git-scm.com
Ionic	ionicframework.com
Apache Cordova	cordova.apache.org

Installing Node.js

The foundation for Ionic is built atop Node.js (often referred to simply as Node). Node is a platform that enables you to run JavaScript outside the browser. This has enabled developers to create applications and solutions that are written in JavaScript and can be run almost anywhere. Both the Ionic and Cordova CLIs are written using Node. Because of this requirement, we need this framework installed first.

To install Node, go to Node website (*http://nodejs.org*) and download the installer for your development platform. If you already have Node 6.X installed, you can skip this step. You will want to use the 6.X version of Node. If you have an additional need to use a later version of Node, you might want to look at Node Version Manager (*https://www.npmjs.com/package/nvm*) to allow you to easily switch between node versions.

Once Node has been installed, open the Terminal and enter **node -v**. This command tells Node to report back the currently installed version:

```
$ node -v
$ v6.9.2
```

If you encounter an issue with the installation, review the documentation.

You should also make sure that NPM—a package manager for node modules is up to date (note: NPM actually does not stand for "node package manager"). When you install Node.js this is automatically done for you. But if you want to check which version of npm you installed:

```
$ npm -v

$ 3.10.9
```

If you need to update your installation of NPM, the command is:

```
$ npm install npm -g
```

With Node and NPM successfully installed, we will now install Git.

Installing Git

While you are free to choose any version control solution (Perforce, SourceSafe, or Git), the Ionic CLI leverages Git for the management of templates. In addition, I have found that for Windows users, using Git Bash makes it easier to follow along with the examples in this book.

Go to *http://git-scm.com*, and click the Download button. Go ahead and open the package file and follow the default installation.

Once the installation is complete, launch the Terminal window and verify it.

In Terminal, type **git --version** and press Enter:

```
$ git --version
$ git version 2.8.4 (Apple Git-73)
```

With Git now installed on our system, we can install the Apache Cordova CLI.

Installing the Apache Cordova CLI

Although we can install both Cordova and Ionic at the same time, I recommend installing each one individually in case there is an issue during the installation process.

The installation of Cordova CLI uses the Node package manager (NPM) to perform the installation. To install it, open either your Terminal window or Git Bash, and enter the following command:

```
$ npm install -g cordova
```

Depending on your internet connection, this can take a while. For macOS users, you may encounter an issue with permissions during the installation. There are two options: rerun the npm command, but preface it with the sudo command. This will allow the node modules to run as the root user. Alternatively, you can configure your system (*http://bit.ly/2mfUjSe*) to solve this permission problem:

```
$ cordova -v
$ 6.4.0
```

With these tools in place, we can finally install the Ionic CLI on to our system.

Installing Ionic CLI

Just like the installation of the Cordova CLI, the Ionic CLI is also installed via NPM. In your Terminal window, enter the following command:

```
$ npm install -g ionic
```

This install will also take some time to complete. Once the Ionic CLI has completed its installation, we will again check it by issuing the **ionic -v** command in our terminal:

```
$ ionic -v
$ 2.1.18
```

Now we have our base installation in place for Ionic development. However, we eventually will want to test our applications either in a device emulator or on an actual device. We will take a look at the installation of these tools shortly. But first, let's set up a sample app and see how to preview it in our browser.

Starting a New Ionic Project

The Ionic CLI provides an easy command to enable you to set up an Ionic project: ionic start. This CLI command will generate a basic Ionic application in the active directory. The Ionic Framework can scaffold this project via a collection of starter templates. These can come from a named template, a GitHub repo, a Codepen, or even a local directory. The named templates are *blank*, *sidemenu*, and *tabs*. We will explore those later in this book. For now, run the following command to create an Ionic project:

```
$ ionic start testApp --v2
```

Since we did not define a starter template, the Ionic CLI will default to the tabs template. The CLI will now begin the process of downloading the template and configuring the various components. It may ask you if you wish to create an Ionic.io account. For now, we can ignore this, but we will be exploring the Ionic services later in this book. Once the process is completed, we need to change the working directory to the *testApp* directory that the CLI generated:

```
$ cd testApp
```

Let's take a quick look at the elements that were installed in this directory.

Ionic Project Folder Structure

The project directory contains quite a number of files and additional directories. Let's take a moment to understand each item and its role:

src	This directory will contain the actual application code that we will be developing. In earlier versions of Ionic v2, this was the *app* directory.
hooks	This directory contains scripts that are used by Cordova during the build process.
node_modules	Ionic now uses npm as its module management system. The supporting libraries can be found here.
resources	The default icons and splash screens for both iOS and Android are included.
platforms	This directory contains the specific build elements for each installed build platform.
plugins	This directory contains Cordova plugins.

www	This directory contains the *index.html* that will bootstrap our Ionic application with the transpiled output from the *app* directory.
.gitignore	A default gitignore file is generated.
config.xml	Used by Cordova to define various app-specific elements.
ionic.config.json	Used by the Ionic CLI to define various settings when executing commands.
package.json	A list of all the npm packages that have been installed for the project.
tsconfig.json	The *tsconfig.json* file specifies the root files and the compiler options required to compile the project.
tslint.json	TypeScript linter rules.

This is the standard structure of any Ionic 2 project. As we add platforms and plugins, additional subdirectories and files will be created.

Hidden Files

Any file starting with a dot on macOS will not be visible in Finder.

Changes from Ionic 1 to Ionic 2

If you have used Ionic 1, there are a number of changes that you might want to be aware of. First, Ionic is no longer using Bower for its package management. Instead, this is now handled through node modules. But the biggest difference is instead of writing your app directly within the *www* directory, your development is now done in the *src* directory.

We will explore the various elements in the project folder in a later chapter. For now, let's just test previewing our application in a browser and ensure that we have a working development environment. For more information on migrating from Ionic 1 to Ionic 2, see Appendix A.

Previewing in the browser

One of the advantages of building hybrid applications is that much of the development and testing can be done locally in the browser. In a traditional native application workflow, you would have to compile your application, then either run it in the emulator or go through the process of installing it on a device. The Ionic CLI has a built-in command to run the application locally in a browser. With the working directory still the one that was created by the `ionic start` command, enter the following command: **`ionic serve`**. This will start a simple web server, open your browser, and load the application for us. It will also listen to changes and auto-refresh the browser whenever a file is saved.

Setting the Port Address

In most cases, `ionic serve` will prompt you to choose an IP address. You should usually just select the local host choice. If port 8100 is in use, you can select an alternate port by passing in the `--p` flag followed by the port number you wish to use.

We should now see the starter tab Ionic application running in our browser. The Ionic tab template contains several screens, and we can navigate through them and explore some of the various components in the Ionic Framework (Figure 2-1).

Figure 2-1. Our Ionic tabs sample application

Since you are viewing your Ionic app in a browser, you can use all the developer tools that you normally use.

Browser Options

While you are free to use whichever browser you are comfortable with, I recommend sticking with Google Chrome. Although this is not exactly the same browser that your content will run in on your mobile devices, it is similar, and you will have fewer issues between the desktop testing and the mobile versions.

Platform Tools Installations

While we have a working development environment, eventually we will need to continue our development in emulators, and finally on-device. To do this we will need to install the native application platform tools. This section will be a bit more complex than the previous installation and specific to each platform we need to install. Thankfully, this is a one-time process; so give yourself time to complete this section.

Currently, Ionic officially supports iOS, Android, and Windows Universal.

iOS

If you plan to develop for iOS, you will need to use Xcode for both emulation and distribution of your app. Xcode is only available for Mac. While there are some solutions that sidestep the need for a Macintosh (PhoneGap Build and Ionic Package), I recommend having at least an entry-level Mac computer available for development.

To install Xcode, simply open the App Store and search for "Xcode". The download is quite large (well over 3 GB), so make sure you have a good internet connection and disk space for installation.

Android

Unlike iOS, development for Android can be done on Windows, Mac, and Linux systems. Installation of the Android SDK can be done either via Android Studio or via the standalone SDK tools. If you want a complete IDE for Android, then download Android Studio, but we only need the SDK for our development. To download either option, go to the Android Developer website (*http://developer.android.com/sdk/instal ling/index.html*). Personally, we prefer to have the full IDE installed instead of just the SDK.

Installing the Android Studio or SDK will require the installation of the Java Development Kit as well. These additional installation instructions can be viewed on the Android Studio page (*http://bit.ly/2mLjVCx*).

Windows Universal

If you wish to build Windows Universal applications, you will have to do this on a Windows machine. Download and install Visual Studio 2015 Community Edition (*http://bit.ly/2mgeSOh*).

During the installation, select "Tools for Cross Platform Development" as well as the SDK for Windows Universal Apps.

Setting Emulators

With the base mobile SDKs installed, we can continue the installation process. For both iOS and Android development, we need to set up the appropriate device emulators. These emulators will allow you to run a virtual mobile device on your computer. We can use them to test our application quickly on various versions of an OS or device type without needing a physical device. They are slower to work with than directly testing in your browser but can enable the ability to test device specific features, such as working with the Contact database.

Emulators require some additional installation and configuration. Let's look at the steps for each platform.

iOS

Technically, the iOS emulator is a simulator as it does not actually run the native OS, but rather simulates its execution. To install our iOS simulators, launch Xcode, then choose Preferences from the Xcode menu. In the Downloads tab, you will find a list of available simulators that can be installed. Please note that each simulator is over 1 GB is size, so make sure you have the disk space and internet connection for the download and installation. We typically only have the last two releases installed on our development machine.

Once this installation is complete, we also need to install the Command Line Tools for Xcode. From the Xcode menu, select Open Developer Tool, then the More Developer Tools option. Then locate the Command Line Tools for Xcode for your version of Xcode and download and install it.

The last piece to work with iOS simulator is to install the ios-sim node module. Open a terminal window and enter the following command:

```
$ npm install -g ios-sim
```

You might need to issue this command with sudo depending on your configuration.

The ios-sim tool is a command-line utility that launches an iOS application in Simulator.

Now we will be able to run our Ionic apps in the iOS simulator. We will look at this in just a bit.

Android

Before we can configure our Android emulator, we need to install and set up the SDK packages. If you are using the SDK only, run the following from the command line:

```
$ android sdk
```

This will launch the standalone SDK manager. This tool will allow you to download the platform files for any version of Android. Like, iOS we recommend only downloading the last two releases packages and tools.

You need to choose the following items:

- Android Platform SDK for your targeted version of Android
- Android Platform-Tools
- Android SDK build-tools version 19.1.0 or higher
- Android Support Repository (found under "Extras")

If you are using Android Studio, from the welcome screen, select Configure, then choose SDK Manager. Then install the same components as the standalone option.

With the SDKs installed, along with the corresponding platform tools, we can now configure the Android emulator. While we can create and configure our virtual android devices within Android Studio, you need to have an active project to do this. Rather, I suggest just using the command line to configure your virtual devices:

```
$ android avd
```

This will open the Android Virtual Device (AVD) Manager. Once it has launched, select the Device Definitions tab to choose a known device configuration. Select the Nexus 5 definition, then click the Create AVD button. A new window will open with a variety of configurations and additional details that you can set for your virtual device—screen size, which version of Android to run, etc. Once you are satisfied with your device, click OK to finish the process. You can have as many virtual devices as you would like.

Android Emulators

The Android emulators are known to be slow to launch and use. This process has improved greatly in recent releases of the default emulator. However, you might want to look at an alternate solution from Genymotion (*https://www.genymotion.com*) for your virtual Android needs.

Setting Up Your Devices

At some point, you will have to actually test your application on your mobile devices. Each platform has a different set of requirements for this.

iOS

While anyone can test their iOS app in the iOS simulator for free, you must be a paid member of the iOS Developer Program in order to test on a device. In the past, provisioning your iOS device for development was a complex process. Thankfully recent changes to Xcode have simplified this process.

1. First, directly connect your iOS device to your Mac. This process can not work via a wireless connection. Next, we need to create a temporary Xcode project. In Xcode, select New→Project from the File menu. The New Project assistant will open, then select the Single View Application choice. On the next screen, enter Demo as the Project Name, then click Next. The settings aren't important because we are going to delete this project once we have configured the device. Select a location for the project, then click Create.

   Xcode will now display the configuration window for our project. We now need to set the active scheme to our device. This is set via the Scheme control near the top-left of the Xcode window.

2. With your device unlocked and displaying its Home Screen, select it from the Scheme dropdown. You should have a warning that there is No Signing Identity Found. Instead of letting Xcode fix this issue, we should manually address it.

3. In the General settings, in the Identity panel, select your team's name (which is probably just your name) from the drop-down list.

   If you do not see your team's name listed, you will need to add your team's account to Xcode. To do this, select Add Account in the drop-down list. The Accounts preferences window will now open. Enter your Apple ID and password that is associated with your iOS Developer Program account, and click Add.

4. Once Xcode has finished logging you in and refreshing its list, close the Accounts window. Select your newly added team from the Team drop-down list.

   Xcode will now display a new warning about No Matching Provisioning Profiles Found. Click the Fix Issue option and Xcode will resolve this issue.

   In order to configure the provisioning profile, Xcode will need some additional information and permissions. You can just answer the question with the defaults.

5. Let's validate that everything is configured correctly. Click the Run button, located in the top-left of the Xcode window, making sure that you have your iOS

device selected as the target. After a few moments, this test app should launch on your device!

Now, to integrate this into our command-line tool chain, we need to install another node tool, ios-deploy. From the command line, enter the following command:

```
$ npm install -g ios-deploy
```

 Installation on El Capitan

If you are running macOS 10.11 El Capitan, you may need to add the --unsafe-perm=true flag when running npm install or else it will fail. For more information on this issue see GitHub (*http://bit.ly/2mgapLq*).

For additional assistance, refer to Apple's documentation (*https://developer.apple.com/xcode/*).

Android

Setting up an Android device is almost the complete opposite from setting up an iOS device. The first step is to enable developer mode on your device. Since each Android device's user interface can vary, these are the general instructions:

1. Open the Settings and scroll to the About Phone item.
2. There should be a Build Number—you must tap it seven times to enable the developer mode. As you get closer to seven taps, the device should notify you how many taps are left.
3. Once this is complete, you can go back to the Settings list and you'll see a new Developer Options item.

If you encounter an issue enabling Developer Mode on your device, review the device's user guide. Next, we need to enable USB debugging in order to deploy our apps. In the Developer Options screen, locate the USB debugging option and enable it.

Your Android device is now ready for development. You may be prompted with a dialog to confirm the pairing when you connect the device to the computer for the first time.

Adding Mobile Platforms

Although the Ionic CLI will scaffold much of our application, we might need to add in the target mobile platforms. In order to view our app in either the emulator or on-device, the corresponding platform must be installed. Open your terminal window, and make sure that your working directory is your Ionic project directory. The Ionic CLI command is `ionic platform add [platform name]`.

To add the project files for Android:

```
$ ionic platform add android
```

To add the project files for iOS:

```
$ ionic platform add ios
```

To add the project files for Windows:

```
$ ionic platform add windows
```

By default, the iOS platform is added if you are running on a Mac, so you rarely need to install that platform manually. This command will generate all the needed files for each specific platform.

Previewing on Emulator

With a mobile platform added to our Ionic project, we can now verify that we can preview our app in the platform emulator. To run our app in an emulator, use the following command:

```
$ ionic emulate [platform]
```

The Ionic CLI will begin building your app for use on that platform's emulator. You will see a lot of output in the terminal as it goes through the process. Once it is finished, the emulator will automatically launch and run your application.

If you need to target a specific emulated device, append the command to include the `-target` switch. For example, if I wanted to emulate an iPad Air, I would use:

```
$ ionic emulate ios --target="iPad-Air"
```

For a list of iOS device types, use:

```
$ ios-sim showdevicetypes
```

For a list of Android devices, you will need to refer to the AVD Manager for the device names.

Once you already have the emulator up and running, you can run the `emulate` command again without closing the emulator. This is faster than exiting the emulator and relaunching it every time you change files because the emulator doesn't have to reboot the OS each time.

The Ionic CLI has another very powerful feature that allows you to reload the app instantly using the live reload flag, `--livereload`. This feature was a huge timesaver when working with emulators during our Ionic 1 development workflows. However, recent device security changes have currently disabled it, and it is not clear if a solution will be found.

You can also output the console logs to Terminal so you can read them more easily (see the Ionic blog post (*http://blog.ionic.io/live-reload-all-things-ionic-cli/*) about this feature):

```
$ ionic emulate ios -l -c
```

```
$ ionic emulate android -l -c
```

Previewing on Device

Although the emulators do a fine job, eventually you will need to install your application on a physical device. The Ionic CLI makes it extremely easy to do so with the run command. In your terminal, enter `ionic run platform`.

The Ionic CLI will then begin the process of compiling the app for installation on your device. When it is finished, it will automatically install the app on the connected device. Be aware that each installation will overwrite the existing installation of the app.

For iOS deployment, you will also need the ios-deploy node module installed; otherwise, you will have to manually perform the installation via Xcode:

```
$ ionic run ios -l -c
```

If you are developing for Android on a Windows machine, you might need to download and install the appropriate USB driver for your device. Check the Android Studio website (*https://developer.android.com/tools/extras/oem-usb.html*) to see if one is needed for your device. No additional drivers should be needed for macOS to deploy to an Android device:

```
$ ionic run android -l -c
```

If a device is not found, the Ionic CLI will then deploy your app to an emulator/simulator for that platform.

Summary

This chapter covered all the steps needed to set up your Ionic development environment. We built a first test app and previewed it locally in our browser, in an emulator, and finally on our device.

CHAPTER 3

Understanding the Ionic Command-Line Interface

One of the key tools that we will be using while developing our Ionic applications is the Ionic command-line interface, or CLI. We touched briefly upon this tool during our initial setup, but this chapter will explore the various options this utility gives us.

First, if you have not installed the Ionic CLI, you can use npm to do so. If you are on a Macintosh, launch the Terminal application. For Windows users, launch Git Bash (or another command prompt). Then enter the following command:

```
$ npm install -g ionic
```

This will install the latest version of the Ionic CLI. The Ionic CLI is fully backward compatible with version 1 projects, which is helpful if you have already done some Ionic development.

 macOS users might need to prepend the npm command with sudo for the installations to work.

Once the installation of the Ionic CLI is complete, we can test its installation by building our first test application:

```
$ ionic start myApp [template name] --v2
```

This command will create a new Ionic application in a new directory named *myApp* using the template that we pass to the command. Let's explore the various template options that we can use.

Ionic currently has three named starter templates: *blank*, *sidemenu*, and *tabs*. If no template is passed as a parameter, then the tabs template will be used (Figure 3-1).

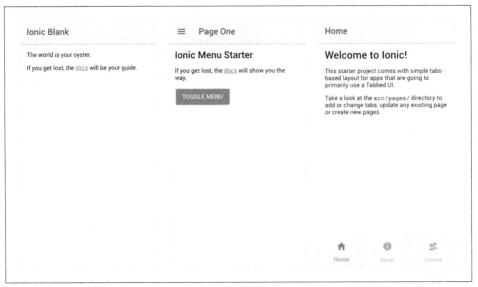

Figure 3-1. The Ionic templates: blank, sidemenu, and tabs

Besides using the three named templates, you can also pass a URL to your own template that could be hosted at GitHub, CodePen, or some other web address. In fact, these named templates are actually just aliases to repositories on GitHub. Here is an example of creating an Ionic app using a template from GitHub:

```
$ ionic start myApp https://github.com/driftyco/ionic2-starter-blank  --v2
```

If you do not want to host a template externally, you can also pass in either a relative or absolute directory as a source location of your template files.

Since the Ionic CLI supports both version 1 and version 2, we need the ability to tell it which version to create. This is done using the --v2 flag. By passing this flag to the command, the Ionic CLI will scaffold our Ionic application to use version 2 of the framework:

```
$ ionic start myIonic2App --v2
```

The --ts Flag

If you used earlier versions of Ionic 2, you might be familiar with the --ts flag, which told the CLI to use TypeScript as the development language. Starting with beta 8, the decision was made to only support TypeScript. Thus, the need to include this flag was removed.

There are some additional command-line flags that you can pass to the command as well. By default, the `ionic start` command will take the name of the directory that is created and set that as the app's name in the *config.xml* file. You are free to change this within *config.xml* at any time, but instead you can use either the -appname or -a flag followed by the actual application name. Since your appname will probably include spaces, your will need to use quotes around the name for this to work:

```
$ ionic start myApp -a "My Awesome Ionic App"
```

Another flag you will wish to change is the app ID. App IDs are the unique names that each platform uses as to identify each app. The recommended format for an app ID is a reverse-domain style naming. By default, the `ionic start` command will auto generate an app ID in the format com.ionicframework.[your application name] + a random number. It is doubtful that this would be the app ID you would want your app to be known by the internals of the various app stores. To change this, you can use either the --id or -i flags followed by the package name. This will change the id attribute in the widget node of the *config.xml* file:

```
$ ionic start myApp -i com.mycompany.appname
```

The last flag that you can include is the --no-cordova or -w flag. This will tell the `ionic start` method not to include any of the Cordova elements when creating the project. You might be wondering why you would even want to do something like that —aren't we building mobile applications and don't we need to use Cordova as part of the process? Yes. However, you might want to use Ionic as the framework for a mobile, web-only application, so you could avoid using Cordova. Another option might be using Ionic as the UI framework for an Electron-based desktop app (*http:// electron.atom.io*). In either case, it is an option that is available if you need it.

Define Your Build Platforms

Once the base Ionic application has been scaffolded, we next need to add the target platform we will want to build for. The command to do this is:

```
$ ionic platform add [platform name]
```

Common Mistake

If you try to run this command without changing your active directory into the project directory that was just created, you will get an error. Always remember to issue cd [*app name*] before running any of the other Ionic CLI commands.

macOS users will have the iOS platform automatically added to the project. This platform is not available if you are running the CLI on Windows. But if you ever need to manually add the iOS platform, the command is:

```
$ ionic platform add ios
```

To build for the Android platform, you will need to add it to the project:

```
$ ionic platform add android
```

To build for the Windows Universal platform, you will need to add it to the project:

```
$ ionic platform add windows
```

Remember for iOS, Android, and Windows Universal, their respective SDKs must be installed on the local machine in order to actually build for that platform. This Ionic command only configures the local project files for use by the SDKs.

If for some reason you need to remove a platform from your project, you can use:

```
$ ionic platform remove [platform name]
```

Occasionally, something might go wrong during an installation of a plugin or during an update. One common solution is to remove the platform, then reinstall it into the project.

Managing Cordova Plugins

The installation of Cordova plugins is often one of the first things you will do after including your build platforms. Although we will touch upon using Cordova plugins and Ionic Native in a later chapter, the basic command is:

```
$ ionic plugin add [plugin id]
```

Usually, the plugin ID is the npm domain name—for example, `cordova-plugin-geolocation`. However, it could reference a local directory or a GitHub repo.

To remove an installed plugin, the command is simply:

```
$ ionic plugin rm [plugin id]
```

If you ever need to see a listing of all the plugins you have installed in your project, use:

```
$ ionic plugin ls
```

Ionic Generator

Although the Ionic CLI will scaffold your application via the `ionic start` command, you can then extend your app with new pages, components, providers, pipes, and more via the CLI. The `generate` command allows you to quickly create a boilerplate version of the element you need:

```
$ ionic g [page|component|directive|pipe|provider|tabs] [element name]
```

For example, if we want to create a new page for an application, the command is simply:

```
$ ionic g page myPage
```

The Ionic CLI will then create a new directory in our app directory, and generate the HTML, SCSS, and TS files for us.

 A Quick Note on Naming Conventions

Ionic 2 uses kebob-casing for file names (e.g., *my-about-page.html*) and CSS classes (e.g., *.my-about-page*). It uses PascalCasing for JavaScript classes in TypeScript (e.g., *MyAboutPage*).

Previewing Your Application

Often, early development can be previewed and tested locally in a browser. Although the Ionic CLI does make it fairly easy to launch your application in an emulator or on an actual mobile device, the ability to preview and debug in what is probably a very familiar environment, your browser is a real advantage.

The *ionic serve* command will start a local development server, then automatically load your application into the browser. In addition, the command will start a LiveReload watcher, so as you make changes to the application, it will be automatically reloaded in the browser without you needing to manually reload it (Figure 3-2).

```
$ ionic serve
```

Figure 3-2. The Ionic tab template being run in a browser

The Ionic lab Command

With the `--lab` flag passed to `ionic serve`, your application will be displayed in an iOS frame, an Android frame, and a Windows frame in the same browser window. This feature will let you quickly see the various platform-specific differences that may exist. To use this simply type the following (see Figure 3-3):

```
$ ionic serve --lab
```

Figure 3-3. Ionic serve running in --lab mode

In this mode, each instance of the Ionic app will run as if on that mobile platform. So any platform-specific CSS or JavaScript will be executed. This feature can be a real timesaver during the early part of the development cycle, but it is in no way a substitute for testing on actual devices.

Specifying an IP Address to Use

If you need to specify what address the LiveReload server will run on, you can pass that value via the `--address` flag, followed by the IP address:

```
$ ionic serve --address 112.365.365.321
```

Emulating Your Ionic App

The `ionic emulate` command will build your Ionic application and then load and run your app on the specified emulator or simulator:

```
$ ionic emulate android
$ ionic emulate ios
$ ionic emulate windows
```

Emulators are useful for testing portions of the application that require actual device features. When launching and previewing your application in an emulator, it takes some time to initialize and then load your app.

Emulating iOS Devices

In order for the Ionic CLI to communicate with the iOS simulator, an additional node package will need to be installed. If you did not install the ios-sim package earlier, please do it now:

```
$ npm install -g ios-sim
```

Once this package is installed, the Ionic CLI will be able to compile the app and run it within the iOS simulator. If you need to target a specific iOS model, you can set the --target flag to the specific device.

For a list of your installed devices, use the following code:

```
$ ios-sim showdevicetypes
```

Table 3-1 shows the possible device types.

Table 3-1. iOS simulator device types

iPhone-5, 10.0	iPhone-6s-Plus, 10.0	iPad-Air-2, 10.0
iPhone-5s, 10.0	iPhone-7, 10.0	Apple-TV-1080p, tvOS 10.0
iPhone-6, 10.0	iPhone-7-Plus, 10.0	Apple-TV-1080p, tvOS 9.1
iPhone-6-Plus, 10.0	iPad-Retina, 10.0	Apple-Watch-38mm, watchOS 2.1
iPhone-6s, 10.0	iPad-Air, 10.0	Apple-Watch-42mm, watchOS 2.1

Supported iOS Devices

Although both the Apple TV and Apple Watch are listed by ios-sim, these platforms are not supported by Apache Cordova nor Ionic.

Emulating Android Devices

To emulate your Ionic application in the Android emulator, you first must have manually created an Android virtual device (AVD) to be used by the emulator. If you did not do this in the previous chapter, use:

```
$ android avd
```

This will launch the AVD manager, a tool that you can use to create and manage various AVDs. Once you have created an AVD, the Ionic CLI will be able to launch the Android emulator and run your application. This process can take quite some time as the emulator boots up.

To target a specific Android device, you can use `--target=NAME` to run the app in the specific device you created; otherwise, the default emulator is used.

Performance Tips

If you are using the Android emulator, one tip for improved performance is to not close the emulator, but keep it running, and just reload the app.

Although the performance of the emulator has improved, many developers have opted for a solution from Genymotion (*https://www.genymotion.com*) as an alternate to the standard Android emulator.

Running Ionic App on a Device

The Ionic CLI can also compile your Ionic application so it can run on a properly configured device:

```
$ ionic run [platform name]
```

If no device is found to be connected to the computer, the Ionic CLI will then attempt to deploy to the emulator for that platform.

If you are deploying to an iOS device, there is an additional node module that you will need to install, ios-deploy:

```
$ npm install -g ios-deploy
```

You must also configure your iOS device for development. If you're working with an Android device, you only need to set it to development mode.

Logging

Both the `emulate` and `run` commands support the ability to remap the console logs, as well as the server logs to the Ionic CLI. To enable console logging, pass in either the `--consolelogs` flag, or the short version `--c`. If you want to capture the server logs, pass in the `--serverlogs` flag, or the short version `--s`.

CLI information

If you ever need to see the entire state of the Ionic CLI and its supporting tooling, use:

```
$ ionic info
```

Here is what my system looks like:

```
Your system information:
```

```
Cordova CLI: 6.5.0
Ionic CLI Version: 2.1.18
Ionic App Lib Version: 2.1.9
ios-deploy version: 1.9.0
ios-sim version: 5.0.13
OS: macOS El Capitan
Node Version: v6.9.2
Xcode version: Xcode 8.0 Build version 8A218a
```

When debugging an issue, this information can often be quite useful.

Summary

In this chapter we have touched on the principle Ionic CLI commands that you will typically use during your development process. There are addition commands and settings available. To see the full list, use `ionic --help`.

To recap the key commands that we introduced in the chapter:

1. Learn to scaffold your initial Ionic application with `ionic start`.

2. Manage mobile platforms to the project with `ionic platform`.

3. Preview the application in the browser, in the emulators, and on-device with `ionic run/emulate`.

CHAPTER 4

Just Enough Angular and TypeScript

With our basic system configured for Ionic development, we can explore another set of foundational technology that Ionic is built atop, Angular. Just as Ionic leverages Apache Cordova to act as the bridge to the native mobile platform, it uses Angular as the underpinnings of its interface layer. Since the beginning, the Ionic Framework has been built on the Angular framework.

Why Angular 2?

Angular 2 is the next version of Google's incredibly popular MV* framework. This new version of Angular was announced at the ngEurope conference in October 2014. The Angular team revealed that this version of Angular would be a significant revision. In many ways, this new Angular was a completely new framework, sharing only its name and some notional references to the original version. This announcement certainly generated a lot of concern and uncertainty about the future of the framework. This was equally true with the Ionic community and within the Ionic team itself. What were the changes that would be required? How much relearning would existing Ionic developers need to undertake to continue to work with Angular?

But as the shock wore off, it became clearer that this evolution of the Angular framework was for the better. The framework was becoming faster, cleaner, more powerful, and also easier to understand. The Angular 2 team also took another bold gamble and looked at the web to come, not the web that was. So they decided to embrace many of the latest and emerging web standards and develop it in next generation of JavaScript.

At ngConf 2016, the Angular team announced that with release candidate 1, the framework will be simply known as Angular instead of Angular 2. For the purposes of this book, we will still refer to it as Angular 2.

So let's take a look at some of these changes to Angular in more detail.

Components

One of the biggest changes from Angular 1 to Angular 2 is the fact that we no longer rely on scope, controllers, or to some degree directives. The Angular team adopted a component-based approach to building elements and their associated logic. Those who have developed applications with more traditional frameworks are very familiar with this type of model. The fact is that we are developing on a platform originally designed to read physics papers and not to build applications upon.

Here is what a sample Angular component looks like:

```
import { Component } from '@angular/core';

@Component({
  selector: 'my-first-component',
  template: `<div>Hello, my name is {{name}}.
  <button (click)="sayMyName()">Log my name</button></div>`
})

export class MyComponent {
  constructor() {
    this.name = 'Inigo Montoya'
  }
  sayMyName() {
    console.log('Hello. My name is ',this.name,'. ↵
                You killed my father. Prepare to die.')
  }
}
```

This is the exact same model that Ionic uses to generate its component library. In fact, there is nothing that prevents you from extending your Ionic application to use your own custom components.

Let's look at this code snippet in greater detail.

First, the code imports the Component module from the Angular library. In Angular this is how dependency injection is handled. With Release Candidate 1 (RC1), the Angular team broke the library into smaller modules, as well as dropped the "2" suffix in the library.

Next, we use the @Component decorator to provide some metadata about our code to the compiler. We define the custom HTML selector to use. So when we use <my-first-component></my-first-component>, the associated template will be inserted into the DOM. Templates can come into two fashions: inline as shown here, or as an external reference. If you need to span your template across multiple lines for readability, make sure you use the backtick (`) instead of a single quote (') to define the template string. We will look at templates in more detail later in this chapter.

After the decorator, we export the class definition itself, MyComponent. Within this constructor of this class, the code sets the name variable to "Inigo Montoya". Unlike Angular 1, and JavaScript in general, Angular 2 has a much tighter control over the scope of variables.

Finally, this sample class has a public method of sayMyName that will write a string to the console. As you work more with Ionic and Angular 2, this new method of creating components and pages will become more familiar and natural to you.

Inputs

Since Angular 2 is built using a component model, it needs a mechanism to pass information into the component itself. This is handled via Angular's Input module. Let's look at a simple component, <current-user>, that will need to know about a user argument in order for it to perform its code. The actual markup would look like this:

```
<current-user [user]="currentUser"></current-user>
```

while the component itself would look like this:

```
import { Component, Input } from '@angular/core';

@Component({
    selector: 'current-user',
    template: '<div>{{user.name}}</div>'
})

export class UserProfile {
    @Input() user;
    constructor() {}
}
```

Within the class definition, there is now an @Input binding to the user variable. With this binding in place, Angular will pass in the currentUser variable into the component, thus enabling the template to render out the user.name value.

This is how Ionic's components also function. We will pass in data and configuration parameters using the same system as this example.

Templates

Templates are HTML fragments that Angular combines with specific elements and attributes to generate the dynamic content. For the most part, the templating system in Angular 2 did not change that much.

{ }: Rendering

```
<div>
  Hello, my name is {{name}}.
</div>
```

However, unlike Angular 1, this data binding is one way. By doing so, the number of event listeners that were generated have been reduced, and thus, performance improved.

[ ]: Binding properties

When a component needs to resolve and bind a variable, Angular now uses the [] syntax. We touched on this earlier in this chapter when covering Inputs.

If we have this.currentColor in our component, we would pass this variable into our component, and Angular would ensure that the values would stay updated:

```
<card-header [themeColor]="currentColor"></card-header>
```

( ): Event handling

In Angular 1, we would use custom directives to listen for user events, like clicking an element (like ng-click). Angular 2 has taken a cleaner approach and just wraps the event you want to listen for in parentheses and then assigns that to a function in the component:

```
<my-component (click)="onUserClick($event)"></my-component>
```

[( )]: Two-way data binding

By default, Angular no longer establishes two-way data binding. If you do need to have this functionality, the new syntax is actually a shorthand notation of the binding property and the event-handling syntaxes:

```
<input [(ngModel)]="userName">
```

The this.userName value of your component will stay in sync with the input value.

*: The asterisk

The use of the asterisk before certain directives tells Angular to treat our template in a special fashion. Instead of rendering the template as is, it will apply the Angular directive to it first. For example, ngFor takes our <my-component> and stamps it out for each item in items, but it never renders our initial <my-component> since it's a template:

```
<my-component *ngFor="let item of items">
</my-component>
```

Events

Events in Angular 2 use the parentheses notation in templates and trigger methods in a component's class. For example, assume we have this template:

```
<button (click)="clicked()">Click</button>
```

and this component class:

```
@Component(...)
class MyComponent {
  clicked() {
  }
}
```

Our `clicked()` method in the component will be called when the button is clicked.

In addition, events in Angular 2 behave like normal DOM events. They can bubble up and propagate down.

If we need access to the event object, simply pass in the `$event` as a parameter in the event callback function:

```
<button (click)="clicked($event)"></button>
```

and the component class would become:

```
@Component(...)
class MyComponent {
  clicked(event) {
  }
}
```

Custom events

What if your component needs to broadcast a custom event to another component? Angular 2 makes this process quite easy.

In our component, we import the `Output` and `EventEmitter` modules. Then we define our new event, `userUpdated`, by using the `@Output` decorator. This event is an instance of an `EventEmitter`:

```
import {Component, Output, EventEmitter} from '@angular/core';

@Component({
  selector: 'user-profile',
  template: '<div>Hi, my name is </div>'
})
export class UserProfile {
  @Output() userDataUpdated = new EventEmitter();

  constructor() {
    // Update user
```

```
  // ...
  this.userDataUpdated.emit(this.user);
  }
}
```

When we want to trigger the broadcast of the event, you simply call the `emit` method on the custom event type and include any parameters to be transmitted with the event.

Now when we used this component elsewhere in our app, we can bind the event that `user-profile` emits:

```
<user-profile (userDataUpdated)="userProfileUpdated($event)"></user-profile>
```

When we import our `UserProfile` component into our new component, it can now listen for the `userProfileUpdated` event that is broadcasted:

```
import {Component} from '@angular/core';
import {UserProfile} from './user-profile';

export class SettingsPage {
  constructor(){}

  userProfileUpdated(user) {
    // Handle the event
  }
}
```

Life cycle events

Both the Angular app and its components offer life cycle hooks that give developers access to each of the critical steps as they occur. These events are usually related to their creation, their rendering, and their destruction.

NgModule

The Angular team reworked the method of bootstrapping your application through the use of the `NgModule` function. This was done toward the end of the release candidate cycle for Angular, so it might come as a surprise to some. The `@NgModule` takes a metadata object that tells Angular how to compile and run module code. In addition, `@NgModule` allows you to declare all your dependencies up front, instead of having to declare them multiple times in an app:

```
import { NgModule }      from '@angular/core';
import { BrowserModule } from '@angular/platform-browser';
import { AppComponent }  from './app.component';

@NgModule({
  imports:      [ BrowserModule ],
  declarations: [ AppComponent ],
  bootstrap:    [ AppComponent ]
```

```
})

export class AppModule { }
```

This code sample shows a basic `app.module.ts` file that will use the `BrowserModule` to enable the Angular app to properly run in a browser, then both declare and bootstrap the AppComponent.

This module is in turned used by the *main.ts* file to perform the actual bootstrapping:

```
import { platformBrowserDynamic } from '@angular/platform-browser-dynamic';
import { AppModule } from './app.module';

const platform = platformBrowserDynamic();

platform.bootstrapModule(AppModule);
```

This sample code initializes the platform that your application runs in, then uses the platform to bootstrap your AppModule. The Ionic starter templates will generate the necessary modules for you.

Another benefit of this system is it enables us to use the Ahead of Time (AoT) compiler, which provides for much faster applications.

Component init event

When a component is created, its constructor function is called. Within the constructor, any initialization we might need to perform on the component can occur. However, if our component is dependent on information or properties from a child component, we will not have access to that data.

Angular provides the `ngOnInit` event in order to handle this need to wait until the component initialization is truly complete. Our component can wait for this method to be triggered by the framework. Then all our properties are resolved and available to be used by the component.

Component life cycle events

Beyond, *ngOnInit*, there are several other life cycle events for a component:

ngOnDestroy
> This method is called before the component is destroyed by the framework. This would be where you unsubscribe observables and detach event handlers to avoid memory leaks.

ngDoCheck
> This method provides the ability to perform custom change detection.

ngOnChanges(changes)

This method is called when one of the component's bindings have changed during the checking cycle. The method's parameter will be an object in the format:

```
{
    'prop': PropertyUpdate
}
```

ngAfterContentInit()

Unlike `ngOnInit`, which is called before the content has been rendered, this method is called once that content is first rendered on the view.

ngAfterContentChecked

This method is called after Angular checks the bindings of the external content that it projected into its view.

ngAfterViewInit

After Angular creates the component's view(s), this method is triggered.

ngAfterViewChecked

The final method during the component initialization process, this will be call once all the data bindings are resolved in the component's views.

Ionic Events

Although you can use the Angular events outlined, it is recommended that you use the Ionic events instead. Table 4-1 lists a description of their triggers.

Table 4-1. A list of Ionic events and their descriptions

Event	Description
`ionViewDidLoad`	Runs when the page has loaded. This event only happens once per page being created. If a page leaves but is cached, then this event will not fire again on a subsequent viewing.
`ionViewWillEnter`	Runs when the page is about to enter and become the active page.
`ionViewDidEnter`	Runs when the page has fully entered and is now the active page. This event will fire, whether it was the first load or a cached page.
`ionViewWillLeave`	Runs when the page is about to leave and no longer be the active page.
`ionViewDidLeave`	Runs when the page has finished leaving and is no longer the active page.
`ionViewWillUnload`	Runs when the page is about to be destroyed and have its elements removed.
`ionViewCanEnter`	Runs before the view can enter. This can be used as a sort of "guard" in authenticated views where you need to check permissions before the view can enter.
`ionViewCanLeave`	Runs before the view can leave. This can be used as a sort of "guard" in authenticated views where you need to check permissions before the view can leave.

Pipes

Pipes, previously known as "Filters," transform a value into a new value, like localizing a string or converting a floating-point value into a currency representation:

```
<p>The author's birthday is {{ birthday | date }}</p>
```

If the birthday variable is a standard JavaScript `Date` object, it will look like `Thu Apr 18 1968 00:00:00 GMT-0700 (PDT)`. Certainly not the most human-readable format. However, within the interpolation expressed in our template, our birthday value is passed through the pipe operator (|) to the `Date` pipe function on the right, thus rendering the author's birthday as April 18, 1968.

Angular comes with a set of commonly used pipes such as `DatePipe`, `UpperCasePipe`, `LowerCasePipe`, `CurrencyPipe`, and `PercentPipe`. They are all immediately available for use in any template.

@ViewChild

Often we need to read or write child component values or call a child's component's method. When the parent component *class* requires that kind of access, we *inject* the child component into the parent as a `ViewChild`:

```
import {Component, ViewChild} from '@angular/core';
import {UserProfile} from '../user-profile';

@Component({
  template: '<user-profile (click)="update()"></user-profile>',
  directives: [UserProfile]
})

export class MasterPage {
  // we pass the Component we want to get
  // assign to a public property on our class
  // give it the type for our component
  @ViewChild(UserProfile) userProfile: UserProfile
  constructor() { }
  update(){
    this.userProfile.sendData();
  }
}
```

Both the `ViewChild` module and `UserProfile` component are injected from the Angular Core. Within the `Component` decorator, we also must set the `directives` property to include a reference to our injected component. Our constructor contains our `ViewChild` decorator that set our `userProfile` variable to our injected component.

With those code elements in place, we are able to interact with our child component's `sendData` method.

Understanding ES6 and TypeScript

Over the past few years, web developers have seen an explosion in attempts to create "better" or more developer-centric versions of JavaScript. CoffeeScript, AtScript, Dart, ES6, TypeScript, and so on have sought to improve on standard JavaScript. Each of these languages sought to extend JavaScript by providing features and functionality aimed at modern application development. But each solution had to deal with the fact that our modern browsers use a version of JavaScript known formally as ECMAScript 5 (ES5), meaning that each solution would need to output its efforts into standard JavaScript.

In order to use either of these modern language options, our code will have to be *transpiled* into ES5-based JavaScript. If you have never heard of the term "transpiling" before, it is a process of taking the code written in one language and converting into another.

Currently, there are two primary choices if you want to use next-generation JavaScript: ES6 or TypeScript. ES6 is the next official version of JavaScript and was formally approved in June 2015, and over time it will be supported natively in our browsers. The other language option is TypeScript. Typescript is Microsoft's extension of JavaScript that comes with powerful type-checking abilities and object-oriented features. It also leverages ES6 as part of its core foundation. TypeScript is a primary language for both Angular and Ionic application development.

Although none of our current browsers support either option, our code can be transpiled using tools like Babel or tsc. We don't have to worry about setting up this system, as it is built into the default Ionic build process.

Variables

With ES6, the way we can define our variables has improved. We can now specify a variable by using the keyword `let` .

In ES5, variables could only be defined using the keyword `var`, and they would be scoped to the nearest function. This was often problematic, as a variable could be accessible outside of the function that it was defined in.

```
for (var i = 0 ; i < 10; i++) {
  console.log(i);  //Output 0-9
}
console.log(i); // Outputs 10
```

The variable i is still available after the loop has finished, which is not quite the expected behavior.

By using the let keyword, this issue is no longer a problem, and the variable is scoped to its nearest block:

```
for (let i = 0 ; i < 10; i++) {
  console.log(i); //Outputs 0-9
}
console.log(i); // Uncaught ReferenceError: i is not defined
```

Now, after the loop has executed, i is not known to the rest of the code. Whenever possible, use let to define your variables.

Classes

JavaScript classes have been introduced in ES6 and are syntactical sugar over JavaScript's existing prototype-based inheritance. The class syntax is *not* introducing a new object-oriented inheritance model to JavaScript. If you have developed using another object-oriented language like C# or Java, this new syntax should look familiar. Here is an example:

```
class Rocket {
  landing(location) {
  }
}

class Falcon extends Rocket {
  constructor() {
    super();
    this.manufacturer = 'SpaceX';
    this.stages = 2;
  }
  landing(location) {
    if ((location == 'OCISLY') || (location == 'JRTI')){
      return 'On a barge';
    } else {
      return 'On land';
    }
  }
}

class Antares extends Rocket {
  constructor() {
    super();
    this.manufacturer = 'OrbitalATK';
    this.stages = 2;
  }
  landing(location) {
      console.log('In the ocean');
```

```
        }
    }
```

Promises

The `Promise` object is used for deferred and asynchronous computations. A `Promise` represents an operation that hasn't completed yet, but is expected in the future. This is exactly the type of functionality we need when interacting with remote servers or even loading local data. It provides a simpler method to handle asynchronous operations than traditional callback-based approaches.

A Promise can be in one of three states:

Pending
> The Promise's outcome hasn't yet been determined because the asynchronous operation that will produce its result hasn't completed yet.

Fulfilled
> The asynchronous operation has completed, and the Promise has a value.

Rejected
> The asynchronous operation failed, and the Promise will never be fulfilled. In the rejected state, a Promise has a *reason* that indicates why the operation failed.

The primary API for a Promise is its `then` method, which registers callbacks to receive either the eventual value or the reason the Promise cannot be fulfilled.

Assuming we have a function `sayHello` that is asynchronous and needs to look up the current greeting from a web service based on the user's geolocation, it may return a Promise:

```
var greetingPromise = sayHello();
greetingPromise.then(function (greeting) {
    console.log(greeting);    // 'Hello in the United States'
});
```

The advantage of this method is that while the function is awaiting the response from the server, the rest of our code can still function.

In case something goes wrong, like if the network goes down and the greeting can't be fetched from the web service, you can register to handle the failure using the second argument to the Promise's then method:

```
var greetingPromise = sayHello();
greetingPromise.then(function (greeting) {
    console.log(greeting);    // 'Hello in the United States'
}, function (error) {
    console.error('uh oh: ', error);    // 'Drat!'
});
```

If `sayHello` succeeds, the greeting will be logged, but if it fails, then the reason (i.e., error) will be logged using `console.error`.

Observables

Many services with Angular use Observables instead of Promises. Observables are implemented through the use of the RxJS library (*https://github.com/ReactiveX/RxJS*). Unlike a Promise, which resolves to a single value asynchronously, an observable resolves to (or emits) multiple values asynchronously (over time).

In addition, Observables are cancellable and can be retried using one of the retry operators provided by the API, such as `retry` and `retryWhen`. Promises require the caller to have access to the original function that returned the Promise in order to have a retry capability.

Template Strings

One of the features of Angular is its built-in templating engine. In many cases, these templates are stored as external files. However, there are times when keeping them inline makes more sense. The difficulty has been writing long inline templates without having to resort to using concatenation or needing to escape any single or double quotes in the string.

ES6 now supports the use of backticks at the start and end of the string:

```
let template = `
  <div>
    <h2>{{book.name}}</h2>
    <p>
      {{book.summary}}
    </p>
  </div>
`;
```

Template strings do not have to remain static. You can perform string interpolation by using $(`expression`) placeholders:

```
let user = {name:'Rey'};
let template = `
  <div>Hello, <span>${ user.name }</span></div>
`;
```

Template Expressions: ES6 versus Angular

ES6's template expression are only meant for string replacement. If you need to evaluate a function or test a condition, use Angular template expressions instead.

Arrow Functions

Arrow functions make our code more concise and simplify function scoping and the `this` keyword. By using arrow functions, we avoid having to type the `function` keyword, `return` keyword (it's implicit in arrow functions), and curly brackets.

In ES5, we would have written a simple `multiply` function like this:

```
var multiply = function(x, y) {
  return x * y;
};
```

But in ES6, using the new arrow function formation, we can write the same function this way:

```
var multiply = (x, y) => { return x * y };
```

The arrow function example allows us to accomplish the same result with fewer lines of code and approximately half the typing.

One common use case for arrow functions is array manipulations. Take this simple array of objects:

```
var missions = [
  { name:'Mercury', flights:6 },
  { name:'Gemini', flights:10 },
  { name:'Apollo', flights:11 },
  { name:'ASTP', flights:1 },
  { name:'Skylab', flights:3 },
  { name:'Shuttle', flights:135 },
  { name:'Orion', flights: 0 }
];
```

We could create an array of objects with just the names or flights by doing this in ES5:

```
// ES5
console.log(missions.map(
  function(mission) {
    return mission.flights;
  }
)); // [6, 10, 11, 1, 3, 135, 0]
```

Rewriting this using the arrow function, our code is more concise and easier to read:

```
// ES6
console.log(missions.map(
  mission=>mission.flights
)); // [6, 10, 11, 1, 3, 135, 0]
```

Types

TypeScript is a data-typed language that gives you compile-time checking. By default, TypeScript supports JavaScript primitives: `string`, `number`, and `boolean`:

```
let num: number;
let str: string;
let bool: boolean;

num = 123;
num = 123.456;
num = '123'; // Error

str = '123';
str = 123; // Error

bool = true;
bool = false;
bool = 'false'; // Error
```

TypeScript also supports typed arrays. The syntax is basically postfixing [] to any valid type annotation (e.g., boolean[]):

```
let booleanArray: boolean[];

booleanArray = [true, false];
console.log(booleanArray[0]); // true
console.log(booleanArray.length); // 2
booleanArray[1] = true;
booleanArray = [false, false];

booleanArray[0] = 'false'; // Error!
booleanArray = 'false'; // Error!
booleanArray = [true, 'false']; // Error!
```

Special Types

Beyond the primitive types, there are a few types that have special meaning in Type-Script. These are any, null, undefined, and void:

```
let someVar: any;

// Takes any and all variable types
someVar = '123';
someVar = 123;
```

The null and undefined JavaScript literals are effectively treated as the same as the any type:

```
var str: string;
var num: number;

// These literals can be assigned to anything
str = undefined;
num = null;
```

Typing Functions

Not only can you type variables, but you can also type the results of a function call:

```
function sayHello(theName: string): string {
    return 'Hello, '+theName;
}
```

If you try to call sayHello and assign the result to an incorrect data type, the compiler will throw an error.

:void

Use :void to signify that a function does not have a return type:

```
function log(message): void {
    console.log(message);
}
```

Summary

There is much more to cover in both Angular and TypeScript than this chapter's very simple introduction. In all likelihood, you will be using additional resources for both of these technologies as you begin to develop more feature-complete applications. But let's look at some of the key points we have covered in this chapter.

We looked at Angular's new component model, its templating, the new data-binding methods, and the component life cycle. Beyond that, we also explored some new capabilities in ES6 and TypeScript, including classes, Promises, and arrow functions, as well as the ability to assign types to our variables and functions.

CHAPTER 5

Apache Cordova Basics

The Ionic Framework is built upon two other technologies: Angular and Apache Cordova. In this chapter, we will explore what Apache Cordova is and how it interacts with Ionic.

Apache Cordova is an open source framework that enables mobile app developers to use their HTML, CSS, and JavaScript content to create a native application for a variety of mobile devices. Let's look further at how this works.

Cordova takes your web application and renders it within a native web view. A web view is a native application component (like a button or a tab bar) that is used to display web content within a native application. You can think of a web view as a web browser without any of the standard user interface chrome, like a URL field or status bar (see Figure 5-1). The web application running inside this container is just like any other web application that would run within a mobile browser—it can open additional HTML pages, execute JavaScript code, play media files, and communicate with remote servers. This type of mobile application is often called a hybrid application.

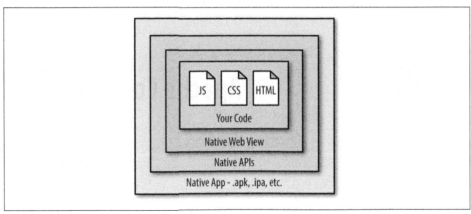

Figure 5-1. How Cordova applications are composited to create fully native applications

Typically, web-based applications are executed within a sandbox, meaning that they do not have direct access to various hardware and software features on the device. A good example of this is the contact database on your mobile device. This database of names, phone numbers, emails, and other bits of information is not accessible to a web app. Besides providing a basic framework to run a web app within a native application, Cordova also provides JavaScript APIs to allow access to a wide variety of device features, like the contacts database. These capabilities are exposed through the use of a collection of plugins. We will explore their use later in this book, but plugins provide a bridge between our web application and the device's native features. There is a core set of plugins that is maintained by the Cordova project, as well as a large collection of third-party plugins that offer even more functionality (NFC communication, Force Touch, and Push Notifications, just to name a few)—see Table 5-1.

Table 5-1. Core plugins

Plugin	Function
Battery status	Monitors the status of the device's battery
Camera	Captures a photo using the device's camera
Console	Provides an improved console log
Contacts	Works with the device's contact database
Device	Gathers device-specific information
Device motion (accelerometer)	Taps into the device's motion sensor
Device orientation (compass)	Obtains the direction the device is pointing to
Dialogs	Visual device notifications
File	Hooks into native filesystem through JavaScript
File transfer	Allows your application to upload and download files
Geolocation	Makes your application location aware
Globalization	Enables representation of objects specific to a locale

Plugin	Function
InAppBrowser	Launches URLs in another in-app browser instance
Media	Records and plays back audio files
Media capture	Captures media files using device's media capture applications
Network connection	Quickly checks the network state and cellular network information
SplashScreen	Shows and hides the application's splash screen
StatusBar	An API for showing, hiding, and configuring status bar background
Vibration	An API to vibrate the device
Whitelist	Implements a whitelist policy for navigating the application WebView

The History of Cordova (aka PhoneGap)

Developers are often confused by the difference between Apache Cordova and PhoneGap. In an attempt to clear up this confusion, we need to understand the origins of
this project. In late 2008, several engineers from Nitobi attended an iPhone development camp at the Adobe offices in San Francisco. They explored the idea of using the
native web view as a shell to run their web applications in a native environment. The
experiment worked. Over the next few months, they expanded their efforts and were
able to leverage this solution to create a framework. They named the project Phone-
Gap, since it allowed web developers the ability to bridge the gap between their web
apps and the device's native capabilities. The project continued to mature, and more
plugins were created, enabling more functionality to be accessed on the phone. Other
contributors joined the effort, expanding the number of mobile platforms it supported.

In 2011, Adobe bought Nitobi, and the PhoneGap framework was donated to the
Apache Foundation. The project was eventually renamed Cordova (which is actually
the street name of Nitobi's office in Vancouver, Canada).

Apache Cordova versus Adobe PhoneGap

Since there is both Apache Cordova and Adobe PhoneGap, it is quite easy to confuse
the projects. This naming issue can be a source of frustration when researching an
issue during development and having to search using both Cordova and PhoneGap as
keywords to find the solutions, or even reading the proper documentation, as the two
projects are so intertwined.

A good way to understand the difference is to think about how Apple has its Safari
browser, but it is based on the open source WebKit engine. The same is true here:
Cordova is the open source version of the framework, while PhoneGap is the Adobe-
branded version. But in the end, there is little difference between the two efforts.
There are some slight differences in the command-line interfaces, but the functionality is the same. The only thing you cannot do is mix the two projects in the same

application. While not as dangerous as when the Ghostbusters crossed their streams, using both Cordova and PhoneGap in the same project will produce nothing but trouble.

PhoneGap or Cordova?

We tend to use PhoneGap as our primary search term since that was its original name when researching issues.

The main difference between the projects is that Adobe has some paid services under the PhoneGap brand, most notably the PhoneGap Build (*https://build.phonegap.com*) service. This is a hosted service that enables you to have your application compiled into native binaries remotely, eliminating the need to install each mobile platform's SDKs locally. The PhoneGap CLI has the ability utilize this service, while the Cordova CLI does not.

The other difference is the PhoneGap CLI can be used in tandem with the PhoneGap developer app (*http://app.phonegap.com*). This free mobile app allows for your app to run on-device without the need to first compile it. This provides a very easy method to test and debug your application on-device. Don't worry, there is an Ionic equivalent (*http://view.ionic.io*) for us to leverage, and we will be using it during our development cycle.

In this book, we will be using the Cordova command-line tool when we are not using the Ionic command-line tool. This is in part due to the fact the Ionic CLI is based on the Cordova CLI, not the PhoneGap CLI.

A Deep Dive into Cordova

In the past, configuring a Cordova project was a difficult task. It meant first creating a native application project in each platform's IDE, then modifying it to support the interfaces for Cordova. With the release of the command-line tool, this process became easier. The CLI scaffolds a basic project and configures it to work with any supported mobile platform you can use. The Cordova CLI also allows us to have easy integration and management of the plugins for our project. Finally, the CLI enables us to quickly compile our app to run in a simulator or on an actual device. We will be exploring these commands further as we work through our sample applications.

Configuring Your Cordova App

Each Cordova application is defined by its *config.xml* file. This global configuration file controls many of the aspects of the application, from app icons, plugins, and range of platform-specific settings. It is based on the W3C's Packaged Web Apps

(Widgets) specification (*http://www.w3.org/TR/widgets/*). The Ionic CLI will generate a starter *config.xml* file during its scaffolding process.

As you develop your Ionic application, you will need to update this file with new elements. Some common examples of this are adjusting the app name, the app ID string, or adding a platform-specific setting like `android-minSdkVersion`.

A deeper exploration of the *config.xml* can be found in Appendix A.

Device Access (aka Plugins)

Some of the real power of Cordova comes from its extensive plugin library. At the time of this writing, there were over 1,250 plugins (*http://cordova.apache.org/plugins/#/*). But what is a Cordova plugin? Here is how the Cordova website defines them:

> A plugin is a bit of add-on code that provides JavaScript interface to native components. They allow your app to use native device capabilities beyond what is available to pure web apps.

As mentioned earlier, there are two sets of plugins: core and third-party. Time for another brief history lesson. Up to version 3.0 of PhoneGap (pre-Cordova), the code base contained both the code to use the WebView and its communication to the native app, along with some of the "key" device plugins. Starting with version 3.0, all the plugins were separated out as individual elements. That change means that each plugin can be updated as needed, without having to update the entire code base. These initial plugins are known as the "core" plugins.

But what about the other 1,220 or so plugins—what do they provide? An incredibly wide range of things: Bluetooth connectivity, push notifications, TouchID, and 3D Touch, just to name a few.

Interface Components: The Missing Piece

While Cordova provides a lot of functionality to the developer in terms of being able to leverage code across multiple platforms, extend beyond the web, and use native device features, it is missing one critical component: user interface elements. Beyond just the basic controls that HTML provides by default, Cordova does not offer any components like those found in a native SDK. If you want to have a tab bar component, you are either going to have to create the HTML structure, write the needed CSS, and develop the JavaScript to manage the views, or use a third-party framework, like Ionic.

This lack of a UI layer has often been one of the difficulties in working with Cordova. With the release of the Ionic Framework, developers now have a first-rate interface toolkit with which they can author their mobile applications. There are other solutions available for a Cordova application, but this book is focused on Ionic. If you would like to look at some other options, you might look at OnsenUI, Framework7, or ReactJS as an option. For me, I have been very pleased with what I have been able to build with the Ionic framework and its services.

Why Not Cordova?

Although Cordova is an incredibly powerful solution for building mobile applications, it is not always the right choice. Understanding the advantages and disadvantages of the framework is critical in how well your application will perform. Our Cordova application is several layers away from the actual native layer. So, great care must be taken to develop a performant Cordova application. This was very true during the early days of PhoneGap, when devices were relatively low powered. Current mobile devices have much more computing power that can be used.

With that said, you are not going to develop the next *Angry Birds* or *Temple Run* using Cordova. But you might be able to build the next *Quiz Up*, *Untappd*, or *Trivia Crack*.

Understanding Web Standards

Another thing to consider is what the WebView is actually capable of. Although most mobile WebViews are fairly current with recognized web standards, it is always worthwhile to understand there might be issues or quirks. If you have been doing any modern web development, there is a good chance you have used *http://caniuse.com*.

This is an excellent resource to check if a particular HTML5 feature is available, or if a CSS property is supported. For example, if we wanted to use scalable vector graphics (SVGs) in our application to assist in dealing with a range of screen sizes and densities, we can go to *http://caniuse.com* and see when each mobile platform began supporting it (Figure 5-2).

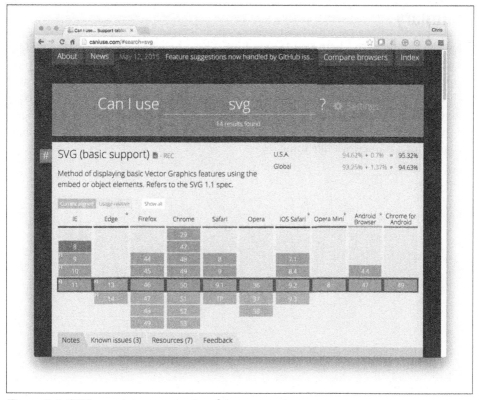

Figure 5-2. SVG support across various browsers

In this case, we can see that while iOS has had support for several versions, the Android platform only recently enabled support for this format.

It is worth noting exactly where the WebView that Cordova uses comes from. When you compile your application, Cordova does not actually include a WebView into the application. Instead, it will use the WebView that is included on the device as part of its OS. That means current iOS devices get a version of WebKit, while certain Android devices will be using Chromium, and others might still be using WebKit.

Although, recently active development was halted, the Crosswalk Project (*https:// crosswalk-project.org*) is still an worthwhile solution if you need to release your application for older Android devices. This plugin replaces the default WebView in your Cordova project with the latest version of Google Chromium, thus giving you the latest browser support. Although using this solution will increase the size of your application, it can help in normalizing the web features that you can use. If your application will be used by older Android devices, using Crosswalk can great resolve some of the browser issues that exist.

Summary

Now you should have a better understanding of how Apache Cordova works and how it enables you to use your web technology skills to create mobile applications. In this chapter, we looked at how Cordova bridges between the native layer and the web technology layer. It's plugin architecture was introduced, which will allow us to access native device features in our hybrid applications. We touched on whether this solution was the right choice for your development needs. Finally, we covered why there is a need for a framework like Ionic.

CHAPTER 6

Understanding Ionic

Let's now take a deeper look at what makes up the foundation of an Ionic page. Each Ionic page is formed from three base files: an HTML file which defines the components that are displayed; a Sass file which defines any custom visual styling for those components; and a TypeScript file which will provide the custom functions for those components. Since Ionic is built upon web technologies, we can use many of the same solutions that we might use in developing a traditional web application or web page (Figure 6-1).

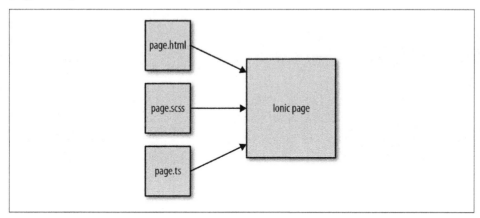

Figure 6-1. Basic Ionic page structure

HTML Structure

Unlike in a traditional HTML file, you do not need to include the <head> tag and any elements like importing CSS files or other code libraries. You also do not include the <body> tag nor even the <!DOCTYPE html> or <html lang="en" dir="ltr"> tags.

The contents of this HTML file are rendered within our application container, so we do not need them. We just define the actual components that will be shown to the user. These components are a mixture of traditional HTML tags, as well as custom tags that are used to define the Ionic components. Here is a sample of an Ionic page's markup.

```
<ion-header>
  <ion-navbar>
    <ion-title>
      Ionic Blank
    </ion-title>
  </ion-navbar>
</ion-header>

<ion-content padding>
  The world is your oyster.
  <p>
    If you get lost, the <a href="http://ionicframework.com/docs/v2">
    docs</a> will be your guide.
  </p>
</ion-content>
```

The rendered Ionic page is shown in Figure 6-2.

You can see the markup is a blend of standard HTML (<p> and <a>) and Ionic tags (<ion-header>, <ion-content>, etc).

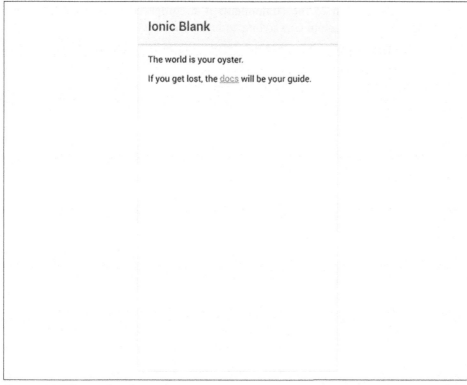

Figure 6-2. The rendered page

Ionic Components

One of Angular's features is the ability to extend the vocabulary of HTML to include custom tags. The Ionic Framework leverages this capability and has created an entire set of mobile components. These include components like <ion-card>, <ion-item-sliding>, and <ion-segment-button>. For a complete summary of the Ionic component library, see Appendix C, as well as the Ionic documentation (*http://ionicframework.com/docs/v2/*). All of the Ionic components have the prefix ion-, so they are easy to spot in the markup.

Autocompleting Ionic Tags

Most code editors offer some form of autocomplete or code-hinting that can be extended. There is usually a downloadable plugin for your editor that enables code hinting for the Ionic Framework.

Behind the scenes, each of the components is decomposed at runtime into basic HTML tags with their custom CSS styling and functionality.

Just like standard HTML tags, Ionic components also accept various attributes to define their settings, such as setting their ID value or defining additional CSS classes. But Ionic components are also extended through additional attributes like:

```
<ion-item-options side="left">
```

or using Angular directives:

```
<button ion-button color="dark">
```

As we build our sample applications, you will become more familiar with the Ionic component library.

Understanding the SCSS File

The visual definition of an Ionic application is defined by CSS. However, this CSS is actually generated by Sass, or Syntactically Awesome Style Sheets. If you have never worked with Sass, it provides several advantages over writing CSS directly. These include the ability to declare variables like `$company-brand: #ff11dd`. You can reference this variable instead of directly assigning the color. Now if we had to change our color, we only have to do it in one location and not across multiple files.

CSS Variable Naming

It is often tempting to give the variable a name like `$company-red`, but consider what happens if the branding changes and instead of red, the color is actually green?

All of Ionic's components are styled using Sass variables. For example, we can change the `$list-background-color` by adding our value in the *app.variables.scss* file. The team has done an incredible job in ensuring that each Ionic component is easy to style. Refer to the Ionic documentation for a complete list of all the configurable Sass variables.

Sass also supports an improved syntax for writing nested CSS. Here is an example of this:

```
nav {
  ul {
    margin: 0;
    padding: 0;
    list-style: none;
  }

  li { display: inline-block; }
```

```
  a {
    display: block;
    padding: 6px 12px;
    text-decoration: none;
  }
}
```

When transformed, it becomes:

```
nav ul {
  margin: 0;
  padding: 0;
  list-style: none;
}

nav li {
  display: inline-block;
}

nav a {
  display: block;
  padding: 6px 12px;
  text-decoration: none;
}
```

This method of writing CSS shorthand can be a real timesaver.

Typically, the screen's *.scss* file is where you will define any page-specific CSS—for example, if you need to have a slightly different button style for a login screen. By defining it in the associated *.scss* file, you keep the associated elements package together in a more logical fashion. For any application-wide theming, that styling should be defined in the *app.core.scss* files.

We will explore theming in greater detail when we are building our sample applications.

Understanding TypeScript

The last element needs to create an Ionic screen is the associated TypeScript (*.ts*) file. This where all the Angular/TypeScript code to control the interactions of this page will be written.

The file will define any code modules we need to import for our screen to function. Typically, these would be components that we might need to programmatically interact with (like navigating to a new screen) or Angular modules that offer needed functions (like making an HTTP request). It will also define the base component that is actually our screen. As we need to add functions to respond to user input, that code will also be added into this file. Here is what a basic Ionic *.ts* file looks like:

```
import { Component } from '@angular/core';
import { NavController } from 'ionic-angular';

@Component({
  selector: 'page-home',
  templateUrl: 'home.html'
})

export class HomePage {

  constructor(public navCtrl: NavController) {

  }

}
```

This TypeScript code just defines the HomePage component and links it the template.

We will be working a lot of TypeScript code throughout our sample applications, so we will not go any further in exploring this element.

Summary

You should have a better understanding of the three key elements that make up a single Ionic screen: the HTML file, the Sass file, and the *.ts* file. Let's move on to building our first actual Ionic application.

CHAPTER 7

Building Our Ionic2Do App

With our development environment configured, some initial exposure to Angular 2, and a foundation in Apache Cordova, we are finally ready to start creating our first Ionic 2 application. As not to break with tradition, we are going to be building the classic to-do list management application. You might wonder why we would build something that has been built so many times before. Part of the reason is that for many of you, building something familiar will let you begin to map how Ionic works to whatever language or framework you might be more familiar with. Another reason is that a to-do app has more complexity that simply printing out "Hello World" on a screen.

To get started we need to create a new Ionic project. We will use the blank template as our basis:

```
$ ionic start Ionic2Do blank --v2
```

Make sure you include the --v2 flag; otherwise you will create an Ionic version 1 application. The --v2 flag will tell the Ionic CLI that you want a version 2 project.

The CLI will begin downloading the various elements for the project: the TypeScript components, the Node modules, and finally the required Cordova components. This process may take a few minute, depending on your internet connection. If you have done Ionic v1 development, you will notice that this process is a bit longer than before.

Once all the packages have been downloaded, the CLI will happily inform you that your Ionic app is ready to go!

Next, you need to make sure you change the working directory into your newly created Ionic project's directory:

```
$ cd Ionic2Do
```

More than once I have forgotten this simple step and wondered why my next Ionic command would fail. The CLI itself provides a gentle reminder when it finishes, as well.

Adding our Platforms

If you are building on a Mac, the Ionic CLI will automatically include the iOS platform for us. Since building for that platform is not an option in Windows, the CLI will not attempt to add it. Since Android can be built on either a Mac or PC, we will add that platform as well to our project:

```
$ ionic platform add android
```

This will add a platforms directory to our project, as well as the *platforms.json* file. The platforms directory will have subdirectories of each of the platforms that we include. If you look at the *platforms > android* directory, you will see all the platform-specific elements needed to build our application for the Android OS: the Gradle files, the *AndroidManifest.xml*, and so on.

To add the iOS platform, we just need to change the platform name in CLI command:

```
$ ionic platform add ios
```

And now the platforms directory will now contain an iOS directory that houses the iOS-specific elements, like the Xcode project file.

Previewing Our Ionic2Do App

Let's go ahead and take a quick look at what the Ionic2 blank template looks like in our browser. Although there is an *index.html* file located inside the *www* directory, we actually cannot open it directly in our browser. Instead, this file needs to be served from an actual web server. Luckily, we do not need to upload this to an actual server; the Ionic CLI has a command that will spin up a local web server and allow us to preview our app:

```
$ ionic serve
```

The Ionic CLI will begin the process of compiling and bundling the dependencies. Then it will compile the Sass files into CSS, insert the IonIcon font library, and then copy the HTML files. A web server is started, Google Chrome is launched (or if already running, a new tab will be created), and our Ionic app is displayed (Figure 7-1).

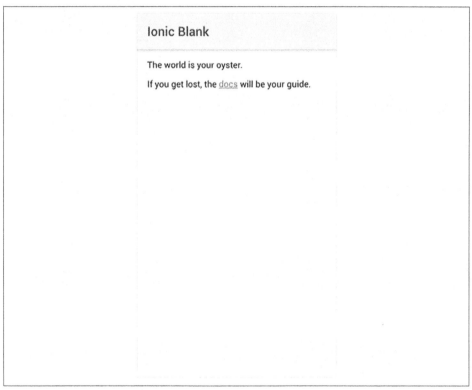

Ionic Blank

The world is your oyster.

If you get lost, the docs will be your guide.

Figure 7-1. Ionic's blank template

The server will now watch the project files for changes and reload the app once you have saved a file.

In addition, you can start the server with the console logging enabled by adding a `--c` flag, as well as enabling the server logs with the `--s` flag

But the flag I usually enable is the `--lab` flag. This will tell the server to create three copies of our Ionic app in the browser: one will have the platform flag set to iOS, another set to Android, and the third set to Windows. This will allow you to quickly preview the differences in the UI between the three platforms and provide a simpler way to test any CSS changes you might be applying to your project (Figure 7-2).

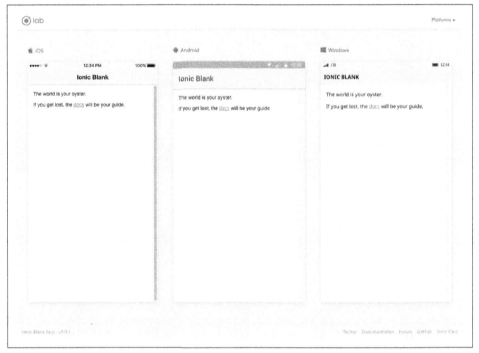

Figure 7-2. Ionic serve using the --lab flag

To quit the server, just type **control-c** into the terminal window.

Previewing a Specific Platform

When using just $ `ionic serve` , your app will use Android as its platform of choice. To see your application as it would be rendered on a different platform, just append `--platform=platformname` to end of the command. The values are `ios`, `android`, and `windows`.

Let's return to the project directory and look at some additional files and how they are related.

Understanding the index.html File

The first file I want to look at is the *www/index.html*. With Ionic 1, there was actually a lot of content that was placed in this file. Here is a portion of one of my Ionic 1 app's script tags:

```
<!-- ionic/angularjs js -->
<script src="lib/ionic/js/ionic.bundle.js"></script>
<script src="lib/ionic-service-core/ionic-core.js"></script>
<script src="lib/ionic-service-analytics/ionic-analytics.js"></script>
```

```
<!-- ngCordova -->
<script src="lib/ngCordova/dist/ng-cordova.min.js"></script>
<!-- cordova script (this will be a 404 during development) -->
<script src="cordova.js"></script>
<!-- App js -->
<script src="js/app.js"></script>
<!--Factories/Services-->
<script src="js/hikedata.js"></script>
<script src="js/mapdata.js"></script>
<script src="js/appStatus.js"></script>
<script src="js/geoLocService.js"></script>
<!--Controllers-->
<script src="views/home/home.js"></script>
<script src="views/hikes/hike.js"></script>
<script src="views/hikelist/hikelist.js"></script>
<script src="views/hikedetails/hikedetails.js"></script>
<script src="views/map/map.js"></script>
<script src="views/about/about.js"></script>
```

As you can see, there are a whole lot of script tags that were added into the *index.html* file during development. With Ionic 2, all of this JavaScript loading management is baked into the CLI and the build process. We now just have three script tags—certainly a much more manageable list. In fact, we no longer have to remember to add script tags for every Angular element; the build process now generates a single *main.js* file with all our code merged together:

```
<!-- cordova.js required for cordova apps -->
<script src="cordova.js"></script>

<!-- The polyfills js is generated during the build process -->
<script src="build/polyfills.js"></script>

<!-- The bundle js is generated during the build process -->
<script src="build/main.js"></script>
```

If we look at the actual content within the <body> tag, we will just find one tag, <ion-app>. Through the use of this one component, our entire app will be bootstrapped

Another change from Ionic 1 to Ionic 2 is the CSS is generated from the Sass files by default. With Ionic 1, you had to enable this process. Now in Ionic 2, everything is built from the Sass files into a single CSS file:

```
<link href="build/main.css" rel="stylesheet">
```

With the shift to a component-focused development paradigm, almost all the real code is now within the App component. Let's explore the new *src* directory in more detail.

Within the *src* directory, we find four directories: *app*, *assets*, *pages*, and *theme*. We also find four files, a *declarations.d.ts* file, an *index.html* file, a *manifest.json* file, and a *service-worker.js* file.

Exploring the app Directory

During the beta releases of Ionic 2, there was an *app.ts* file that contained the general bootstrapping Angular code for the application. With the shift to NgModule, and Angular itself stabilizing its recommended directory structures, the Ionic directory structure followed suit. Now, the initial app files are stored within the *app* directory, while the rest of the app is located in the *pages* directory.

Inside the app directory, we will find five files. Table 7-1 is a brief summary of them.

Table 7-1. File summary

app.component.ts	This file contains the base component that our app will initially use.
app.html	This file declares the initial app HTML tag.
app.module.ts	This file declares the initial modules, providers, and entry components.
app.scss	This file defines any global CSS styles.
main.ts	This TypeScript file is used during development to load our app.

Let's explore each of these files in a bit more depth to understand their role. First, open *app.module.ts* in your editor.

Visual Studio Code

The relationship between a developer and his code editor is a special one. In working with Ionic 2, I personally have found using Microsoft's Visual Studio Code as my editor of choice. It is a free download from https://code.visualstudio.com/. It obviously has support for TypeScript, as well as Cordova and Ionic.

This file declares what the NgModule function will do when called as Angular/Ionic runs:

```
import { NgModule, ErrorHandler } from '@angular/core';
import { IonicApp, IonicModule, IonicErrorHandler } from 'ionic-angular';
import { MyApp } from './app.component';
import { HomePage } from '../pages/home/home';

import { StatusBar } from '@ionic-native/status-bar';
import { SplashScreen } from '@ionic-native/splash-screen';

@NgModule({
  declarations: [
    MyApp,
    HomePage
  ],
  imports: [
    IonicModule.forRoot(MyApp)
  ],
```

```
    bootstrap: [IonicApp],
    entryComponents: [
      MyApp,
      HomePage
    ],
    providers: [
      StatusBar,
      SplashScreen,
      {provide: ErrorHandler, useClass: IonicErrorHandler}
    ]
})
export class AppModule {}
```

There are several Ionic-specific things to note here. First, importing IonicApp and IonicModule from the ionic-angular library. The IonicModule's forRoot method is called to define the root app component. We can pass a config object into IonicMod ule. This object allows us to define such items like the back button text, the icon mode, or even the tab placement. Since we are not changing any of these settings, we will leave them as their platform defaults. Check out the complete list of all the configuration settings (*http://bit.ly/2nh22zo*).

We also define NgModule's bootstrap parameter to use IonicApp for the actual bootstrap process.

For the entryComponents parameter, we define an array that contains all the components used by our application. In this case, the MyApp and HomePage components are included. By doing this, the Ahead of Time (AoT) compiler can use this and improve our application's performance.

Now, let's explore the *app.component.ts* file in more depth. At the start of the file are the import statements. If you recall, this is how Angular 2 handles its dependency injection:

```
import { NgModule, ErrorHandler } from '@angular/core';
import { IonicApp, IonicModule, IonicErrorHandler } from 'ionic-angular';
import { MyApp } from './app.component';
import { HomePage } from '../pages/home/home';

import { StatusBar } from '@ionic-native/status-bar';
import { SplashScreen } from '@ionic-native/splash-screen';
```

The first import statement loads the Component module from Angular core.

What About the @App Component?

In earlier versions of Ionic 2, the application was bootstrapped using the App module. With the release of beta 8, the Ionic team shifted away from this custom module to use the generic Compo nent module instead.

The next import statement loads the Platform module from the Ionic Framework libraries. The third import statement loads the StatusBar and Splashscreen plugins from the Ionic Native library. The final import statement loads our HomePage component that is defined in the *home* directory inside the *pages* directory. We will touch on this module in a bit.

Next, comes the actual @Component decorator:

```
@Component({
  templateUrl: 'app.html'
})
```

What Is a Decorator?

Decorators are simply functions that modify a class, property, method, or method parameter.

Within our Component decorator, we will specify the template to render. The template can be declared in one of two forms: inline, or as an external file and referenced using templateUrl instead.

If the template is short, we could just include it inline. For example, the *app.component.ts* file had the template declared inline. Here is what it used to look like:

```
template: `<ion-nav [root]="rootPage"></ion-nav>`
```

For more complex HTML templates, you will want to keep them in a separate file.

Let's look at the *app.html* file next. This template is just the <ion-nav> component:

```
<ion-nav [root]="rootPage"></ion-nav>
```

Just as in Ionic 1, this is a basic navigation container for our content. We will look at the Navigation components in a bit. Also included in our template is set the root page for the component. We use Angular 2's new one-way data-binding syntax of [ ] to set the root property to the rootPage variable. Returning to the *app.component.ts* file, we can see that variable is set within the class definition:

```
export class MyApp {
  rootPage = HomePage;

  constructor(platform: Platform, statusBar: StatusBar, splashScreen:
  SplashScreen) {
    platform.ready().then(() => {
      // Okay, so the platform is ready and our plugins are available.
      // Here you can do any higher level native things you might need.
      statusBar.styleDefault();
      splashScreen.hide();
    });
```

```
    }
  }
```

The Ionic CLI automatically names this class MyApp. Next, it defines the rootPage variable to be the HomePage component. Since this is TypeScript, we also define the variable type, in this case, we are setting it to be of type any.

The component's constructor has the Ionic Platform component passed as a parameter. Within the constructor, a JavaScript Promise is made from the platform.ready function. Once Ionic and Cordova are done bootstrapping, this Promise will be returned, and any device specific code will be safe to execute.

DeviceReady Event

If you have done any Cordova or PhoneGap development in the past, then you are probably familiar with the deviceReady event that Cordova will fire once the web-to-native bridge has finished initializing. It is similar to the documentReady event that traditional web development listens for.

In earlier versions of Ionic 2, we would have made a call to ionicBootstrap, but this is now handled within the NgModule function.

The next file within our *app* directory is the *app.scss* file. This file serves as a global Sass file for our app. If you are not familiar with Sass, it is a stylesheet language that compiles to CSS. We will explore styling and theming later. For now, we can leave this file as is.

The final file, *main.ts*, is the entry point to our application. By default our app is running in development mode. Here is what is in the *main.ts* looks like:

```
import { platformBrowserDynamic } from '@angular/platform-browser-dynamic';

import { AppModule } from './app.module';

platformBrowserDynamic().bootstrapModule(AppModule);
```

The platformBrowserDynamic module is loaded, as is our AppModule. Then the bootstrapModule function is called and our AppModule passed in. For the production version of *main.ts*, the enableProdMode module is loaded and called before we make the bootstrap call.

Remember, these files are about the initial start of the application. You should not need to interact with these files much except to override a configuration or a global styling change. When we are ready to test or release our application, we will build our application with an additional flag that will enable the build to switch to production mode.

The pages directory

The Ionic CLI will also generate a *pages* directory. With Ionic 1, it was common to keep the HTML templates in one directory and the related *controller.js* file in another directory. Now, it is considered best practice to keep all the associated files together. So within the *pages* directory, we will find a *home* directory. Inside this folder, we will find *home.html*, *home.scss*, and *home.ts*. As you build out your Ionic 2 application, you will create new directories for each page and place them within the *pages* directory.

The home.html file

Looking at the HTML code of this file, we will see that all the tags begin with <ion-. One of the original reasons the Ionic Framework was built atop the Angular Framework was the ability to extend the HTML language to include markup that represented the mobile components that were needed. This is still true with Ionic 2:

```
<ion-header>
  <ion-navbar>
    <ion-title>
       Ionic Blank
    </ion-title>
  </ion-navbar>
</ion-header>

<ion-content padding>
  The world is your oyster.
  <p>
    If you get lost, the <a href="http://ionicframework.com/docs/v2">
    docs</a> will be your guide.
  </p>
</ion-content>
```

In order for our <ion-navbar> to be above the content and remain fixed during page transitions, it must be placed within a <ion-header> tag. Now within the <ion-navbar>, we find the <ion-title> tag that sets the title of the Navbar. This component is platform-aware. On iOS, the text is centered within the Navbar, as with the Apple iOS Human Interface guidelines; but on Android or WindowsPhone the text is aligned left. This is a great example of defining the base component and Ionic doing the heavy lifting of applying the platform-specific styling.

Beneath the navbar is the <ion-content>. This defines the main container that we will place most of our app's interface. It has one Angular directive, padding, to provide some CSS padding to the container. The blank template has some text, a <p> tag, as well as, an <a> tag. This is a great example of just using basic HTML to define your content.

The home.ts file

This TypeScript file contains very little code. In fact, this is the bare minimum to create an Ionic page:

```
import { Component } from '@angular/core';
import { NavController } from 'ionic-angular';

@Component({
  selector: 'page-home',
  templateUrl: 'home.html'
})
export class HomePage {

  constructor(public navCtrl: NavController) {

  }
}
```

We first import the `Component` module from the Angular core library. Just as the `App` component was standardized to `Component`, so was the `Page` component standardized to `Component`. Next we import the `NavController` component from the Ionic-Angular library. One of the biggest things you have to remember when you are developing with Angular 2 is you have to import the components and features from Angular and Ionic in order to use them. The entire library is no longer available for use by default.

Our `Component` decorator defines its `templateUrl` as `'home.html'` and the selector to be `page-home`.

The build directory

Before the first release candidate of Ionic 2, the Ionic CLI generated a running version of our app by building the finished app in a slightly different manner. It used to take all the HTML files and copy them into a build directory within the *www* directory. Any changes to Sass files—the *.scss* files—that we have generated will be compiled and appended to each platform's CSS file. Our TypeScript is transpiled to ES5 and packed with the Angular and Ionic code and saved as *app.bundle.js*.

Although there is still a build directory within the *www*, you will not find your HTML files within it anymore. Now, when the Ionic CLI generates a running version of our app, the HTML templates are pre-compiled and included within the *main.js* file. The build directory now stores four files: *main.css*, *main.js*, *main.js.map*, and *polyfills.js*. All of the *.scss* files are compiled and merged into *main.css*. Our TypeScript is still transpiled into ES5 and packed with the Angular and Ionic code and saved as *main.js*. The *main.js.map* files assist with any debugging we may need to do, while the *polyfill.js* address any cross-browser compatibility issues that need to be addressed.

The theme directory

The next top-level element within the *src* directory is the *Theme* directory. Here we find a Sass file that we can modify to override any default CSS used by Ionic. We won't spend much time here now, other than to say that with Ionic2 the ability to customize our app's visual styling is much easier.

The assets directory

This directory was added in RC0. The goal of this directory is to house the various assets your app can need, such as fonts and images.

The declarations.d.ts file

Because TypeScript utilizes static types, we need to be able to "describe" code we want to use and import. This is handled through type definitions, and there is a fairly large collection of them managed by the TypeScript team. If for some reason you are unable to find the types for the third-party library, you can create a shorthand type definition in the *declarations.d.ts* file. The *.d.ts* denotes that the file is a definition file and not actual code. Within the file, we can add a line to declare our module:

```
declare module 'theLibraryName';
```

This line tells the TypeScript compiler that the module is found, and it is an object of any type. This will allow the library to be used freely without the TypeScript compiler giving errors.

The manifest.json file

Since Ionic can be used to create progressive web apps (PWAs), a default *manifest.json* file is included. We will discuss this file and PWAs in more detail in Chapter 13.

The service-worker.js file

The final item in the *src* directory is the *service-worker.js* file, another component of creating PWAs. We will ignore it for now and return to it in earnest in Chapter 13.

Now that we have had a brief survey of the basic files created by the Ionic CLI for this template, let's get to work modifying them for our Ionic2Do app.

Updating the Page Structure

While Home, as an initial page name, might be acceptable for some projects, I want to update our structure to be more reflective of what this page is: a list of our tasks. Let's go through our files and directories and update the reference to tasklist. We will start with the *app.component.ts* file:

```
import { Component } from '@angular/core';
import { Platform } from 'ionic-angular';
import { StatusBar } from '@ionic-native/status-bar';
import { SplashScreen } from '@ionic-native/splash-screen';

import { TaskListPage } from '../pages/tasklist/tasklist';

@Component({
  templateUrl: 'app.html'
})
export class MyApp {
  rootPage = TaskListPage;

  constructor(platform: Platform, statusBar: StatusBar, splashScreen:
  SplashScreen) {
    platform.ready().then(() => {
      // Okay, so the platform is ready and our plugins are available.
      // Here you can do any higher level native things you might need.
      statusBar.styleDefault();
      splashScreen.hide();
    });
  }
}
```

Visual Studio Code

If you are using Visual Studio Code as your editor, you will see portions of your code get a red squiggly line underneath them. This is
editor informing you of an issue, such as a missing file or an unre-
ferenced variable.

We also need to update the *app.module.ts* file. Since we are adjusting the starting
component, we need to adjust it to reflect the new component name and directory:

```
import { NgModule, ErrorHandler } from '@angular/core';
import { IonicApp, IonicModule, IonicErrorHandler } from 'ionic-angular';
import { MyApp } from './app.component';
import { TaskListPage } from '../pages/tasklist/tasklist';

import { StatusBar } from '@ionic-native/status-bar';
import { SplashScreen } from '@ionic-native/splash-screen';

@NgModule({
  declarations: [
    MyApp,
    TaskListPage
  ],
  imports: [
    IonicModule.forRoot(MyApp)
  ],
  bootstrap: [IonicApp],
```

```
  entryComponents: [
    MyApp,
    TaskListPage
  ],
  providers: [
    StatusBar,
    SplashScreen,
    {provide: ErrorHandler, useClass: IonicErrorHandler}]
})
export class AppModule {}
```

Save this file, and we will move on to adjusting the directory structure and file names. Within the *page* directory, change the references from 'home' to 'tasklist':

```
import { Component } from '@angular/core';
import { NavController } from 'ionic-angular';

@Component({
  selector: 'page-tasklist',
  templateUrl: 'tasklist.html'
})

export class TaskListPage {

  constructor(public navCtrl: NavController) {

  }
}
```

Switch to *tasklist.scss* file and change the selector from page-home {} to page-tasklist {} then save this file.

If you are still running $ ionic serve, stop it by pressing Ctrl-C while in the terminal. Then run $ ionic serve again, and we should see no visible changes from before.

Let's first update our HTML template by opening *tasklist.html*.

In the <ion-title> tag, change Ionic Blank to Tasks. Next, we add a button to the header that will allow us to add tasks to our list. Adding buttons in either a navbar or its parent component, the toolbar, is a bit different from adding standard buttons.

After the closing </ion-title> tag, add a <ion-buttons> tag. This component acts as a container for a collection of buttons. This component did not exist in Ionic 1, causing some interesting solutions when you wanted a row of buttons within your navbar.

Within this tag we need to included an attribute that controls the placement of the buttons it contains. You can either give it the value of start or end. I want our add item button to be placed at the far left of the header, so set this to end:

```
<ion-buttons end></ion-buttons>
```

Next, we can add a standard button element `<button>` and use the Angular 2 syntax to define the click handler to a function named `addItem()`. We will also add the `ion-button` directive to give the button the proper platform styling. Another change in Ionic 2 is the `icon-left` and `icon-right` directives. These directives will add a small amount of padding to either the left or right of the icon. Otherwise, the icon will appear directly next to the text. If you have an icon only button, then add `icon-only`. This will add padding to all the sides of the icon to give it proper spacing:

```
<ion-header>
  <ion-navbar>
    <ion-title>
      Tasks
    </ion-title>
    <ion-buttons end>
      <button ion-button icon-left (click)="addItem()">Add Item</button>
    </ion-buttons>
  </ion-navbar>
</ion-header>
```

Go ahead and save this file. If `$ ionic serve` is running, we should see our changes applied in the browser (see Figure 7-3).

Figure 7-3. Ionic2Do with the updated header

Ionic ships with a nice collection of icons. They are actually hosted as an independent GitHub project, so you can use them outside of Ionic if you want to.

Ionic 2 made several changes on how we work with the Ionicon library. First, we now have the `<ion-icon>` tag, instead of using `<i>`. Next, instead of referencing the icon we want to use by defining it with a CSS class, we set just the `name` attribute to the icon we want. For the Add Item icon, a standard + icon will work just fine. The markup is:

```
<button ion-button icon-left (click)="addItem()">
  <ion-icon name="add"></ion-icon> Add Item
</button>
```

Many icons have both Material Design and iOS versions. Ionic will automatically use the correct version based on the platform.

However, if you want more control, you can explicitly set the icon to use for each platform. Use the `md` (material design) and `ios` attributes to specify a platform-specific icon:

```
<ion-icon ios="logo-apple" md="logo-android"></ion-icon>
```

If you want to use a specific icon, then simply use the icon's full name. For example, if we wanted to use the iOS outline map icon across all platforms, the markup would be:

```
<ion-icon name="ios-map-outline"></ion-icon>
```

Check the Ionic Framework Ionicons page (*http://bit.ly/2nz02jl*) to find the full icon name, then select the icon. It will display the icon's information (Figure 7-4).

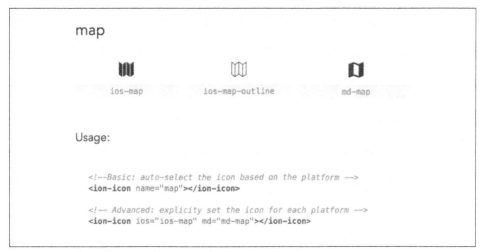

Figure 7-4. The full icon information for the map Ionicon

Now, let's turn our attention to building our list of tasks.

Replace the placeholder content in the `<ion-content>` with this bit of HTML:

```
<ion-content>
  <ion-list>
    <ion-item *ngFor="let task of tasks">{{task.title}}</ion-item>
  </ion-list>
</ion-content>
```

Let's walk through this code fragment. The `<ion-content>` tag serves as our container for content. It will automatically scroll if the content exceeds the viewport. Next, we have the `<ion-list>`, which as you might guess is used to display rows of information. In our case, this will be rows of tasks. Within our `<ion-list>` we define what our list item's template will be, and how to map and bind our data.

With Angular 1, we would use the `ng-repeat` directive to define the array to repeat through to generate our tasks. Angular 2 changed this directive to `*ngFor`. It does essentially the same function. For our sample, we are going to loop through an array named `tasks` and set each item into a locally scoped variable named task. Using the data-binding syntax, {{task.title}}, we will render out each task's title string. Save this file, and open the *tasklist.ts* file.

Within the class, we will define the tasks variable. Since we are using TypeScript, we need to set the type. For now, let's just define the tasks array as an array of any:

```
export class TaskListPage {
  tasks: Array<any> = [];

  constructor(public navCtrl: NavController) {
  }
```

Now, we need to include an actual constructor in our class definition.

Within the constructor, let's set our tasks array to some placeholder content to verify that our template code is working:

```
constructor(public navCtrl: NavController) {
  this.tasks = [
    {title:'Milk', status: 'open'},
    {title:'Eggs', status: 'open'},
    {title:'Syrup', status: 'open'},
    {title:'Pancake Mix', status: 'open'}
  ];
}
```

Save this file. Again, using $ ionic serve , we can preview this running app in our browser (Figure 7-5).

Figure 7-5. Ionic2Do app

Let's turn our attention to being able to add an item to our task list.

If you recall, we already included a click handler, `addItem` in the HTML file, so we now need to write it.

In the *tasklist.ts* file, after the end of the constructor we will add our `addItem` function. For now, we will use the standard `prompt` method to display a dialog to allow the user to enter a new task title. This will be included in a generic object that is pushed onto our `tasks` array:

```
addItem() {
  let theNewTask: string = prompt("New Task");
  if (theNewTask !== '') {
    this.tasks.push({ title: theNewTask, status: 'open' });
  }
}
```

Save the file and wait for the app to be recompiled and reloaded. Switching back to our browser, click the Add Item button in the header and the browser will open a prompt dialog. Next, enter a new task and close the dialog. Angular will automatically update our list (Figure 7-6).

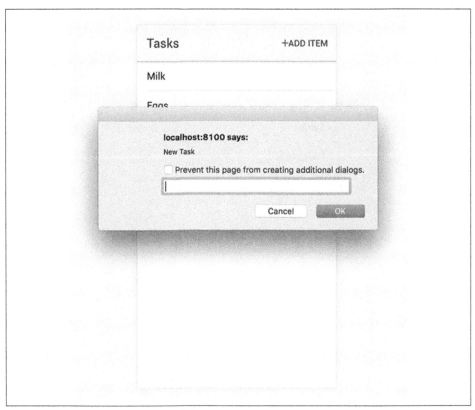

Figure 7-6. Ionic2Do's Add Item dialog

If you launched your preview using $ `ionic serve --lab` , you noticed that only one list was updated with your new tasks. That is because `ionic serve` is actually running two instances of the app.

Now, that we can add items to our task list, let's add a method to mark them as done. A common interface pattern for this is to swipe from right to left on a row to reveal a set of buttons. Ionic 2 provides an `<ion-item-sliding>` component that recreates this user experience.

Replace this code block:

```
<ion-item *ngFor="let task of tasks">
    {{task.title}}
</ion-item>
```

with the following:

```
<ion-item-sliding #slidingItem *ngFor="let task of tasks">
  <ion-item>
    {{task.title}}
```

```
    </ion-item>
  </ion-item-sliding>
```

The ngFor is now placed on the <ion-item-sliding> component instead of the <ion-item>. The elements within the <ion-item> tag will be our visible row items. We also need to include the reference to the slidingItems variable.

Next, we need to use the <ion-item-options> component to contain our buttons that will be shown when we swipe the row. This component supports having these option buttons be on the right, left, or even both sides. Simply add side='right' to the ion-item-options that you want revealed when the user swipes from the right to left. For items that you want to show when the user swipes from left to right, define it as side='left'. If you do not include a side, it will default to the right side.

For this app, we will have a button to mark a task as done, and another button to remove it from the list completely. The markup is just the standard <button> tag. Each button will have a click function and use an icon from the Ionicon library. Here is the snippet:

```
<ion-list>
  <ion-item-sliding *ngFor="let task of tasks">
    <ion-item>
      {{task.title}}
    </ion-item>
    <ion-item-options side="right">
      <button ion-button icon-only (click)="markAsDone(task)" color="secondary">
        <ion-icon name="checkmark"></ion-icon>
      </button>
      <button ion-button icon-only (click)="removeTask(task)" color="danger">
        <ion-icon name="trash"></ion-icon>
      </button>
    </ion-item-options>
  </ion-item-sliding>
</ion-list>
```

To mark a task as done, our click handler will call a function named markAsDone, and pass it the reference to that row's task. If you have used Angular before, you know this is a great example of the power of the framework. You can let Angular keep track of each row and let it resolve the management of what task we are interacting with, rather having to do all the bookkeeping ourselves.

For the button content, we will just use the <ion-icon> component. Now, since there is nothing inside the <ion-icon>, you might be tempted to self-close this tag. But Angular requires the tags within a template not be self-closed (Figure 7-7).

Figure 7-7. Ionic2Do's sliding list buttons

Let's switch to the *tasklist.ts* file and add our two functions: markAsDone and remove Task, after our addItem function:

```
markAsDone(task: any) {
    task.status = "done";
}

removeTask(task: any) {
    task.status = "removed";
    let index = this.tasks.indexOf(task);
    if (index > -1) {
        this.tasks.splice(index, 1);
    }
}
```

Before we test our app, let's make it so that when a user marks a task as done, we draw a line through the task. CSS makes this very easy with the text-decoration property. In the *tasklist.scss* file, add the following CSS:

```
.taskDone {text-decoration: line-through;}
```

Angular provides a method of conditionally applying CSS classes to an element. We will have Angular apply the CSS class `taskdone` if the task's status property is done to our `<ion-item>`:

```
<ion-item [ngClass]="{taskDone: task.status == 'done'}" >
```

Angular 1 to Angular 2

This directive is a good example of some of the subtle changes between Angular 1 and Angular 2. In Angular 1, the syntax was `ng-class="expression"`. In Angular 2, the syntax is now `[ngClass]="expression"`.

Make sure all the files are saved, and then test the app in your browser. You should be able to swipe a row and reveal the two option buttons. Click on the checkmark to mark the task as done. You should see the text change to have a line drawn through it. But, the row did not slide back over the option buttons after we clicked. Let's fix this interface issue.

In the *tasklist.html* file, we first need to modify our `import` statement to include the `ItemSliding` component:

```
import {NavController, ItemSliding} from 'ionic-angular';
```

Then we need to modify the `<ion-item-sliding>` component. Add a local template variable `#slidingItem`. The `<ion-item-sliding>` component will set this variable with a reference to each row. Next, pass this variable as the first parameter to both our option button functions. The new code will look like this:

```
<ion-item-sliding *ngFor="let task of tasks" #slidingItem>
  <ion-item [ngClass]="{taskDone: task.status == 'done'}">
    {{task.title}}
  </ion-item>
  <ion-item-options side="right">
    <button ion-button icon-only (click)="markAsDone(slidingItem, task)"↵
    color="secondary">
      <ion-icon name="checkmark"></ion-icon>
    </button>
    <button ion-button icon-only (click)="removeTask(slidingItem,task)"↵
    color="danger">
      <ion-icon name="trash"></ion-icon>
    </button>
  </ion-item-options>
</ion-item-sliding>
```

Save the file, and open the *tasklist.ts* file again. We need to include our new parameter to both the `markAsDone` and `removeTask` functions. This parameter will be typed to `list`:

```
markAsDone(slidingItem: ItemSliding, task: any) {
  task.status = "done";
  slidingItem.close();
}

removeTask(slidingItem: ItemSliding, task: any) {
  task.status = "removed";
  let index = this.tasks.indexOf(task);
  if (index > -1) {
    this.tasks.splice(index, 1);
  }
  slidingItem.close();
}
```

We can call the close method on the list reference, and it will slide our list item back for us.

Ionic 1 to Ionic 2

Ionic 1 also had a similar list component. However, to trigger the close action required injecting a reference to $ionicListDelegate and using it. Ionic 2 cleans up this code and just requires the reference to the list's row be available.

Try our new version out, and you will see that our rows will close after we click either option button.

Adding Full-Swipe Gesture

You have probably used the full-swipe gesture to perform an action on a list item. A great example of this is in the iOS Mail app. If you do a short swipe on the list, the option buttons will reveal themselves. This is what we have working in our application now. But in the iOS Mail app, if you keep swiping, the last option element is automatically triggered. Let's add this functionality to our application.

First, we need to add an event listener for the ionSwipe event. This event will be triggered when the user has performed the full-swipe gesture. We also need to tell it what function to call. Typically, this would be the same function that the last option button would call. So, our <ion-item> will now become:

```
<ion-item-options side="right" (ionSwipe)="removeTask(slidingItem, task)">
```

Second, we need to add an additional property on the button that we want to visually expand as the gesture is performed. Again, since this is typically done on the last item, we will add to our button that deletes the task. The new button is now:

```
<button ion-button icon-only expandable color="danger" ↵
  (click)="removeTask(slidingItem, task)">
```

And with those two additions, we have added support for a full-swipe gesture in our application.

Simple Theming

Besides adapting the components' look to the platform, we can also quickly affect their color. Ionic has five predefined color themes: primary (blue), secondary (green), danger (red), light (light gray), and dark (dark gray). To apply a theme color, we can just add to most Ionic components. Let's add a touch of color to the header by setting its theme color to `primary`:

```
<ion-navbar color="primary">
```

We had already set the theme color to each of the option buttons:

```
<button color="secondary" (click)="markAsDone(slidingItem, task)">
...
<button color="danger" (click)="removeTask(slidingItem, task)">
```

We will explore styling our Ionic apps in further detail in a later chapter. But for now, we have a little color in our app.

Proper Typing

The build scripts for Ionic are rather strict in what they allow in terms of variable typing. That is why the `tasks` variable is typed as `any`, instead of `Object`. Now it is possible to provide some inline typing for an `Object`. To do this for our task, it would be:

```
tasks: Array<{ title: string, status: string }> = [];
```

But if we change the typing on the task parameter in `maskAsDone` and `removeTask` functions to `Object`, the build process will report an error:

```
Typescript Error
Property 'status' does not exist on type 'Object'.
```

This is the TypeScript informing us about the fact that we added the `status` property on to the `Task` object. In earlier versions of the Ionic build scripts, our app would have still functioned; with the existing build scripts, we will need to address it.

The fix is quite simple: we need to create a custom `Task` class and use it instead of the generic `Object`. We could just define the `Task` class directly within the *tasklist.ts* file; but instead we will create a new file named *task.ts* in the same directory as our *tasklist.ts* file. In this file, we will export a class named `Task`. It will have two properties: title, and status, both typed as strings:

```
export class Task {
  title: string;
  status: string;
}
```

In the *tasklist.ts* file, we need to inject this class definition:

```
import { Component } from '@angular/core';
import { NavController, ItemSliding } from 'ionic-angular';
import { Task } from './task';
```

Then change the typing of our task array from:

```
tasks: Array<Object> = [];
```

to:

```
tasks: Array<Task> = [];
```

We also need to adjust the input parameters for both the markAsDone and removeTask functions. The task variables need to now be typed as Task instead of any.

Saving Data

You might have noticed a major flaw in our app. Any tasks that we add are not being saved. If you reload the app, only the four initial tasks are shown. There are options to solve this problem. We could use localStorage to save our data, but there are cases where this data can be cleared out by either the user or the system. WebSQL is an option, but the specification is no longer maintained, so there might be long-term support issues to consider. If we want to use a Cordova plugin, there are several other options to consider. Since our data structure is fairly straightforward, it could be written to the file system as a simple text file and read back in. Not a very elegant solution (nor secure), but it would work. A more advanced option might be to use the SQLite Plugin, maybe in conjunction with PouchDB. We could also look at using the new Storage module from Ionic itself.

But these are one-to-one solutions. In our connected, multidevice, multiplatform world, I want to be able to share and interact with my task list across all my mobile devices.

Creating a FireBase account

One option you can use to quickly have a cloud-based database is FireBase from Google. One of Firebase's services is to provide a real-time JSON database for storing and syncing your app's data. If you do not have an account, you can sign up for a free developer account with Firebase (*https://firebase.google.com*).

There you will be prompted to create a new project. Go ahead give your project the name of "Ionic2Do." Next, select your country or region from the list and click Create

Project. This will create a basic Firebase system for us to use. From this dashboard screen, click the Database choice, which will display our default database.

We will need several configuration elements to connect our application up to Firebase. Firebase makes this fairly simple: locate the "Add Firebase to your web app" button and click it. This will display a complete code sample for connecting our app; however, we are only interested in the config values:

```
var config = {
  apiKey: "your-api-key",
  authDomain: "your-authdomain",
  databaseURL: "https://someurl.firebaseio.com",
  storageBucket: "someurl.appspot.com",
  messagingSenderId: "your-sender-id"
};
```

Save this information to a temporary file, as we will need it later.

But before we can use this database, we need to adjust its security setting. Click the Rules tab to bring up the Rules editor. By default, the database is set to require authorization for both read and write access. Since we are just working on a simple tutorial, we can relax these settings. Change the rules from:

```
{
  "rules": {
    ".read": "auth != null",
    ".write": "auth != null"
  }
}
```

to:

```
{
  "rules": {
    ".read": "auth == null",
    ".write": "auth == null"
  }
}
```

Then click Publish. Our database can now be read and written to without needing authentication.

Installing Firebase and AngularFire2

In order to use Firebase, we need to install some additional node modules that our app will use.

Everything Is in Beta

Both the AngularFire and Firebase libraries are still under active development. The code samples listed here might change as the libraries are updated. Please refer to either the O'Reilly site (*http://oreil.ly/2mQlUtJ*) or this book's website (*http://ionic2book.com*) for updates.

The first node module we need to install is the @types module. In the early development of TypeScript, there were several different type declaration managers for the *.d.ts* files. With the release of TypeScript 2.0, the preferred method is to use the @types module to manage any additional library declarations:

```
$ npm install @types/request --save-dev --save-exact
```

Now, let's install Firebase into our project. From the command line:

```
$ npm install firebase  --save
```

Although we could work with Firebase directly, the AngularFire library was built to make this process even easier. Now with the addition of Observables in Angular 2, the method to interface with Firebase has become even simpler. If you have worked with Angular 1 and Firebase, then you probably used the AngularFire library to provide AngularJS bindings for FireBase. AngularFire 2 is the TypeScript version of this library. This version is still in beta at the time of this writing. To install the Angular-Fire library, execute this from the command line:

```
$ npm install angularfire2 --save
```

Ionic Build System

When we use the Ionic CLI to build our application, it executes a series of scripts collectively known as the Ionic App Scripts.The Ionic App Scripts were recently broken out from the main framework as a standalone GitHub repo, so they can be updated and improved independently of the framework itself. These scripts take our various files, third-party libraries, assets, and whatever else our apps need and produce our runnable application. Throughout the development of Ionic 2, the team changed the build system four times, from Browserify to WebPack to Rollup.js and back to Web-Pack 2. We recommend following the Ionic Blog (*http://blog.ionic.io*) for the latest updates on the Ionic build options.

To install the latest version of the Ionic App Scripts, run the following command from the Ionic project directory:

```
$ npm install @ionic/app-scripts@latest
```

By default, the Ionic App Scripts will do the following steps for us:

- Transpile source code to ES5 JavaScript
- Compile Ahead of Time (AoT) template
- Compile Just in Time (JiT) template
- Inline template for JiT builds
- Bundle modules for faster runtime execution
- Treeshake unused components and dead-code removal
- Generate CSS from bundled component Sass files
- Autoprefix vendor CSS prefixes
- Minify JavaScript files
- Compress CSS files
- Copy *src* static assets to *www*
- Lint source files
- Watch source files for live-reloading

Rather than relying on an external task runner like Grunt or Gulp, these scripts are executed from npm scripts. These scripts perform a wide range of tasks for us, including those in Table 7-2.

Table 7-2. Available Tasks

Task	Description
build	Creates a complete build of the application; uses `development` settings by default; use `--prod` to create an optimized build
clean	Empties the *www/build* directory
cleancss	Compresses the output CSS with CleanCss (*https://github.com/jakubpawlowicz/clean-css*)
copy	Runs the copy tasks, which by default copies the *src/assets/* and *src/index.html* files to *www*
lint	Runs the linter against the source *.ts* files, using the *tslint.json* config file at the root
minify	Minifies the output JS bundle and compresses the compiled CSS.
sass	Creates a Sass compilation of used modules; bundling must have run at least once before Sass compilation
watch	Runs watch for dev builds

In addition to these tasks, the app scripts support the ability for extensive customization to fit within your larger build system. This customization ranges from various config files, config values, or Ionic environmental variables that can be set. You can learn more about the Ionic App Scripts on GitHub (*http://bit.ly/2nh1A4e*).

Adding AngularFire to Our app.module.ts File

There are some changes we need to make to our *app.module.ts* file to use our AngularFire/Firebase solution. First, we need to import the actual components from the angularfire2 package:

```
import { AngularFireModule } from 'angularfire2';
```

The second change is to define our default Firebase configurations. Before the *@NgModule* declaration, add this code (replacing the values that were assigned to you when you created your Firebase account):

```
export const firebaseConfig = {
  apiKey: "your-api-key",
  authDomain: "your-authdomain",
  databaseURL: "https://someurl.firebaseio.com",
  storageBucket: "someurl.appspot.com",
  messagingSenderId: "your-messageSenderID"
};
```

The final change is to the `imports` array within the `@NgModule` declaration. Here we need to add the call to the `AngularFireModule` and initialize it with our config:

```
imports: [
  IonicModule.forRoot(MyApp),
  AngularFireModule.initializeApp(firebaseConfig)
],
```

With that, our initial setup to use AngularFire/Firebase is done. Let's turn our attention to where the real work lies in the *tasklist.ts* file.

Using Firebase Data

Like with the changes to *app.module.ts*, the first thing we need to update is our `import` statements. We need to import the `AngularFire` and `FirebaseListObservable` modules from the AngularFire 2 library:

```
import { AngularFire, FirebaseListObservable } from 'angularfire2';
```

Typically when working with dynamic data, a common solution is to use the `Observable` module from the RxJS library. If you have not heard of the RxJS library before, it is a set of libraries to compose asynchronous and event-based programs using observable collections and Array#extras style composition in JavaScript. The library is actively maintained by Microsoft. You can learn more about this library at GitHub (*https://github.com/Reactive-Extensions/RxJS*).

AngularFire takes the use of `Observable` a bit further and extends to a custom version, `FirebaseListObservable`. This is what we will use for our application.

Next, we need to replace using a local array to store our tasks, to one that will be bound to the Firebase data.

So our `tasks: Array<Task> = [];` will now become `tasks: FirebaseListObserva ble<any[]>;`. This will enable any updates to be applied to our `tasks` variable.

Our component is going to be using the AngularFire library to communicate with our `Firebase` database. In order to do this, we will need to pass a reference to that library as a parameter in our constructor:

```
constructor(public navCtrl: NavController, public af: AngularFire) { … }
```

Since our list of tasks is going to be stored remotely, we can replace our initial `tasks` array with the AngularFire request to return the data in the *tasks* subdirectory.

```
this.tasks = af.database.list('/tasks');
```

At the moment, this array should be empty since our database is empty. Before we can go ahead and perform a spot check on our app by running `$ ionic serve`, we need to add a pipe to our `ngFor` directive in the *tasklist.html*. In order to use the `Fire baseListObservable` array, we need to tell Angular that this data will be asynchro-nously fetched. To do so, we just need to include the `async` pipe. Otherwise, when Ionic/Angular tries to render this template, there isn't any data defined yet and it will throw an error. By adding the `async` pipe, Angular knows how to properly handle this information delay:

```
<ion-item-sliding *ngFor="let task of tasks | async" #slidingItem
  (ionSwipe)="removeTask(slidingItem, task)">
```

What Is a Pipe?

Pipes are functions that will transform data within a template. Angular has several built-in pipes to perform common tasks like changing text case or formatting numbers.

You should be able to add new items to your task list. After you have added a few items, go ahead and quit the server, then relaunch it. You should see your items repo-pulate your list.

Alternatively, you could log into your Firebase account and see your data listed.

You might have noticed that we did not modify the `addItem` function for this to work. Since our `tasks` variable is a `FirebaseListObservable` to our `Firebase` database, adding new items is still done via the `push` method.

However, both the `markAsDone` and `removeTask` methods will need some refactoring in order to properly interact with Firebase. Instead of directly interacting with the specific array item, we must use the AngularFire methods to do this.

In the `markAsDone` function, replace:

```
task.status = "done";
```

with:

```
this.tasks.update(task.$key, { status: 'done' });
```

The `task.$key` is the unique key value that is generated by Firebase when it was added to the database.

In the `removeTask` function, replace:

```
task.status = "removed";
let index = this.tasks.indexOf(task);
if (index > -1) {
  this.tasks.splice(index, 1);
}
```

with:

```
this.tasks.remove(task.$key);
```

Save our file, and run our application again using `$ ionic serve`. Our sliding buttons will now properly update our Firebase dataset.

You might have noticed that the `task.$key` references are being flagged with the following warning: `Property '$key' does not exist on type 'Task' any`. This is a simple fix. Open the *task.ts* file, add a new property $key, and set its type to any.

With that, we have transformed our local to-do application to one that uses a cloud-based one with very few lines of code. We have just barely touched on the power of Firebase and AngularFire2. It would be worth your time to explore the capabilities of these libraries further.

Using Ionic Native

Let's see how our app looks in an emulator. From the command line, either use `$ ionic emulate ios` or `$ ionic emulate android`.

Emulating Android

In case you forgot, launching the default Android emulator can be extremely slow. I recommend using Genymotion as a substitute for any virtual device testing.

Emulating iOS

When you run just `ionic emulate ios`, you might want to target a specific device type and OS. To do this, simply append the command with `--target="devicename, OSType"`. For example, if I wanted to target an iPhone 5s running iOS 10, the command would be `ionic emulate ios --target="iPhone-5s, 10.0"`.

Our app should connect with our `FireBase` database and display our task list. Now, let's add a new task by tapping the Add Item button (Figure 7-8).

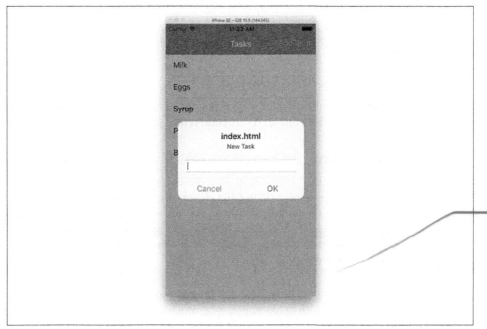

Figure 7-8. JavaScript dialog within our Ionic application

Notice the dialog: it is the same JavaScript dialog that we have been seeing in our browser. Now if we want a native-looking app, we certainly need to address this before releasing it to the app stores.

One of the many plugins that exist for Cordova uses native dialogs in place of the JavaScript version. To support using Cordova plugins with the Ionic 2 framework, they create a curated set of wrappers for many of the most common plugins.

By default, Ionic Native is included, but if you need to manually include Ionic Native into our project, use this command:

```
$ npm install @ionic-native/core --save
```

With Ionic Native installed we will have the interfaces needed to interact with our Cordova plugins.

What About ngCordova?

The ngCordova library (also maintained by the team behind Ionic) was designed for use with Angular 1 and Ionic 1 projects. Ionic Native is the replacement solution for Angular 2 and Ionic 2 projects.

The next step we need to perform is to install the actual plugin. One of the available plugins for Cordova is the Dialogs plugin. This plugin will render native dialogs in our app, instead of the web-based options. From the terminal, we can install it via Ionic CLI:

```
$ ionic plugin add cordova-plugin-dialogs
```

This will download the plugin code for all our installed platforms and update the *config.xml* so our app will now be built with this code reference included.

Plugin Sources

In the past, the plugins were referenced via the org.apache.cordova.* naming system. When the plugin host was moved to npm, the naming system changed to the cordova-plug-* pattern. You might find references to the older system in some documentation, so you will want to replace that reference with the proper npm version of the plugin.

Starting with Ionic Native 3.x, one more step is now required into order to use the plugin in our application. With Ionic Native 2.X, the entire Ionic Native library was loaded into your application (just the interfaces, not the actual plugins). Now, each plugin can be selectively added to your application, thus making your application smaller and hopefully a tiny bit faster to start. This change in how the plugin interfaces are used, does mean we will need to import and add each plugin provider to our @NgModule's provider list.

In the *app.module.ts* file, we need to import and add each plugin provider to our @NgModule declaration. Here is the full @NgModule declaration with our three plugins listed in the providers array:

```
@NgModule({
  declarations: [
    MyApp,
    TaskListPage
  ],
  imports: [
```

```
        IonicModule.forRoot(MyApp)
    ],
    bootstrap: [IonicApp],
    entryComponents: [
      MyApp,
      TaskListPage
    ],
    providers: [
      StatusBar,
      SplashScreen,
      Dialogs,
      { provide: ErrorHandler, useClass: IonicErrorHandler }
    ]
})
```

In the *tasklist.ts*, we will need to import the `Dialogs` module. With the other import statements, add the following:

```
import { Dialogs } from '@ionic-native/dialogs';
```

and in our constructor, we will need to pass in the reference to the `Dialogs` module:

```
constructor(public navCtrl: NavController, public af: AngularFire,
public dialogs: Dialogs) {
```

Then we need to replace these lines of code with:

```
this.dialogs.prompt('Add a task', 'Ionic2Do', ['Ok', 'Cancel'], '').then(
  theResult => {
    if ((theResult.buttonIndex == 1) && (theResult.input1 !== '')) {
      this.tasks.push({ title: theResult.input1, status: 'open' });
    }
  }
)
```

Index Values

You might be wondering why we are comparing to an index value of 1, since typically arrays start counting from 0. The zero value is used to indicate the dismissal of the dialog by not using any of the user defined buttons.

If we want to error-proof our code a bit, we could check that the inputted string was not empty before we added it our list. Figure 7-9 shows what the application's Add Item Dialog now looks like.

Figure 7-9. Add Item dialog using the Cordova dialog plugin

And with that, a basic to-do application was built. We looked at some basic Ionic components and theming, worked with an external library, and incorporated the Ionic Native library. In the next chapter, we will explore more Ionic components and navigation methods.

Summary

With this application we have explored the basic structure of an Ionic 2 project. You learned how to add elements to a header component, work with lists, enable the swipe to reveal function, and use the Ionicon library. We added FireBase support to save our data in the cloud, as well as adding an Ionic Native component for the user dialogs to make our application look native.

CHAPTER 8

Building a Tab-Based App

A very common type of application you might build is one that uses a tab-based navigation system. This design pattern works very well when you have a limited number (five or fewer) of groups (or tabs) of content. We are going to use this design pattern to create an app that will allow you to explore the various US national parks (in honor of them celebrating their centennial in 2016). Figure 8-1 shows what our final app will look like.

We are again going to use the Ionic CLI to scaffold our application. First, create a new directory that we will be building from. I named my directory *IonicParks*:

```
$ ionic start IonicParks --v2
```

Since we are going to be creating a tabs-based app, we did not need to pass in a template name, since the tab template is the default.

Next, change your working directory to the newly created *IonicParks* directory:

```
$ cd IonicParks
```

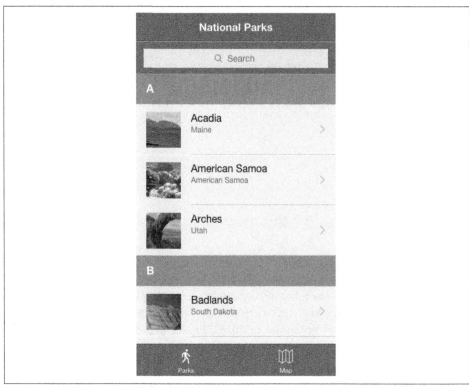

Figure 8-1. Ionic national parks app

Now let's explore the template itself (Figure 8-2) before we get down to business:

```
$ ionic serve
```

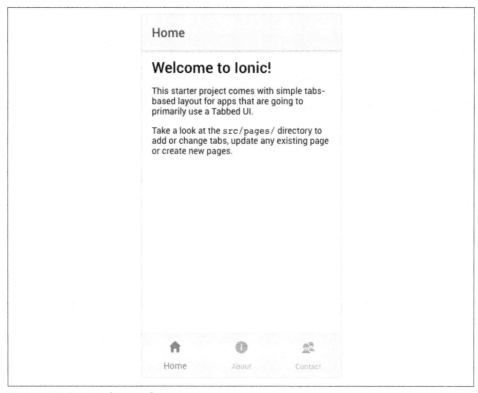

Figure 8-2. Ionic tabs template

Not a lot here, but we can navigate between the three tabs (named Home, About, and Contact), and see the content change.

Taking a look inside the *app.module.ts* file, we see that instead of importing one page, we now are importing four. These four pages comprise the three pages for each tab (HomePage, AboutPage, and ContactPage) and one page (TabsPage) that will serve as the container for the application. Each of these pages is included in the declaration and entryComponents array.

Looking at the *app.component.ts* file, the only change here is that the rootPage is the TabsPage and not a specific tab view.

Now, let's go take a look at the *pages* directory. Inside this directory, we will find four additional directories: *about*, *contact*, *home*, and *tabs*. Open the *home* directory, and within it are the HTML, SCSS, and TS files that define our home tab.

The SCSS file is just a placeholder, with no actual content inside. The HTML file has a bit more content inside.

First, the HTML defines an <ion-navbar> and <ion-title> component:

```
<ion-header>
  <ion-navbar>
    <ion-title>Home</ion-title>
  </ion-navbar>
</ion-header>
```

Next, the code defines the `<ion-content>` tag. The component also sets the `padding` directive within the `<ion-content>` tag:

```
<ion-content padding>
```

The rest of the HTML is just plain-vanilla HTML.

Now, let's take a look at the component's TypeScript file. This file is about as light-weight as possible for an Ionic Page:

```
import { Component } from '@angular/core';
import { NavController } from 'ionic-angular';

@Component({
  selector: 'page-home',
  templateUrl: 'home.html'
})
export class HomePage {

  constructor(public navCtrl: NavController) {

  }
}
```

Our `Component` module is imported into our code from the Angular core. Next, our `NavController` is imported from the ionic-angular library. This component is used whenever we need to navigate to another screen.

In our `Component` decorator, we set our templateURL to the HTML file and the selector to page-home.

The last bit of code is just setting the `HomePage` class to be exported and has the nav-Controller pass into the constructor.

The other two pages are almost identical to this `Page` component. Each exporting out a component respectively named `AboutPage` and `ContactPage`.

Let's look at the tabs themselves. In the *tabs* directory, we see that it contains just a *tabs.html* file and a *tabs.ts* file. Let's look at the HTML file first:

```
<ion-tabs>
  <ion-tab [root]="tab1Root" tabTitle="Home" tabIcon="home">↵
  </ion-tab>
  <ion-tab [root]="tab2Root" tabTitle="About" tabIcon="information-circle">↵
  </ion-tab>
  <ion-tab [root]="tab3Root" tabTitle="Contact" tabIcon="contacts">↵
```

```
    </ion-tab>
  </ion-tabs>
```

Like Ionic 1, Ionic 2 also has an <ion-tabs> and <ion-tab> components. The <ion-tabs> component is just a wrapper component for each of its children, the actual tabs themselves. The <ion-tab> component has a more few attributes that we need to change. Let's start with the two easier ones: tabTitle and tabIcon. These two attributes set the text label of the tab and the icon that will be displayed. The icon names are from the IonIcon library.

You do not need to set both the title and the icon on tab component. Depending on how you want yours to look, only include what you want.

Also, depending on the platform you are running your app on, the tab style and position will automatically adapt (see Figure 8-3).

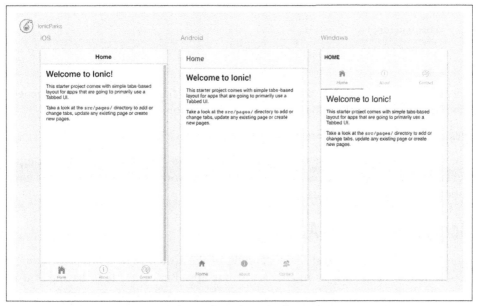

Figure 8-3. Tabs component rendering based on platform type

If you want to force a specific tab placement, there are two options—either directly on the component itself with:

```
<ion-tabs tabsPlacement="top">
```

or globally through the app config options. This is done in the *app.module.ts* file:

```
IonicModule.forRoot(MyApp, {tabsPlacement: 'top'} )
```

For a full list of configuration options, check out the Ionic Framework documentation (*http://ionicframework.com/docs/v2/api/config/Config/*).

The last item to look at in the <ion-tab> is the [root] binding that defines what component should act as that tab's root:

```
import { Component } from '@angular/core';
import { HomePage } from '../home/home';
import { AboutPage } from '../about/about';
import { ContactPage } from '../contact/contact';

@Component({
  templateUrl: 'tabs.html'
})
export class TabsPage {
  // this tells the tabs component which Pages
  // should be each tab's root Page
  tab1Root: any = HomePage;
  tab2Root: any = AboutPage;
  tab3Root: any = ContactPage;

  constructor() {

  }
}
```

We have our now familiar import statements. The first loads the base Component module, and the next three load each of the pages for our tabs.

Next, in our Component decorator, we set the templateUrl to the *tabs.html* file.

The class definition is where we assign each of the tabs to its corresponding components. That is all we need to establish our tabs framework. Ionic will manage the navigation state for each tab for us.

Bootstrapping Our App

Now that we have a general understanding of the structure of a tab-based Ionic 2 application, we can start to modify it for our app. But rather than having you go through all the files and folders and rename them to something meaningful, we are going to take a shortcut. I have already made the initial changes to the template files. In addition, I also included a datafile with the national park data and various images for use in the app.

First, go ahead and delete the *IonicPark* directory that the CLI generated. Now we will be scaffolding our app from a template from my GitHub repo:

```
$ ionic start Ionic2Parks https://github.com/chrisgriffith/Ionic2Parks --v2
```

Once this process is complete, again remember to change your working directory:

```
$ cd IonicPark
```

And if you are targeting Android, don't forget to add that platform:

```
$ ionic platform add android
```

Loading Data via the HTTP Service

Before we start building the app in earnest, let's create a provider to load our local JSON data into our app. This way, we will have actual data to work with as we build out our app.

In the *app* directory, create a new directory named *providers*; and within that directory, create a new file named *park-data.ts*.

As you can expect, using the HTTP service in Angular 2 is slightly different from Angular 1. The main difference is that Angular 2's HTTP service returns Observables through RxJS (*https://github.com/Reactive-Extensions/RxJS*), whereas $http in Angular 1 returns Promises.

Observables give us expanded flexibility when it comes to handling the responses coming from the HTTP requests. As an example, we could leverage an RxJS operator like retry so that failed HTTP requests are automatically re-sent. This can be very useful if our app has poor, weak, or intermittent network coverage. Since our data is being loaded locally, we don't need to worry about that issue.

Returning to our *park-data.ts* file, we will inject three directives into it:

```
import { Injectable } from '@angular/core';
import { Http } from '@angular/http';
import 'rxjs/add/operator/map';
```

Next, we use the @Injectable() decorator. The Angular 2 documentation reminds us to remember to include the parentheses after the @Injectable; otherwise, your app will fail to compile.

We are going to define ParkData as the provider's class. Now add a variable named data, and define its type to any and set it to be null. In the constructor, we will pass in the Http directive that we imported and classify it as a public variable. The class's actual constructor is currently empty:

```
@Injectable()
export class ParkData {
  data: any = null;

  constructor(public http: Http) {}

}
```

Within the class definition, we will create a new method named load. This method will do the actual loading of our JSON data. In fact, we will add in some checks to make sure we only load this data once throughout the lifespan of our app. Here is the complete method:

```
load() {
  if (this.data) {
    return Promise.resolve(this.data);
  }

  return new Promise(resolve => {
    this.http.get('assets/data/data.json')
      .map(res => res.json())
      .subscribe(data => {
        this.data = data;
        resolve(this.data);
      });
  });
}
```

Since we are hardcoding the file's location that we are loading, our method is not taking in a source location—hence, load().

The first thing this method does is check if the JSON data had been loaded and saved into the data variable. If it has, then we return a Promise that resolves to this saved data. We have to resolve our data to a Promise since that is the same return type that the actual loading portion uses in *park-list.ts*. We will look at working with Observables in another chapter.

Let's look at that block of code in detail. If the data has not been loaded, we return a basic Promise object. We set it to resolve after calling the HTTP service and using the get method from our JSON data that is at *assets/data/data.json*. As with all Promises, we need to define its subscription. Again using the fat arrow function, =>, the result is stored in a variable named res. We will take the string and use Angular's built-in JSON converter to parse it into an actual object. Finally, we will resolve our Promise with the actual data.

At this point, we only have written the provider. Now, we need to actually use it in our app. Open *app.component.ts*, and add import { ParkData } from '../provid ers/park-data'; with the rest of the import statements. This will load the provider and assign it to ParkData.

Next, we need to add an array of providers in the @Component declaration:

```
@Component({
  templateUrl: 'app.html',
  providers: [ ParkData ]
})
```

Let's now modify the constructor to load our data. We will pass in the reference to the ParkData provider into the constructor. After the platform.ready code block, we will call the parkData.load() method. This will trigger the provider to load our data-file:

```
    constructor(platform: Platform, statusBar: StatusBar, splashScreen: SplashScreen,
            public parkData: ParkData) {
    platform.ready().then(() => {
        // Okay, so the platform is ready and our plugins are available.
        // Here you can do any higher level native things you might need.
        statusBar.styleDefault();
        splashScreen.hide();
    });
    parkData.load();
}
```

If you want to do a quick test to see if the data is being loaded, wrap the park
Data.load() in a console.log(). The __zone_symbol__value of the ZoneAwarePro
mise will contain an array of the 59 objects that are created.

What Is a Zone?

A zone is a mechanism for intercepting and keeping track of asynchronous work. Since our data is being loaded in an asynchronous
fashion, we need to use zones to keep track of the original context
that we made our request in.

Here is a formated sample of what the each of the park's object data looks like:

```
createDate: "October 1, 1890"
data: "Yosemite has towering cliffs, waterfalls, and sequoias in a diverse↵
      area of geology and hydrology. Half Dome and El Capitan rise from the↵
      central glacier-formed Yosemite Valley, as does Yosemite Falls, North↵
      America's tallest waterfall. Three Giant Sequoia groves and vast ↵
      wilderness are home to diverse wildlife."
distance: 0
id: 57
image: "yosemite.jpg"
lat: 37.83
long: -119.5
name: "Yosemite"
state: "California"
```

Display our Data

Now that the data has been read into the app and is available via our service provider,
let's turn our attention to actually displaying our 59 national parks in a list.

First, we need to add a method on our ParkData service provider to actually return
the data that we have loaded. After the load method, add the following method:

```
getParks() {
    return this.load().then(data => {
        return data;
```

```
    });
  }
```

Two things to note about this method. First, it calls the load method. This is a safety check to ensure that the data is there. If for some reason it is not, it will load it for us. Since our provider is using Promises, constructing a system that can be chained together is quite easy. Second, since this system is Promise based, we have to handle everything in a .then syntax. This is something that you might have to remember to do as you migrate from Angular 1 to Angular 2.

Switching to *park-list.html*, we add the following after the <ion-content> tag:

```
<ion-list>
  <ion-item *ngFor="let park of parks" ↵
            (click)="goParkDetails(park)" detail-push>
    <ion-thumbnail item-left>
      <img src="assets/img/thumbs/{{park.image}}">
    </ion-thumbnail>
    <h2>{{park.name}}</h2>
    <p>{{park.state}}</p>
  </ion-item>
</ion-list>
```

If you recall from the Ionic2Do app, we will define an <ion-list> component, then define the <ion-item> that will be auto-generated for us. The repeated items are being supplied by an array named parks, which we will define shortly. Each element of this array is put into a local variable named park. A click handler is also added to the <ion-item>; it will call a function named goParkDetails and will pass in the park variable as its parameter.

If our app is running in iOS mode, disclosure arrows will automatically be added. On Android and Windows, this icon is not added to the list item. If we want to show the right arrow icon that does not display it by default, we can include the detail-push attribute. Conversely, if we don't want to show the right arrow icon, we can use the detail-none attribute. We will still need to enable this visual state in the *variables.scss* file by adding:

```
$item-md-detail-push-show: true;
```

after we define our $colors variable.

Returning back to the *park-list.html* file, within the <ion-item>, we will insert an <ion-thumbnail> component and set its position in the row by using item-left. The image tag is fairly straight forward. If you used the template for the project, it should have included an *img* directory that also contained a *thumbs* directory. That directory will hold thumbnails for each of our parks. By using Angular's data binding, we can dynamically set the src for each thumbnail with src="assets/img/thumbs/

{{park.image}}". Next, the park name and state are shown with <h2> and <p> tags, respectively, and are also data bound to the park object.

One last thing to do is to remove the padding attribute on the <ion-content> as well. This will enable the list to be the full width of the viewport. With the HTML template updated, we can now focus on the component's code.

Extending parklist.ts

The first thing that we need to do is to inject our service provider into the component with:

```
import { ParkData } from '../../providers/park-data';
```

Initially, the component's class is completely empty. We will replace it with the following code:

```
export class ParkListPage {
  parks: Array<Object> = []

  constructor(public navCtrl: NavController, public parkData: ParkData) {
    parkData.getParks().then(theResult => {
      this.parks = theResult;
    })
  }

  goParkDetails(theParkData) {
    console.log(theParkData);
  }
}
```

Let's define the parks variable that we referenced in our HTML template:

```
parks: Array<Object> = [];
```

Within the parameters of the constructor for the class, we will define a public variable parkData of type ParkData.

Next, we will call the getParks method on the parkData. In the past, we might have written something like this to get our park data:

```
parks = parkData.getParks();
```

But since we are leveraging the power of Promises, we need to actually write our request for this data as such:

```
parkData.getParks().then(theResult => {
    this.parks = theResult;
    }
)
```

That wraps up the changes to the constructor itself. The last bit of code that was added was a placeholder function for the click event from the `<ion-item>`. The method accepts the park data object as a parameter, and simply writes that data to the console. We will focus on this function shortly, but let's view our work so far by using `$ ionic serve` (see Figure 8-4).

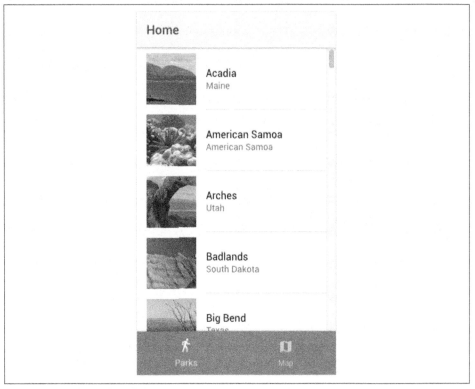

Figure 8-4. National parks app

Once the app has been regenerated, we should see a scrolling list of national parks in a browser, each with a thumbnail, title, and state listed. If you click on an item, the park data will be written out to the JavaScript console. Now that we have this initial screen working, we can turn our attention to creating the details page for that park.

Generating New Pages

With Ionic 2, adding new pages into our app is now a bit more complex. Thankfully, there is a page-generator function available in the CLI. Since we need to generate a park details page, our command will be:

```
$ ionic g page parkDetails
```

The CLI will take our camelCase name and convert it into a kebab-case version. The generator will automatically append Page to the class name for us. So if you open the *park-details.ts* file, you will see this class name:

```
export class ParkDetailsPage { ...
```

We also need to include a reference to the new component in the *app.module.ts* file:

```
import { ParkDetailsPage } from '../pages/park-details/park-details';
```

Then add this module to both the declarations and entryComponents arrays.

Ionic Generators

We also use the Ionic CLI generator to create providers by replacing the page flag with the provider flag. In fact, the provider we wrote earlier in the chapter could have been generated in that fashion.

Now, let's build upon the code in the *park-list.ts* file to enable the navigation to our newly generated page. We need to import some additional modules from the Ionic core. Our first import will become:

```
import { NavController, NavParams } from 'ionic-angular';
```

Next, we will need to import the reference to the page that we are going to navigate to:

```
import { ParkDetailsPage } from '../park-details/park-details';
```

With these modules injected into our component, the goParkDetails function will now navigate to the park details page and pass along the park information:

```
goParkDetails(theParkData) {
    this.navCtrl.push(ParkDetailsPage, { parkData: theParkData });
}
```

Understanding the Ionic 2 Navigation model

Back in Ionic 1, the AngularJS UI-Router was used to navigate between pages. For many apps, this navigation system works fairly well. But if your application has a complex navigation model, using it would become problematic. For example, if we were creating our Ionic Parks app in Ionic 1, we would have to have two distinct URLs for a Parks Details page if we want access it via both a park list screen and a map list screen. These types of issues forced the Ionic team to rebuild their entire navigation model.

The current navigation model is based on a push/pop system. Each new view (or page) is pushed onto a navigation stack, with each view stacking atop the previous one. When the user navigates back through the stack, the current view is removed (popped) from the stack (see Figure 8-5).

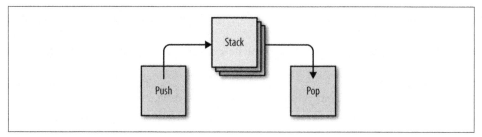

Figure 8-5. Ionic 2 navigation model

This new model makes the navigation model much simpler to work with.

Passing Data Between Pages

In our goParkDetails function, it received the parkData for the clicked list item. By using the NavParams module, we can pass this data to the constructor of the new page.

We need to refactor the *park-details.ts* file to support the incoming data. With generated Ionic pages, the NavParams module from ionic-angular is already included. Next, in the class definition, we need to add a parkInfo variable that is typed to Object.

In this constructor, the navigation parameters are passed in and stored in the variable navParams:

```
import { Component } from '@angular/core';
import { NavController, NavParams } from 'ionic-angular';

@Component({
  selector: 'page-park-details',
  templateUrl: 'park-details.html'
})
export class ParkDetailsPage {
  parkInfo: Object;
  constructor(public navCtrl: NavController, public navParams: NavParams) {
    this.parkInfo = navParams.data.parkData;
    console.log(this.parkInfo);
  }
}
```

For now, let's just write to the console the parkData that has been piggybacked on this parameter. Our selected park's data object is saved on the data method of the navParams. Saving our files and running $ ionic serve, clicking any item should now change our view and write to the console our data.

You will notice that the Ionic Framework handled the screen-to-screen animation, as well as automatically added a back button in our header to enable the user to navigate back through the navigation stack.

Updating the Park Details Page

Since we can now navigate to the park details page, let's turn our attention to taking this dynamic data and displaying it. Figure 8-6 shows what our initial Park Details screen will look like.

Figure 8-6. The national park details screen

The generated HTML page has some basic tags included, but we are going to replace most it. First, let's remove the help comment from the top of the page. For the page title, we will replace it with `{{parkInfo.name}}`:

```
<ion-header>
  <ion-navbar color="primary">
    <ion-title>{{parkInfo.name}}</ion-title>
  </ion-navbar>
</ion-header>
```

```
<ion-content>
    <img src="assets/img/headers/{{parkInfo.image}}">
    <h1 padding>{{parkInfo.name}}</h1>
    <ion-card>
        <ion-card-header>
            Park Details
        </ion-card-header>
        <ion-card-content>
            {{parkInfo.data}}
        </ion-card-content>
    </ion-card>
</ion-content>
```

One new component we are using on this screen is the `<ion-card>`. As the documentation states, "Cards are a great way to display important pieces of content, and are quickly emerging as a core design pattern for apps." Ionic's card component is a flexible container that supports headers, footers, and a wide range of other components within the card content itself.

With a basic park details screen in place, go ahead and preview it with `$ ionic serve`.

Add a Google Map

As you might expect, an app about the national parks would require them each to be shown on a map of some kind. Unfortunately, there is not an official Google Maps Angular 2 module. There are some third-party efforts, but let's work instead with the library directly. To do this we will need to include the library in our *index.html* file. Since the terms of use for the Google Maps SDK forbids the storing of the tiles in an offline fashion, we can reference the remotely hosted version:

```
<!-- Google Maps -->
<script src="http://maps.google.com/maps/api/js"></script>

<!-- cordova.js required for cordova apps -->
<script src="cordova.js"></script>

<!-- The polyfills js is generated during the build process -->
<script src="build/polyfills.js"></script>

<!-- The bundle js is generated during the build process -->
<script src="build/main.js"></script>
```

We can ignore the need for an API key while we are developing our application, but an API key is required for production. You can obtain an API key at the Google Developers page (*https://developers.google.com/maps/signup*). When you get your API key, change the script `src` to include it in the query string.

Adding Additional Typings

Since we are adding in a third-party code library to be used in our app, wouldn't it be nice to have code hinting support and strong typing for that library? We can do this by extending our TypeScript definitions. The command to do this is:

```
$ npm install @types/google-maps --save-dev --save-exact
```

Adding Our Content Security Policy

A Content Security Policy (CSP) is an added layer of security designed to reduce certain types of malicious attacks, including cross-site scripting (XSS). Remember, our hybrid apps are still bound by the same rules that web apps have. As such, we also need to safeguard our applications in a similar manner.

In our *index.html* file, we need to include a CSP:

```
<meta http-equiv="Content-Security-Policy" content="default-src * gap://ready; ↵
img-src * 'self' data:; font-src * 'self' data:; script-src 'self'↵
'unsafe-inline' 'unsafe-eval' *; style-src 'self' 'unsafe-inline'↵
*">
```

Since Google Maps transfers its map tiles via the data URI method, our CSP needs to allow for this type of communication. In addition, we will need to add support of `font-src` as well as for the Ionicons to work properly. This tag should be placed within the <head> tag.

Adjust the CSS to support the Google Map

With our library able to be loaded and related data, let's turn our attention to the map page itself. In *park-map.html*, we need to add a container for the map to be rendered in:

```
<ion-content>
  <div id="map_canvas"></div>
</ion-content>
```

We need to give it either a CSS `id` or `class` in order to apply some CSS styling. Since the tiles are dynamically loaded, our `div` has no width or height when it is first rendered. Even as the map tiles are loaded, the width and height of the container are not updated. To solve this, we need to define this `div`'s width and height. In the *park-map.scss* file, add the following:

```
#map_canvas {
    width: 100%;
    height: 100%;
}
```

This will give the container an initial value, and our map will be viewable.

Rendering the Google Map

We are going to work on this code in three sections. The first will get the Google Map displaying, the second will be to add markers for each of the national parks, and the final section will make clicking on the marker navigate to the Park Details page. Switch to the *park-map.ts* file.

We will need to add the `Platform` module to the `import` statement `from ionic-angular`:

```
import { Platform, NavController } from 'ionic-angular';
```

We will use the `Platform` module to make sure everything is ready before setting up the Google map.

Within the class definition, we will define the `map` variable as a Google Map. This variable will hold our reference to the Google map:

```
export class ParkMapPage {
    map: google.maps.Map;
```

Next, we expand the constructor:

```
constructor( public nav: NavController, public platform: Platform) {
  this.map = null;
  this.platform.ready().then(() => {
    this.initializeMap();
  });
}
```

We make sure that we have reference to `Platform` module, then set up a Promise on the platform ready method. Once the platform ready event has fired, we then call our `initializeMap` function, using the fat arrow syntax:

```
initializeMap() {
  let minZoomLevel = 3;

  this.map = new google.maps.Map(document.getElementById('map_canvas'), {
    zoom: minZoomLevel,
    center: new google.maps.LatLng(39.833, -98.583),
    mapTypeControl: false,
    streetViewControl: false,
    mapTypeId: google.maps.MapTypeId.ROADMAP
  });
}
```

This function will create the new map and assign it to the `div` with the id of "map_can vas". We also define some of the various map parameters. These parameters include the zoom level, the center map (in our case, the center of the continental US), the various map controls, and finally the style of the map. The last object method is a custom method where we will store the park information that we will need later in this chapter.

If we run $ ionic serve, then we should see a map being rendered in the Map tab, as seen in Figure 8-7.

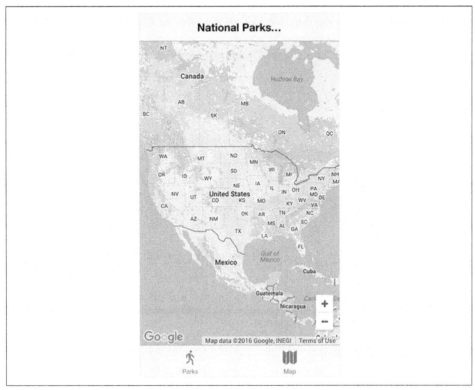

Figure 8-7. Google map within our Ionic app

Add Map Markers

Now that we have a Google map displaying in our mobile app, we can turn to the next task: adding the markers for each national park. The first thing we need to do is inject the ParkData service into our component:

```
import { ParkData } from '../../providers/park-data';
```

Next, we will need to add an array that will hold our park data, as well as ensure the parkData is properly available to the class:

```
export class ParkMapPage {
  parks: Array<Park> = [];
  map: google.maps.Map;
```

```
constructor(
    public nav: NavController,
    public platform: Platform,
    public parkData: ParkData
    ) {
```

Although we could simply type our `parks` array to any, let's properly type to our park's data structure. To do this, we will need to define the interface. Create a new directory named *interfaces* within the *app* directory. Within that new directory, create a new file named *park.ts*. This file will hold our simple definition for our Park interface. The code for this is:

```
export interface Park {
    id: number;
    name: string;
    createDate: string;
    lat: number;
    long: number;
    distance: number;
    image: string;
    state: string;
    data: string;
}
```

This interface will tell the compiler that `Park` data type will have these elements and their associated data types.

Back in the *park-map.ts* file, we will need to import this interface file:

```
import { Park } from '../../interfaces/park';
```

That should resolve any warnings in your editor about the `Park` data type.

Go ahead and also import this interface in the *park-list.ts* file and change this variable:

```
parks: Array<Object> = [];
```

to:

```
parks: Array<Park> = [];
```

Within the `initializeMap` function, we will need to add the code to actually display our markers.

But rather than use the standard Google marker image, let's use a marker that looks like the National Parks Service arrowhead logo:

```
let image = 'assets/img/nps_arrowhead.png';
```

Then we will get the park data from the `parkData` service. Once this Promise is answered, the result will be stored in the `parks` array:

```
this.parkData.getParks().then(theResult => {
    this.parks = theResult;
```

```
    for (let thePark of this.parks) {
      let parkPos:google.maps.LatLng = ↵
          new google.maps.LatLng (thePark.lat, thePark.long);
      let parkMarker:google.maps.Marker = new google.maps.Marker();
      parkMarker.setPosition(parkPos);
      parkMarker.setMap( this.map);
      parkMarker.setIcon(image);
    }
})
```

Our code will loop through this array and generate our markers. Save this file, and if `ionic serve` is still running, the app will reload. Select the Map tab, and you now see icons on our map for each of the national parks. Right now, these markers are not interactive. Let's add that capability.

Making the Markers Clickable

When a user clicks or taps a marker on the map, we want to navigate them to the Park Details page for that markers. To do this we need to inject some of the Navigation modules from Ionic, as well as the actual `ParkDetailsPage` module. Our new import block will now look like this:

```
import { Component } from '@angular/core';
import { Platform, NavController, NavParams } from 'ionic-angular';
import { Park } from '../../interfaces/park';
import { ParkData } from '../../providers/park-data';
import { ParkDetailsPage } from '../park-details/park-details';
```

Within the `for` loop that adds each marker, we will need to add an event listener that will respond to our click, and then navigate to the `ParkDetailsPage` and pass along the marker's park data. Unfortunately, the standard Google Map Marker has none of that information. To solve this, we are going to create a custom Map Marker that we can store our park information.

Create a new file, *custom-marker.ts*, within our *park-map* directory. This new class will extend the base `google.maps.Marker` to have one additional value, our `parkData`. We first need to import the Park interface. Then we will export our new class, `Custom MapMarker`, which is extended from `google.maps.Marker`. Next, we define our `park Data` variable and assign the type of `Park`. Within the class's constructor, we will pass in the actual park data. The critical bit of code is the `super()`. This will tell the class we extended `from` to also initialize:

```
import {Park} from '../../interfaces/park';

export class CustomMapMarker extends google.maps.Marker{
  parkData:Park
  constructor( theParkData:Park
  ){
```

```
    super();
    this.parkData = theParkData;
  }
}
```

Save this file, and return back to *park-map.ts*. If you guessed that we need to import this new class, you would be correct:

```
import { CustomMapMarker } from './custom-marker';
```

Now, our `parkMarker` can use our `CustomMapMaker` class in place of the `google.maps.Marker`. So this line of code:

```
let parkMarker:google.maps.Marker = new google.maps.Marker();
```

becomes this:

```
let parkMarker:google.maps.Marker = new CustomMapMarker(thePark);
```

 We are passing the park's data into the instance, thus saving our park data within each marker.

Now we can assign our event listener for each marker. But how do we reference the actual `parkData` stored within each marker so that we can include it as a `navParam`?

We are going to take a shortcut with this block of code. Since we did not define an interface for our `CustomMapMarker`, our compiler does not know about our additional property. But, we can use the any data type to sidestep this issue. So, if we simply create a local variable, `selectedMarker`, with the type of any and assign the `parkMarker` to it, we will be able to reference the `parkData`. Here is the completed fragment:

```
google.maps.event.addListener(parkMarker, 'click', () => {
  let selectedMarker:any = parkMarker;

  this.navCtrl.push(ParkDetailsPage, {
    parkData: selectedMarker.parkData
  });
});
```

The navigation code should look very familiar from the Park List page. Here is the complete `initializeMap` function:

```
initializeMap() {
  let minZoomLevel:number = 3;

  this.map = new google.maps.Map(document.getElementById('map_canvas'), {
    zoom: minZoomLevel,
    center: new google.maps.LatLng(39.833, -98.583),
    mapTypeControl: false,
```

```
      streetViewControl: false,
      mapTypeId: google.maps.MapTypeId.ROADMAP
    });

    let image:string = 'img/nps_arrowhead.png';

    this.parkData.getParks().then(theResult => {
      this.parks = theResult;

      for (let thePark of this.parks) {
        let parkPos:google.maps.LatLng =↵
            new google.maps.LatLng (thePark.lat, thePark.long);
        let parkMarker:google.maps.Marker = new CustomMapMarker(thePark);
        parkMarker.setPosition(parkPos);
        parkMarker.setMap( this.map);
        parkMarker.setIcon(image);

        google.maps.event.addListener(parkMarker, 'click', () => {
          let selectedMarker:any = parkMarker;

          this.navCtrl.push(ParkDetailsPage, {
            parkData: selectedMarker.parkData
          });
        });
      }
    })
  }
```

Save the file, and we should now be able to click a marker and see the Park Details page (Figure 8-8).

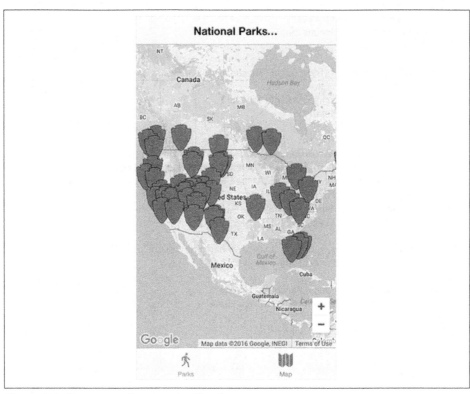

Figure 8-8. Custom markers on our Google map

Adding Search

Let's extend our application a bit further by adding a search bar for the Park List. Ionic has an `<ion-searchbar>` as part of the component library. The search bar component will let the user type in the name of a national park and the list of parks will automatically update (Figure 8-9).

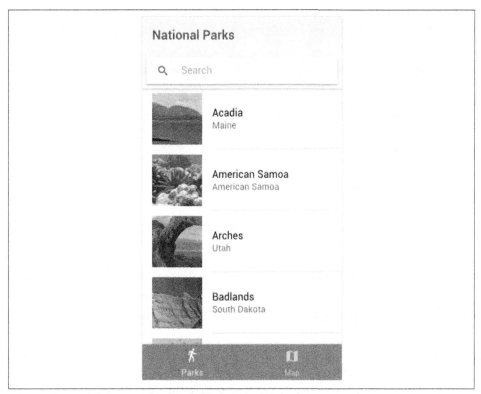

Figure 8-9. Search bar component added to our Ionic app

Since we want the search bar to always be available, we need it to be fixed to the top of the screen. We can use the `<ion-toolbar>` component to handle this. This component just needs to be after the `<ion-navbar>`.

We'll need to define a model to our `<ion-searchbar>` component and bind it to the query string. Also, we need to add a function to handle user input:

```
<ion-toolbar>
  <ion-searchbar [(ngModel)]="searchQuery" (ionInput)="getParks($event)" ↵
                 (ionClear)="resetList($event)">↵
  </ion-searchbar>
</ion-toolbar>
```

If you are wondering what the `[( )]` is doing around `ngModel`, this is a new syntax for Angular's two-way data binding. The square brackets tell Angular that this is a getter, while the parentheses tell Angular that this is a setter. Putting the two together, you have two-way data binding.

Now in the *park-list.ts* file, let's define this variable within our class:

```
export class ParkListPage {
  parks: Array<Park> = []
  searchQuery: string = '';
```

Also in the *park-list.ts* file, we need to add our getParks function:

```
getParks(event) {
  // Reset items back to all of the items
  this.parkData.getParks().then(theResult => {
    this.parks = theResult;
  })

  // set queryString to the value of the searchbar
  let queryString = event.target.value;

  if (queryString !== undefined) {
    // if the value is an empty string don't filter the items
    if (queryString.trim() == '') {
      return;
    }

    this.parkData.getFilteredParks(queryString).then(theResult => {
      this.parks = theResult;
    })
  }
}
```

The first part of the getParks function ensures that we will be using the original list of parks. If you have coded any filtering functions in the past, you are probably aware that you need to make sure that you are working from an unfiltered list.

Next, we get the query string from the search bar, then check that it is neither undefined nor empty.

Finally, we will call a new method on the parkData provider (*park-data.ts*) to do the actual filtering based on the search string, and set the results to the parks:

```
getFilteredParks(queryString) {
  return this.load().then(Parks => {
    let theFilteredParks: any = [];

    for (let thePark of Parks) {
      if (thePark.name.toLowerCase().indexOf(queryString.toLowerCase()) > -1) {
        theFilteredParks.push(thePark);
      }
    }

    return theFilteredParks;
  });
}
```

We first make sure we have the master park data again, then we define a new empty array that will push any matching parks onto it. The code then loops through each park and compares the park's name against the query string. This code does take an additional step, forcing both the park name and query string to lowercase before testing if it can find a match. If a match is found, it is pushed to theFilteredParks array. Once all the parks have been examined, this array is returned and our displayed list automatically updated.

Our search is still not quite functionally complete. The clear button is not working. Although we bound the ionClear event to a resetList function, we haven't written it yet. The function is actually quite simple; we just need to reset our parks array back to the full list:

```
resetList(event) {
  // Reset items back to all of the items
  this.parkData.getParks().then(theResult => {
    this.parks = theResult;
  })
}
```

With that, we should have a fully functioning search bar in our app.

Theming Our Application

Now that we have a functioning app, it certainly could use a touch of color to brighten it up from the default look. There is nothing special about styling an Ionic-based application. The same techniques used in styling a web app or web page apply here.

Ionic uses Sass or Syntactically Awesome Style Sheets as the CSS pre-processor solution. If you have not used a CSS pre-processor before, one of the main reasons to do so is it gives you the ability to abstract your CSS in reusable parts. For example, you can define a variable that is the app's primary color, and let the preprocessor apply it throughout the CSS. So, if you need to change it for some reason, you change it in one place.

Ionic breaks down its Sass files into two files; *src/app/app.scss* for any global app specific styling, and *src/theme/variables.scss* for the predefined theme colors.

The first styling change to make is to assign a forest green color to the header. There are several ways accomplish this: we could directly style each specific component, or modify one of the prebuilt themes. For these components, let's choose the latter solution.

In *variables.scss* file, replace the hex color associated with the primary color with #5a712d. Since we did not assign a theme to either the header or the tabs components, we need to do so. In each of the three pages, update the <ion-navbar> to <ion-navbar color="primary">.

In `tabs.html`, replace `<ion-tabs>` with `<ion-tabs color="primary">`. Saving all these files, run `$ ionic serve`. The headers and tabs should now have a forest green background.

Now let's turn our attention to styling the various content elements in the app. Let's change the general `<ion-content>` background color to a light tan. In the *app.scss* file, add the following CSS:

```
ion-content {background-color: #f4efdd;}
ion-card-header {background-color: #cfcbbb; font-weight: bold;}
ion-card-content{margin-top: 1em;}
ion-item-divider.item {background-color: #ab903c; color: #fff;
    font-size: 1.8rem; font-weight: bold !important;}
.item {background-color: #f4efdd;}
.toolbar-background {background-color: #706d61;}
.searchbar-input-container {background-color: #fff;}
```

As you can see this CSS is a mix of styling the Ionic components directly, such as the `ion-content` and `ion-card-header`, but also setting specific CSS classes. By setting this in the *app.scss*, these will be applied throughout the app. If you needed to set the style of a specific page or component, then you would do that within the *.scss* file for that item. Let's do that now.

The park's name on the Park Details page is a bit too far down from the header photo, and we need to make sure our header image fills the entire width:

```
page-park-details {
  h1{margin-top: 0;}
  img{width: 100%;}
}
```

Now the `<h1>` tag only on the Park Details page will have its top margin set to zero, leaving any other `<h1>` tags we might use styled as they normally would be (see Figure 8-10).

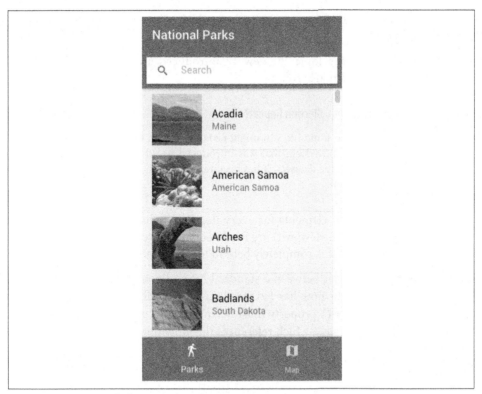

Figure 8-10. Our styled national parks app

The Ionic Framework actually exposes quite a few variables in their SCSS that you can override (*http://bit.ly/2luYIfZ*).

> If you are ever having trouble applying a style, remember this is all just CSS, and the web inspector in your browser can assist in finding either the target you need to address or uncover a cascading issue.

Virtual Scrolling

One of the greatest impacts on the performance of a hybrid application is the number of DOM elements on a given page. Usually this manifests as an issue when scrolling lists of content. Most users can spot a hybrid application by the poor scrolling performance. Knowing this issue, the team at Ionic focused its efforts on creating a scrolling experience that is as native as possible.

Our app only has 59 items, and each row is rather straightforward in the elements it contains. If we expanded our app to include all the national monuments, our list would exceed 400. At this value, we probably would start to see some stutter and jerkiness in the scrolling.

To address this issue, the Ionic Framework introduced a special set of directives, known collectively as Virtual Scrolling.

What About Collection Repeat?

If you used Ionic 1.x, you might be familiar with Collection Repeat. This was the system that was introduced to solve the problem of scrolling large datasets. It has been replaced with the Virtual Scrolling solution.

Instead of creating DOM elements for every item in the list, only a small subset of records (enough to fill the viewport) are rendered and reused as the user scrolls. The Virtual Scroller manages this completely behind the scenes for us.

There are a few differences between a standard list and one that uses Virtual Scrolling. First, the <ion-list> now has [virtualScroll] binding to our data. The data given to the virtualScroll property must be an array. Second, the <ion-item> now has a *virtualItem property, which references the individual item that will be passed into the template.

It is probably easier if you see the revised code for a park's list:

```
<ion-list [virtualScroll]="parks">
  <ion-item *virtualItem="let park" (click)="goParkDetails(park)" detail-push>
    <ion-thumbnail item-left>
      <img src="assets/img/thumbs/{{park.image}}">
    </ion-thumbnail>
    <h2>{{park.name}}</h2>
    <p>{{park.state}}</p>
  </ion-item>
</ion-list>
```

Other than replacing the *ngFor="let park of parks" with the two virtualScroll properties, the code remains the same. However, there is one more change we should make to improve our list's scrolling performance, and that is to replace the <img> tag with <ion-img>:

```
<ion-img src="assets/img/thumbs/{{park.image}}"></ion-img>
```

This tag is designed for use specifically with the Virtual Scrolling system. The <ion-img> tag manages HTTP requests and image rendering. Additionally, it includes a customizable placeholder element which shows before the image has finished loading. While scrolling through items quickly, <ion-img> knows not to make any image requests, and only loads the images that are viewable after scrolling.

Here are some additional performance tweaks that you might consider making to improve performance:

- Do not change the size of the image once it has loaded.
- Provide an approximate width and height so the virtual scroll can best calculate the cell height.
- Avoid changing the dataset, as it requires the entire virtual scroll to be reset, which is an expensive operation.

Custom List Headers

The Virtual Scrolling system also supports dynamic headers and footers. In this sample, our list will have a header inserted after every 20th record:

```
<ion-list [virtualScroll]="items" [headerFn]="customHeaderFn">

  <ion-item-divider *virtualHeader="let header">
    {{ header }}
  </ion-item-divider>

  <ion-item *virtualItem="let item">
    Item: {{ item }}
  </ion-item>

</ion-list>
```

and the supporting function would be:

```
customHeaderFn(record, recordIndex, records) {
  if (recordIndex % 20 === 0) {
    return 'Header ' + recordIndex;
  }
  return null;
}
```

When applied to our list of national parks, our <ion-list> becomes:

```
<ion-list [virtualScroll]="parks" [headerFn]="customHeaderFn">
  <ion-item-divider *virtualHeader="let header">
    {{ header }}
  </ion-item-divider>

  <ion-item *virtualItem="let park" (click)="goParkDetails(park)" detail-push>
    <ion-thumbnail item-left>
      <ion-img src="assets/img/thumbs/{{park.image}}"></ion-img>
    </ion-thumbnail>
    <h2>{{park.name}}</h2>
    <p>{{park.state}}</p>
    </ion-item>
</ion-list>
```

And in our *park-list.ts* file, we can add the following function to insert the first letter of the park's name into our custom header:

```
customHeaderFn(record, recordIndex, records) {
  if ( recordIndex > 0) {
    if ( record.name.charAt(0) !== records[recordIndex-1].name.charAt(0)) {
      return record.name.charAt(0);
    } else {
      return null;
    }
  } else {
    return record.name.charAt(0);
  }
}
```

One last piece will be to provide a little bit of styling on ion-item-divider. Make the change in the *park-list.scss* to:

```
page-park-list {
  ion-item-divider {
    background-color: #ad8e40;
    font-weight: bold;
  }
}
```

So, we now have an app that looks like Figure 8-11.

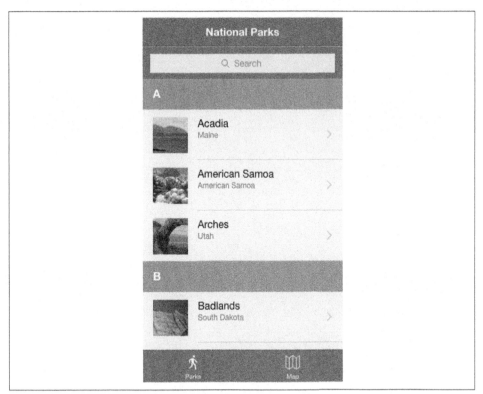

Figure 8-11. Virtual Scrolling with dynamic headers applied

Summary

With this app we have explored how to work with a tab-based design, used a data provider, integrated a Google map, and applied some basic theming. If you want to extend this app some, here are a couple of ideas that you can try.

1. Add a park specific map to the page details screen.

2. Look at adding a photo slide show to each park. Ionic has an `<ion-slides>` component that can do the trick.

3. If you want a real challenge, look at calculating the distance to each park. There is a distance property already in the *data.json* file. You can leverage the Geolocation plugin to find your current latitude and longitude, then use the Haversine formula to calculate the distance.

CHAPTER 9

Building a Weather Application

One of other prebuilt templates that the Ionic Framework provides is the side menu template. This design pattern has become increasingly prevalent over the past few years. Rather than having a fixed number of items in a tab bar (which typically remain on-screen using precious screen real estate), this user interface moves many of the navigation options onto a panel that is kept off-screen until the user taps a menu button of some kind. Often this button is either three horizontally stacked lines (aka the hamburger menu) or in some cases three vertical dots. Now, I am not going to get into the pros and cons of this user interface element. I would encourage you to spend a little time researching it on your own to see if it is right for your project. With that said, this is the design pattern we will use to build our Ionic weather application.

Getting Started

Like the two previous projects, we need to generate our initial app. We use another starter template from a GitHub repo. This base template is just the side menu template, with some additional elements in the assets folder:

```
$ ionic start Ionic2Weather https://github.com/chrisgriffith/Ionic2Weather --v2
```

Once this process is complete, again remember to change your working directory:

```
$ cd Ionic2Weather
```

And if you are targeting Android, don't forget to add that platform:

```
$ ionic platform add android
```

Let's take a look at the template in our browser with:

```
$ ionic serve
```

Figure 9-1 shows what you should see in your browser.

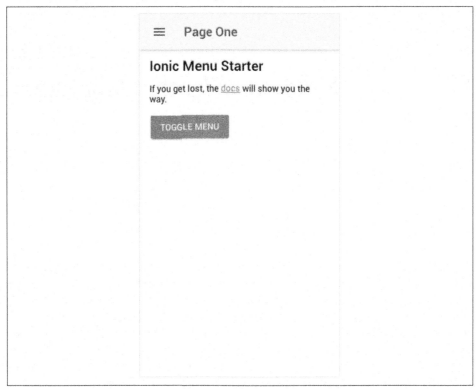

Figure 9-1. The starter side menu template

The template is fairly straightforward. The main screen demonstrates two methods to reveal the side menu: either by the menu icon in the navbar or by the button in the content section. Once you tap either item, the menu animates onto the screen, and the existing content is masked by a semi-transparent overlay. The exact animation will mirror the platform the app is running on. This animation can be overriden, of course.

The side menu itself contains two sections: its own navbar, here labeled Menu, and its own content, here showing a list of two items (Page One and Page Two). If you tap outside the side menu, Ionic will automatically dismiss the side menu for you. If you tap on either the Page One or Page Two, the main content of our app will update, and the side menu will be dismissed.

Exploring the Side Menu Template

The side menu template is a bit more complex than the other two templates, so let's take a long look at the base template before we build our Ionic weather app. There are no changes to the default *index.html* file, so there is no need to explore it. Instead, we will start with the *app.html* file. This file can be found in the *src/app* directory. This is our initial HTML that is rendered by our app. Unlike the other two templates, this template's app component references an external HTML template (*app.html*) instead of having the template written inline. As we'll see, since this template is a bit more complex than the blank or tab templates, it makes sense to have it as an external reference. Here is what the template looks like:

```
<ion-menu [content]="content">
  <ion-header>
    <ion-toolbar>
      <ion-title>Menu</ion-title>
    </ion-toolbar>
  </ion-header>

  <ion-content>
    <ion-list>
      <button menuClose ion-item *ngFor="let p of pages" (click)="openPage(p)">
        {{p.title}}
      </button>
    </ion-list>
  </ion-content>

</ion-menu>

<!-- Disable swipe-to-go-back because it's poor UX to combine STGB
with side menus -->
<ion-nav [root]="rootPage" #content swipeBackEnabled="false"></ion-nav>
```

There are quite a few changes from Ionic 1's side menu structure. Most notably, <ion-side-menus> and <ion-side-menu-content> tags have been removed and replaced with <ion-menu> and the new page reference system.

Let's look at the <ion-menu> tag in detail. This tag sets up the content that will be displayed within our side menu. But there is a critical attribute that is also set within this tag, the [content]="content". Here we are setting the content property of the ion-menu to the variable content and not a string. If you look at the last tag in the template you will see a reference to #content, which defines it as a local variable. Now our <ion-menu> can reference it properly and use it for its main content. We will come back to the rest of the attributes of <ion-nav> in a bit.

Next, our template defines the header of the side menu by using the <ion-toolbar> tag. This component is a generic bar that can be placed above or below the content, much like the <ion-navbar>, but without the navigation controls:

```
<ion-toolbar>
    <ion-title>Menu</ion-title>
</ion-toolbar>
```

Then, we define the side menu content in the <ion-content> tag:

```
<ion-content>
  <ion-list>
    <button menuClose ion-item *ngFor="let p of pages" (click)="openPage(p)">
      {{p.title}}
    </button>
  </ion-list>
</ion-content>
```

The template uses an `<ion-list>` to loop through the pages array and create a list of buttons that are labeled with the object's title property. It also sets up a click handler, `openPage` to respond to the user tapping on the button.

Now, let's return to the `<ion-nav>` tag and explore it in more detail:

```
<ion-nav [root]="rootPage" #content swipeBackEnabled="false"></ion-nav>
```

The root property is set to `rootPage`. This is defined in the *app.component.ts* file, and will be the property we will update when we need to change our main content. Now let's turn our attention to the *app.component.ts* file and how these elements are linked together in code.

Exploring the app.component.ts File

Just like the side menu's HTML template was a bit more complex, so is its *app.components.ts* file. First, we have several more import statements than before:

```
import { Component, ViewChild } from '@angular/core';
import { Nav, Platform } from 'ionic-angular';
import { StatusBar, Splashscreen } from 'ionic-native';

import { Page1 } from '../pages/page1/page1';
import { Page2 } from '../pages/page2/page2';
```

In addition to the `Component` module being imports, we are also importing the `View Child` component from `@angular/core`. Including this import enables our code to use the property decorator `@ViewChild` to define a reference to a child element. This is the underlying mechanism that allows us to properly reference our nav element.

The next two import statements should look fairly familiar to you. We need the `Nav` and `Platform` directives imported from Ionic and the reference to the StatusBar from Ionic Native.

The final two imports are the two sample content pages in the template. Since our *app.component.ts* handled the side menu navigation, it needs to have a reference to any screen it may navigate to.

Our `@Component` decorator should also look familiar. As pointed out earlier, it references an external template.

Next, we define our `rootPage` variable to be of data type `any`, and set it initially to the `Page1` component:

```
rootPage: any = Page1;
```

For the side menu's list of pages, that array is defined, as is the structure of its contents:

```
pages: Array<{title: string, component: any}>
```

Here is a great example of how TypeScript can provide some code safety by defining the element types.

The constructor then initializes the app (which for the moment handles a status bar call on iOS, once the platform is ready), and sets the `pages` array to our two sample pages.

Finally, we define the `openPages` function that is called from the side menu buttons:

```
openPage(page) {
    // Reset the content nav to have just this page
    // we wouldn't want the back button to show in this scenario
    this.nav.setRoot(page.component);
}
```

This function takes the page object that is passed into the function and then tells the nav controller to set its root property to the `page.component`. By setting the navigation root, we reset the navigation stack history. In doing so, we also prevent Ionic from automatically adding a back button.

Side Menu Options

You might have noticed we actually have not set any options for our side menu.

The menu can be placed either on the left (default) or the right. To change the placement of the side menu, set the side property to the position you want:

```
<ion-menu side="right" [content]="content">...</ion-menu>
```

The side menu supports three display types: `overlay`, `reveal`, and `push`. The Ionic Framework will use the correct style based on the currently running platform. The default type for both Material Design and Windows mode is `overlay`, and `reveal` is the default type for iOS mode.

If you want to change it directly on the `<ion-menu>` tag, use this:

```
<ion-menu type="overlay" [content]="content">...</ion-menu>
```

However, you can set the side menu type globally via the app `config` object. This is set in the *app.module.ts* file. The following code snippet sets the base style to `push`, and then sets the `menuType` style to `reveal` for `md` (Android) mode:

```
  imports: [
    IonicModule.forRoot(MyApp, { menuType: 'push',
    platforms: {
     md: {
       menuType: 'reveal',
     }
    }})
  ]
```

Displaying the Menu

To actually display our side menu, we can use the `menuToggle` directive anywhere in our template. Let's look at the *page1.html* file (*src/pages/page1*), and you will find the HTML block that defines the `<ion-navbar>`:

```
<ion-header>
  <ion-navbar>
    <button ion-button menuToggle>
      <ion-icon name="menu"></ion-icon>
    </button>
    <ion-title>Page One</ion-title>
  </ion-navbar>
</ion-header>
```

On the `<button>` element, you will see the `menuToggle` directive has been applied. This is all we need to do in order for Ionic to display our side menu. This does not define the visible element for our side menu button. That is done in this example by the `<ion-icon>` and setting the name to *menu*.

In fact, if you look further in the *page1.html* code, you will see this:

```
<button ion-button secondary menuToggle>Toggle Menu</button>
```

Here, the button element has the `menuToggle` directive applied to it, thus allowing it to open the side menu as well. Although the Ionic Framework handles a modest amount of work for us in opening and closing the side menu, there may be times when we need to directly close the side menu. We add this functionality by using the `menuClose` directive on our element:

```
<button ion-button menuClose="left">Close Side Menu</button>
```

That covers most of the basics of the side menu template. Let's get started building our actual application.

Converting the Template

Before we begin converting the template to our needs, let's generate our two pages that our app will use, as well as the data providers:

```
$ ionic g page weather
```

```
$ ionic g page locations
```

Next, let's add in our two providers. The first provider will eventually be the provider that will pull live weather data from darksky.net (formerly Forecast.io):

```
$ ionic g provider WeatherService
```

Once the command has finished generating the template provider, we need to create our second provider. This provider will be used to take a human-friendly location, like San Diego, and turn it into a corresponding latitude and longitude required by darksky.net. We will touch on both of these providers later in this chapter:

```
$ ionic g provider GeocodeService
```

Now, with our new base pages and providers in place, let's convert this template to use them. Open *app.module.ts* in your editor.

In the import section, we can remove the reference to Page1 and Page2 and add in the imports to our two newly created pages:

```
import { WeatherPage } from '../pages/weather/weather';
import { LocationsPage } from '../pages/locations/locations';
```

Also, update the declarations and entryComponents arrays to reflect these new pages.

After those imports, we can import our two providers:

```
import { WeatherService } from '../providers/weather-service';
import { GeocodeService } from '../providers/geocode-service';
```

In the providers array, we will need to add our two providers:

```
providers: [
  StatusBar,
  SplashScreen,
  Geolocation,
  { provide: ErrorHandler, useClass: IonicErrorHandler },
  WeatherService,
  GeocodeService
]
```

With those changes made, we can turn to *app.component.ts* and begin to update it. First, replace the two Page imports with our new pages:

```
import { WeatherPage } from '../pages/weather/weather';
import { LocationsPage } from '../pages/locations/locations';
```

Continuing further down in the file, we will see the line of code that defines the root Page variable for our application. We need to change this to reference our Weather Page instead of Page1:

```
rootPage: any = WeatherPage;
```

Our next bit of code to modify is the `pages` array. We are going to be extending this array quite a bit over the course of building our app, but for now, we will do just the basics.

Since this app is written in TypeScript, we need to be careful when modifying templates that we properly update any variable definitions. For example, the `pages` variable is defined to be an array that contains objects with a title property that is of type `string`, and component property that is of type `any`. Since we would like to display an icon next to each item in my side menu list, we will need to update the definition to:

```
pages: Array<{title: string, component: any, icon: string}>
```

Let's update the `pages` array to reference the proper component, as well as add an icon value and change the title. Here is the new array:

```
this.pages = [
  { title: 'Edit Locations', component: LocationsPage, icon: 'create' },
  { title: 'Current Location', component: WeatherPage, icon: 'pin' }
];
```

Later, we will extend this array to hold our saved locations and their latitudes and longitudes.

If you ran the app in its current form, you would only see the weather page and have no ability to access the side menu. Let's address that issue now and make a few other changes to the navbar.

Open *weather.html* in your editor.

First, we need to add in the side menu button within the `<ion-navbar>`:

```
<button ion-button menuToggle>
  <ion-icon name="menu"></ion-icon>
</button>
```

Next, change the `<ion-title>` to display `Current Location`. Once we have geolocation enabled, we will return to this tag later and have it display the actual location name:

```
<ion-title>Current Location</ion-title>
```

If you save the file now, you should see the menu icon on the left and have the ability to display our side menu. Let's update the header in the *locations.html* as well:

```
<ion-header>
  <ion-navbar>
    <button ion-button menuToggle>
      <ion-icon name="menu"></ion-icon>
    </button>
    <ion-title>Edit Locations</ion-title>
  </ion-navbar>
</ion-header>
```

Now, with that code added, this page will be able to display the side menu as well. Switch back to the *app.html* file and update the code to show our icons next to each list item. We just need to add a <ion-icon> tag and set its name to the icon property of the list element. We will also need to add some padding to the right of the icon so that the text is not directly next to the icon itself. The quickest way is to just add a space between the end tag </ion-icon> and the opening mustache tags of {{p.title}}:

```
<ion-list>
  <button menuClose ion-item *ngFor="let p of pages" (click)="openPage(p)">
    <ion-icon name="{{p.icon}}"></ion-icon> {{p.title}}
  </button>
</ion-list>
```

If we wanted better control over the spacing between the icon and the location name, we could have set it in our CSS.

Another minor tweak is to set the <ion-title> to:

```
<ion-title>Ionic Weather</ion-title>
```

instead of the default Menu.

Our final tweak is to add a reference to where we are getting the weather data from (because you actually read the terms and conditions, right?). After the <ion-list>, add this bit of markup:

```
<p><a href="https://darksky.net/poweredby/">Powered by Dark Sky</a></p>
```

Save this file, and our side menu should now show our icons and have the ability to navigate to our two pages.

Mocking Up Our Weather Provider

Our next step is to get some weather data that we can use in our application. We are going to approach this in two phases. We are going to first load in static weather data. This will allow us to do some initial screen layout. Then we will hook our application up into a live data source.

There is a static data file that you can use that is included in the *assets* directory. This file is a snapshot of some darksky.net weather data.

Now, let's update the weather provider code to have a method to get this data. Open the *weather-service.ts* file and replace it with this code:

```
import { Injectable } from '@angular/core';
import { Http } from '@angular/http';
import 'rxjs/add/operator/map';

@Injectable()
```

```
export class WeatherService {
  data: any = null;

  constructor(public http: Http) {
    console.log('Hello WeatherService Provider');
  }

  load() {
    if (this.data) {
      return Promise.resolve(this.data);
    }

    return new Promise(resolve => {
      this.http.get('assets/data/data.json')
        .map(res => res.json())
        .subscribe(data => {
          this.data = data;
          resolve(this.data);
        });
    });
  }
}
```

After the load method, add in this function:

```
getWeather() {
  return this.load().then(data => {
    return data;
  });
}
```

Although the method does call the load function, I like having it as a separate method. This gives us some flexibility later if our application requires it.

Now, we just need to have the app tell this provider to load the data. Back in the *app.component.ts* file, we will need to make a few changes to call our provider.

First, we need to import this provider into the component:

```
import { WeatherService } from '../providers/weather-service';
```

In the constructor, we need to pass in reference our WeatherData provider:

```
constructor(publice platform: Platform,
public weatherService: WeatherService) {...}
```

Now, within the initializeApp function we can call this service and load our weather data:

```
initializeApp() {
    this.platform.ready().then(() => {
      // Okay, so the platform is ready and our plugins are available.
      // Here you can do any higher level native things you might need.
      this.statusBar.styleDefault();
```

```
        this.splashScreen.hide();
    });
  }
```

With our data now available, let's work on actually displaying it.

Laying Out the Weather Data

Before we can display our mock weather data, we need to have access to it within the context of that page. Open the *weather.ts* file. The first thing we will need to do is import the `WeatherData` provider:

```
import { WeatherService } from '../../providers/weather-service';
```

Next, we need to add three variables to hold our weather data with the class definition. We will type these as `any`, so it will not generate any TypeScript errors:

```
theWeather: any = {};
currentData: any = {};
daily: any = {};
```

The reason there are `currentData` and `daily` variables is that the actual JSON data structure from darksky.net is a bit nested. So rather than having to traverse this in our template, we can define the `currentData` and `daily` variables as pointers.

Next, pass a reference to our WeatherService into our constructor:

```
constructor(public navCtrl: NavController, public navParams: NavParams,
public weatherService: WeatherService) { }
```

Now, within our constructor we can call the `getWeather` method on the `weatherData` provider:

```
this.weatherService.getWeather().then(theResult => {
  this.theWeather = theResult;
  this.currentData = this.theWeather.currently;
  this.daily = this.theWeather.daily;
});
```

With the data now loaded, let's turn our attention to the HTML template. Open *weather.html* again so we can begin updating the template to show our weather data.

For the layout of our data, we are going to use the Ionic Grid component. From the Ionic documentation:

> Ionic's grid system is based on flexbox, a CSS feature supported by all devices that Ionic supports. The grid is composed of three units — grid, rows and columns. Columns will expand to fill their row, and will resize to fit additional columns.

To begin, we will add a `<ion-grid>` tag. Next, we will define our first row that will contain the current temperature and conditions:

```
<ion-row>
  <ion-col col-12>
    <h1>{{currentData.temperature | number:'.0-0'}}&deg;</h1>
    <p>{{currentData.summary}}</p>
  </ion-col>
</ion-row>
```

If you take a look at the actual *data.json* file, you will see the temperature values are actually saved out to two decimal places. I doubt we need this level of accuracy for our app. To solve this, we can use one the of the built-in Pipe functions in Angular to round our values for us.

What Is a Pipe?

A pipe takes in data as input and transforms it into the desired output. Angular includes several stock pipes such as DatePipe, Upper-CasePipe, LowerCasePipe, CurrencyPipe, and PercentPipe.

By adding **| number:'.0-0'** after the data binding for currentData.temperature, our data will go from 58.59 to 59.

Next, we will add another row that will display the high and low temperatures for the next three days:

```
<ion-row>
  <ion-col col-4>
    {{daily.data[0].temperatureMax | number:'.0-0'}}&deg;<br>
    {{daily.data[0].temperatureMin | number:'.0-0'}}&deg;
  </ion-col>
  <ion-col col-4>
    {{daily.data[1].temperatureMax | number:'.0-0'}}&deg;<br>
    {{daily.data[1].temperatureMin | number:'.0-0'}}&deg;
  </ion-col>
  <ion-col col-4>
    {{daily.data[2].temperatureMax | number:'.0-0'}}&deg;<br>
    {{daily.data[2].temperatureMin | number:'.0-0'}}&deg;
  </ion-col>
</ion-row>
```

Now if you save the file and try to run the app, you will encounter an error. This error occurs because our data is being loaded via a Promise and is not initially available to the template. To fix this issue, we can add an ngIf directive to tell the template not to display our grid until we have our data. However, we could have set our variables to some initial values, and thus allowed the template to render. Any of our non–data-bound elements would be shown, like the ° symbol. By wrapping the entire grid in an ngIf, we can control the display of everything. So our <ion-grid> tag becomes:

```
<ion-grid *ngIf="daily.data != undefined">
```

Saving the file again, our template will correctly render once the data has been properly loaded.

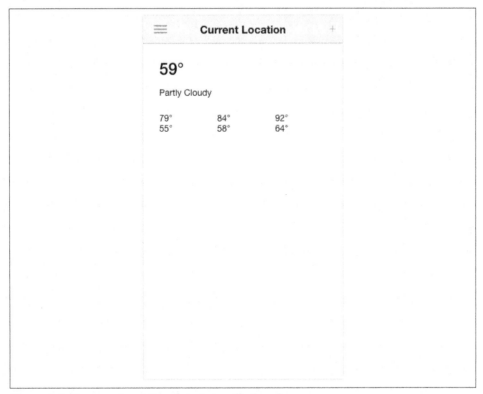

Figure 9-2. Our mock weather data being displayed

Loading Feedback: Loading Dialogs and Pull to Refresh

It would be nice if there was some feedback that the app was loading the weather data. Although the load time might be brief when using our mock data, once we hook it up to a live data source, it might take a moment or two.

Ionic has a `LoadingController` component that we can easily add into our app. Update the import statement for ionic-angular to include Loading.

```
import { NavController, NavParams, LoadingController } from 'ionic-angular';
```

Next, in the class definition add in a loading variable of type `Loading`:

```
export class WeatherPage {
  theWeather: any = {};
  currentData: any = {};
  daily: any = {};
  loader: LoadingController;
```

We will also need to pass this module into our constructor:

```
constructor(public navCtrl: NavController,
            public navParams: NavParams,
            public weatherService: WeatherService,
            public loadingCtrl: LoadingController) {...
```

Now we can create our loading dialog component instance. Add this code before making the weatherService.getWeather() call:

```
let loader = this.loadingCtrl.create({
  content: "Loading weather data...",
  duration: 3000
});
```

We are setting a duration for the dialog for the moment for testing purposes since our data is still being loaded locally. By setting it to three seconds, it gives us a chance to see it before it is dismissed. To display the loading dialog, we need to simply tell the loader instance to show the dialog via the present method:

```
loader.present();
```

For more information about the Loading component, see the Ionic Framework website (*http://bit.ly/2nzeYxU*).

By saving this file and running the app, the loading dialog will appear for three seconds and then dismiss itself (Figure 9-3).

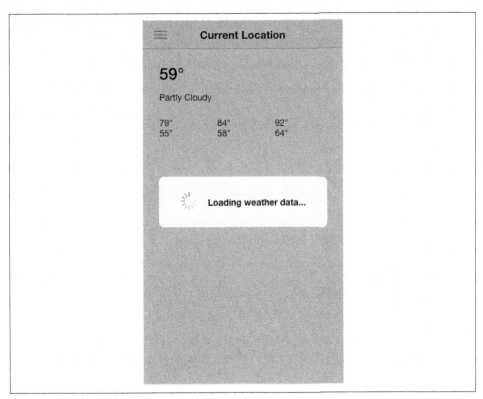

Figure 9-3. The loading dialog

Since we are working with dialogs and data updates, let's add in the code to allow us to use the Refresher component (aka Pull To Refresh). This is a popular UX method to allow users to force a data refresh without having to have an on-screen control to enable it.

In the *weather.html* file, after the `<ion-content>`, we can add:

```
<ion-refresher (ionRefresh)="doRefresh($event)">
  <ion-refresher-content
    pullingIcon="arrow-dropdown"
    pullingText="Pull to refresh"
    refreshingSpinner="circles"
    refreshingText="Refreshing...">
  </ion-refresher-content>
</ion-refresher>
```

This will define the `<ion-refresher>` and `<ion-refresher-content>`. Beyond setting the text that is displayed, you can also define which spinner animation you want. The built-in options are `ios`, `ios-small`, `bubbles`, `circles`, `crescent`, and `dots`.

When the pull to refresh component is triggered it will call the doRefresh method. Let's add in the doRefresh method to the *weather.ts* file.

First, we need to include this component as part of the imports from Ionic:

```
import { NavController, NavParams, LoadingController, Refresher } from
'ionic-angular';
```

Then include a variable to reference the Refresher in the class definition:

```
export class WeatherPage {
  theWeather: any = {};
  currentData: any = {};
  daily: any = {};
  loader: LoadingController;
  refresher: Refresher;
```

Now we will add in the doRefresh method to our class:

```
doRefresh(refresher) {
  setTimeout(() => {
    refresher.complete();
  }, 2000);
}
```

For the moment, we are just triggering a simple timeout call for two seconds. We will return to this method once we have live data enabled, but this will allow us to see the Refresher's UI in action.

Adding GeoLocation

The Dark Sky API requires us to pass in a latitude and longitude value in order to get the weather forecast. We can obtain this set of data through the use of Cordova's Geolocation plugin. To add this plugin to our app, we need to use this command in the terminal:

```
$ ionic plugin add cordova-plugin-geolocation
```

The CLI will add the plugin for all the install platforms. Note that this command only installs the plugin itself; it does not write any of the actual code to use this plugin. In the *app.module.ts* file, we need to import and add the Geolocation plugin provider to our @NgModule declaration.

Open *weather.ts*, and first, let's import the Geolocation module from Ionic Native:

```
import { Geolocation } from '@ionic-native/geolocation';
```

as well as adding to our parameters in the constructor.

If you recall, Ionic Native acts as an Angular wrapper for your Cordova plugins.

Next, in the constructor, we will call the `getCurrentPosition` function on the Geolocation module. For the moment, it will just write out your current latitude and longitude to the console:

```
Geolocation.getCurrentPosition().then(pos => {
    console.log('lat: ' + pos.coords.latitude + ', lon: ' + pos.coords.longitude);
});
```

Since making GPS requests are battery consuming, we should save this result and use it instead. Instead of saving this to a generic object, let's define a variable that implements the CurrentLoc interface.

To do this, we need to define that interface. Create a new directory named *interfaces* within the *app* directory. Within that new directory, create a new file named *current-loc.ts*. This file will hold our simple definition for our CurrentLoc interface. The code for this is:

```
export interface CurrentLoc {
    lat: number;
    lon: number;
    timestamp?: number;
}
```

This interface will tell the compiler that it needs both a `lat` and `long` property with their allowed values as numbers. It also tells the compiler that an optional property `timestamp` can be passed. This is done by adding in the ? after the property name.

Returning to *weather.ts*, we need to import this interface for use in our class:

```
import { CurrentLoc } from '../../interfaces/current-loc';
```

Now, we can create a `currentLoc` variable that implements the CurrentLoc interface:

```
currentLoc: CurrentLoc = {lat:0 , lon: 0};
```

Our `getCurrentPosition` call can now save our result into our `currentLoc` variable:

```
Geolocation.getCurrentPosition().then(pos => {
    console.log('lat: ' + pos.coords.latitude + ', lon: ' + pos.coords.longitude);
    this.currentLoc.lat = pos.coords.latitude;
    this.currentLoc.lon = pos.coords.longitude;
    this.currentLoc.timestamp = pos.timestamp;
});
```

We will save the timestamp in case we want to check the age of the data and trigger a refresh. I will leave that to you as a programming challenge once the app is complete. Now that we know where on this planet you are, let's find out your weather.

Accessing Live Weather Data

There are a variety of weather services you can use, but for this app, we will use the Dark Sky service. Sign up for a developer account on the Dark Sky register page (*https://darksky.net/dev/register*).

Once you have signed up, you will be issued an API key. We will need this to use the API. Currently, the API allows up to 1,000 calls per day before you have to pay for usage.

The call to the API is actual quite simple:

```
https://api.darksky.net/forecast/APIKEY/LATITUDE,LONGITUDE
```

If we just replaced our local data call in the *weather-data.ts* file with this URL (replacing the APIKEY with your API key, and also hardcoding a location), you would find that it will not work. Opening the JavaScript console, you would see an error like this:

```
XMLHttpRequest
cannot load https://api.darksky.net/forecast/APIKEY/LATITUDE,LONGITUDE.
No 'Access-Control-Allow-Origin' header is present on the requested resource.
Origin 'http://localhost:8100' is therefore not allowed access.
```

This error happens due to the browser's security policies, which are essentially a way to block access to data from other domains. It is also referred to as CORS (Cross-Origin Resource Sharing). Typically, solving this issue during development requires setting up a proxy server or some other workaround. Thankfully, the Ionic CLI has a built-in workaround.

In *ionic.config.json* (which can be found at the root level of our app), we can define a set of proxies for `ionic serve` to use. Just add in a `proxies` property and define the path and the proxyUrl. In our case it, will look like this:

```
{
  "name": "Ionic2Weather",
  "app_id": "",
  "v2": true,
  "typescript": true,
  "proxies": [
    {
      "path": "/api/forecast",
      "proxyUrl": "https://api.darksky.net/forecast/APIKEY"
    }
  ]
}
```

Replacing the APIKEY in the proxyURL with your actual API key.

Save this file, making sure to restart $ `ionic serve` for these changes to take effect.

Returning back to the *weather-service.ts* file, we can update the http.get call to be:

```
this.http.get('/api/forecast/43.0742365,-89.381011899')...
```

Our application will be able to now properly call the Dark Sky API, and our live weather data will be returned to our app.

Connecting the Geolocation and Weather Providers

Currently our latitude and longitude values are hardcoded into the Dark Sky request. Let's address this issue.

Obviously, we need to know our current position. We have that code already in place with the Geolocation function. Since we are using the Ionic Native wrapper to the Cordova plugin, this is already sent up as a Promise. One of the advantages of using Promises is the ability to chain them together, which is exactly what we need to do here. Once we have our location, then we can call Dark Sky and get our weather data.

To chain Promises together, you just continue on using the .then function:

```
geolocation.getCurrentPosition().then(pos => {
  console.log('lat: ' + pos.coords.latitude + ', lon: ' + pos.coords.longitude);
  this.currentLoc.lat = pos.coords.latitude;
  this.currentLoc.lon = pos.coords.longitude;
  this.currentLoc.timestamp = pos.timestamp;
  return this.currentLoc;
}).then(currentLoc => {
  weatherService.getWeather(currentLoc).then(theResult => {
    this.theWeather = theResult;
    this.currentData = this.theWeather.currently;
    this.daily = this.theWeather.daily;
    loader.dismiss();
  });
});
```

Besides adding .then, we have to add the return this.currentLoc within the Geolocation Promise. By adding a return, it enables us to pass this data along the Promise chain.

Demo Code Warning

We are being a bit sloppy here and not accounting for any errors. With any network calls to a remote system, you should always expect failure and code for that case.

This is a great example of how using Promises can make work with asynchronous processes so much easier.

Another minor tweak to the app is to remove the duration value in our loading dialog:

```
let loader = this.loadingCtrl.create({
  content: "Loading weather data..."
});
loader.present();
```

We will let the loading dialog now stay up until we finally get our weather data. Once we do, we can simply call `loading.dismiss()` and remove the loading dialog.

Now we need to update our *weather-service.ts* to support dynamic locations.

First, import our custom location class:

```
import { CurrentLoc } from '../interfaces/current-loc';
```

Next, change the `load` function to accept our current location:

```
load(currentLoc:CurrentLoc) {
```

Then modify the `http.get` call to reference this information:

```
this.http.get('/api/forecast/'+currentLoc.lat+','+currentLoc.lon)
```

Finally, we also need to adjust the `getWeather` method as well to support using a location:

```
getWeather(currentLoc:CurrentLoc) {
  this.data = null;
  return this.load(currentLoc).then(data => {
    return data;
  });
}
```

We also clear the weather data that was previously retrieved by the service before we load new data. Here is the revised *weather-service.ts* file:

```
import { Injectable } from '@angular/core';
import { Http } from '@angular/http';
import 'rxjs/add/operator/map';
import { CurrentLoc } from '../interfaces/current-loc'

@Injectable()
export class WeatherService {
  data: any = null;

  constructor(public http: Http) {
    console.log('Hello WeatherService Provider');
  }

  load(currentLoc:CurrentLoc) {
    if (this.data) {
      return Promise.resolve(this.data);
    }

    return new Promise(resolve => {
      this.http.get('/api/forecast/'+currentLoc.lat+','+currentLoc.lon)
```

```
      .map(res => res.json())
      .subscribe(data => {
        this.data = data;
        resolve(this.data);
      });
    });
  }

  getWeather(currentLoc:CurrentLoc) {
    this.data = null;
    return this.load(currentLoc).then(data => {
      return data;
    });
  }
}
```

One last change is to remove the call to `this.weatherData.load()` in *app.compo-nent.ts file*. Save the files, reload the application, and live local weather information will be shown on the page.

Getting Other Locations' Weather

It is nice to know the weather where you are, but you might also want to know the weather in other parts of the world. We will use the side menu to switch to different cities, as in Figure 9-4.

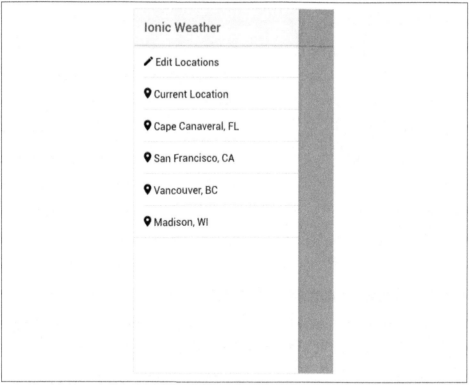

Figure 9-4. Ionic weather app's side menu

The first set of changes we are going to make is to the `pages` array in the *app.compo‐nent.ts* file. First, let's import our `CurrentLoc` class:

```
import { CurrentLoc } from '../interfaces/current-loc';
```

Next, we need to include the location's latitude and longitude data that we can refer‐ence to look up the weather. Since neither the Edit Locations nor the Current Loca‐tions will have predefined locations, this new property will be declared as optional:

```
pages: Array<{title: string, component: any, icon: string, loc?:CurrentLoc}>;
```

Next, we will fill this array with some locations:

```
this.pages = [
  { title: 'Edit Locations', component: LocationsPage, icon: 'create' },
  { title: 'Current Location', component: WeatherPage, icon: 'pin' },
  { title: 'Cape Canaveral, FL', component: WeatherPage, icon: 'pin', ↵
    loc: {lat:28.3922, lon:-80.6077} },
  { title: 'San Francisco, CA', component: WeatherPage, icon: 'pin', ↵
    loc: {lat:37.7749, lon:-122.4194} },
  { title: 'Vancouver, BC', component: WeatherPage, icon: 'pin', ↵
    loc: {lat:49.2827, lon:-123.1207} },
```

```
{ title: 'Madison, WI', component: WeatherPage, icon: 'pin', ↵
    loc: {lat:43.0742365, lon:-89.381011899} }
];
```

Now, when we select one of the four cities, we now know its latitude and longitude. But we need to pass this data along to our weather page. In Ionic 1, we would have used $stateParams to do this; but in Ionic 2, we can just pass an object as a parameter to the NavController. So, our openPage function will now pass this data (assuming it is there):

```
openPage(page) {
  // Reset the content nav to have just this page
  // we wouldn't want the back button to show in this scenario
  if (page.hasOwnProperty('loc') ) {
    this.nav.setRoot(page.component, {geoloc: page.loc});
  } else {
    this.nav.setRoot(page.component);
  }
}
```

Go ahead and save this file, and open *weather.ts*. Retrieving the data is actually just a simple get() call. We will assign the data to a variable named loc. Add this code after we display the loading dialog:

```
let loc = this.navParams.get('geoloc');
```

If this variable is undefined, we will make the call to the Geolocation method like before. But, if this value is defined, then we will use that data to call the weather service with it:

```
geolocation.getCurrentPosition().then(pos => {
  console.log('lat: ' + pos.coords.latitude + ', lon: ' + pos.coords.longitude);
  this.currentLoc.lat = pos.coords.latitude;
  this.currentLoc.lon = pos.coords.longitude;
  this.currentLoc.timestamp = pos.timestamp;
  return this.currentLoc;
}).then(currentLoc => {
  weatherService.getWeather(currentLoc).then(theResult => {
    this.theWeather = theResult;
    this.currentData = this.theWeather.currently;
    this.daily = this.theWeather.daily;
    loader.dismiss();
  });
});
} else {
  this.currentLoc = loc;
  weatherService.getWeather(this.currentLoc).then(theResult => {
    this.theWeather = theResult;
    this.currentData = this.theWeather.currently;
    this.daily = this.theWeather.daily;
    loader.dismiss();
```

```
    });
  }
```

If we have a location, we will first assign it to the currentLoc variable, then call our getWeather function.

Save this file and test it out. Hopefully, the weather is different in each of the locations.

However, our page title is not updating after we switch locations. This is actually another simple fix. First, we need to pass the location's name along with its location. In *app.component.ts*, change:

```
this.nav.setRoot(page.component, {geoloc: page.loc});
```

to:

```
this.nav.setRoot(page.component, {geoloc: page.loc, title: page.title});
```

In *weather.ts*, we need to make two changes. First, we need a variable to store our page title in so the template can reference it. In the class constructor, we will add this:

```
pageTitle:string = 'Current Location';
```

Then, within our code block that gets the weather for the other locations, we can get the other NavParam and assign it to the `pageTitle`:

```
this.pageTitle = this.navParams.get('title');
```

The last minor change is to the template itself. We need to update the `<ion-title>` tag to reference the `pageTitle` variable:

```
<ion-title>{{pageTitle}}</ion-title>
```

And with that, our page title should now display our current location's name.

Pull to Refresh: Part 2

You might have been wondering why we bothered to set the currentLoc to the location that was passed in. We can add it directly into our `getWeather` function. Remember that pull to refresh component we added? Yeah, that one. We actually never had it do anything except close after two seconds. Let's update this code to actually get new weather. All we have to do is replace the `setTimeout`, so the `doRefresh` function becomes:

```
doRefresh(refresher) {
  this.weatherService.getWeather(this.currentLoc).then(theResult => {
    this.theWeather = theResult;
    this.currentData = this.theWeather.currently;
    this.daily = this.theWeather.daily;
    refresher.complete();
```

```
    });
}
```

API Limits

Within the `doRefresh` would be a great place to check that time-stamp property to prevent API abuse.

Unfortunately, I doubt you will see any changes to the weather data, as weather usually does not change that quickly. Let's turn our attention to the Edit Location screen.

Editing the Locations

This screen will be where we can add a new city to our list, or remove an existing one. Here is what our final screen will look like Figure 9-5.

Figure 9-5. The Add City dialog

Open the *locations.html* file and let's add in our add city button after the `<ion-content>`. You should remove the `padding` attribute as well:

```
<ion-content>
  <button ion-button icon-left clear color="dark" item-left
  (click)="addLocation()">↵
    <ion-icon name="add"></ion-icon>Add City</button>
</ion-content>
```

For this button, we are applying the clear and dark styles to it. The clear attribute will remove any border or background from the button, while the dark attribute will color the icon with the dark color. We will have the click event call a function named addLocation.

After the <button> tag, we are going to add in our <ion-list> that will display the list of our saved locations:

```
<ion-list>

  <ion-list-header>
    My Locations
  </ion-list-header>

  <ion-item *ngFor="let loc of locs">
   <button ion-button icon-left clear color="dark"
   (click)="deleteLocation(loc)">
     <ion-icon name="trash"></ion-icon>
   </button>{{loc.title}}
  </ion-item>

</ion-list>
```

We are using the <ion-list-header> to act as our list header rather than just a regular header tag. Hopefully, the <ion-item> tag looks a bit familiar to you. It is just going to iterate over an array of locs and render out each location. Next, we set up a button that will allow us to delete a location. Again, we will use the clear and dark attributes for the button styling. The click event will call a function named deleteLocation that we have yet to write. We will wrap up the code block by binding the text to the title value with {{loc.title}}.

With the HTML in place, we can focus on the changes we need to make in our code. We will start with *locations.ts* and add in the elements needed to get the template to work at a basic level.

We will again import our CurrentLoc class:

```
import { CurrentLoc } from '../../interfaces/current-loc';
```

Within the class definition, we need to create our locs array. This array is actually going to be the same content as our pages array does in the *app.component.ts* file:

```
export class Locations {
  locs: Array<{ title: string, component: any, icon: string,
  loc?: CurrentLoc }>;
```

But whenever you find yourself repeating elements like this, you should always pause and consider if this is something that should be abstracted. In this case, our answer is going to be yes. Instead of listing out our array's structure, we will move into the object to an interface and simply use it instead.

Create a new file named *weather-location.ts* inside the *interfaces* directory. Here we will define our WeatherLocation interface. Since the `loc` property uses the `CurrentLoc` interface, we need to make sure we import that module as well:

```
import { CurrentLoc } from './current-loc';

export interface WeatherLocation {
  title: string;
  component: any;
  icon: string;
  loc?: CurrentLoc;
}
```

The actual interface will define the location's title, its page component, its icon, and an optional element of a `CurrentLoc` type.

With this interface created, switch back to *locations.ts* and import that interface:

```
import { WeatherLocation } from '../../interfaces/weather-location';
```

Then, we can update the `locs` array to be a properly typed array:

```
locs: Array<WeatherLocation>;
```

Next, let's add the two placeholder functions for the adding and deleting of locations after the constructor:

```
deleteLocation(loc) {
  console.log('deleteLocation');
}

addLocation() {
  console.log('addLocation');
}
```

Let's work on populating our `locs` array with our saved places. We could simply copy over the pages array that is used in the side menu, and our template should render it out just fine. But any changes we make to our `locs` array will not be reflected in the `pages` array. We need to move this data into something that both components can reference.

For this, we will create a new provider named `LocationsService`. Instead of using the `ionic generate` command, which creates a provider that is aimed at getting remote data, will we just manually create our provider.

Create a new file named *locations-service.ts* within the *providers* directory.

The first thing we need to do is define our imports. We will need `Injectable` from Angular, as well as our `WeatherLocation` interface and `WeatherPage` component:

```
import { Injectable } from '@angular/core';
import { WeatherLocation } from '../interfaces/weather-location';
import { WeatherPage } from '../pages/weather/weather';
```

Next, we need to include the `@Injectable()` decorator:

```
@Injectable()
```

Now we can define our service, the `locations` Array (properly typed to `WeatherLocation`), then initialize that array with our default locations:

```
export class LocationsService {
  locations: Array<WeatherLocation>;

  constructor() {
    this.locations = [
      { title: 'Cape Canaveral, FL', component: WeatherPage, icon: 'pin', ↵
        loc: { lat: 28.3922, lon: -80.6077 } },
      { title: 'San Francisco, CA', component: WeatherPage, icon: 'pin', ↵
        loc: { lat: 37.7749, lon: -122.4194 } },
      { title: 'Vancouver, BC', component: WeatherPage, icon: 'pin', ↵
        loc: { lat: 49.2827, lon: -123.1207 } },
      { title: 'Madison, WI', component: WeatherPage, icon: 'pin', ↵
        loc: { lat: 43.0742365, lon: -89.381011899 } }
    ];
  }
```

We can wrap our service with the functions that we will need: one to get the locations, one to add to the locations, and one function to remove a location:

```
getLocations() {
    return Promise.resolve(this.locations);
}

removeLocation(loc:WeatherLocation) {
    let index = this.locations.indexOf(loc)
    if (index != -1) {
        this.locations.splice(index, 1);
    }
}

addLocation(loc: WeatherLocation) {
    this.locations.push(loc);
}
```

As with all providers, we need to make sure they are included in our provider array in *app.module.ts*:

```
import { LocationsService } from '../providers/locations-service';
...
providers: [
```

```
        StatusBar,
        SplashScreen,
        Geolocation,
        { provide: ErrorHandler, useClass: IonicErrorHandler },
        WeatherService,
        GeocodeService,
        LocationsService
    ]
```

Returning back to *locations.ts*, we can import this service into the component:

```
import { LocationsService }  from '../../providers/locations-service';
```

We also need to add this module into our constructor, call that service's `getLocations` method to get our default locations, and save the result into our `locs` array:

```
constructor(public navCtrl: NavController,
            public navParams: NavParams,
            public locationsService: LocationsService) {
    locationsService.getLocations().then(res => {
      this.locs = res;
    });
  }
```

Saving the file, and navigating to the Edit Locations screen, you should now see our four default cities listed.

Deleting a City

Let's implement the actual `deleteLocation` function in the *locations.ts* file. We already have the stub function in place in our component. All we need to do is simply call the `removeLocation` method on the `LocationsService`:

```
deleteLocation(loc:WeatherLocation) {
    this.locationsService.removeLocation(loc);
  }
```

Adding a City

Adding a city is a bit more complex. If you recall, the Dark Sky weather service uses latitude and longitudes to look up the weather data. I doubt you will ask, "How is the weather in 32.715, −117.1625 ?" but rather, "How is the weather in San Diego?" To translate between a location and its corresponding latitude and longitude we need to use a geocoding service.

Using a Geocoding Service

For this app, we will use the Google Maps Geocoding API (*http://bit.ly/2kxYQKF*).

In order to use this API, we will need to be registered with Google as a developer and have an API key for our application. Go to the Google Maps API page (*http://bit.ly/2lv31rK*) and follow the instructions to generate an API key for the geocoding API. Save this 40 character string, as we will need it shortly:

```
export class GeocodeService {
  data: any;
  apikey:String = 'YOUR-API-KEY-HERE';
  constructor(public http: Http) {
    this.data = null;
  }

  getLatLong(address:string) {
    if (this.data) {
      // already loaded data
      return Promise.resolve(this.data);
    }

    // don't have the data yet
    return new Promise(resolve => {
      this.http.get('https://maps.googleapis.com/maps/api/geocode/↵
json?address='+encodeURIComponent(address)+'&key='+this.apikey)
        .map(res => res.json())
        .subscribe(data => {
          if(data.status === "OK") {
            resolve({name: data.results[0].formatted_address, location:{
                    latitude: data.results[0].geometry.location.lat,
                    longitude: data.results[0].geometry.location.lng
            }});
          } else {
            console.log(data);
            //reject
          }
        });
    });
  }
}
```

The first change is the new variable named `apikey`. You will need to set its value to the key you just generated.

The constructor just sets the data variable to `null`. The heart of this class is actually the `getLatLong` method. This method accepts one parameter named `address`.

The method will then make this request:

```
this.http.get('https://maps.googleapis.com/maps/api/geocode/json?↵
address='+encodeURIComponent(address)+'&key='+this.apikey)
```

Note that we have to use the `encodeURIComponent` method to sanitize the address string before we can make the call to the Google Maps Geocoding API.

Once the data is returned from the service, we can check if a named place was located using the `data.status` value. Then we can traverse the JSON, get the needed data, and resolve the Promise.

Now that we have a way to turn San Diego into 32.715, –117.1625, we can return back to *locations.ts* and finish our `addLocation` function.

We will need to import our new geocode service:

```
import { GeocodeService } from '../../providers/geocode-service';
```

Also include it with the constructor:

```
constructor(public navCtrl: NavController,
            public navParams: NavParams,
            public locationsService: LocationsService,
            public geocodeService: GeocodeService) {
```

Instead of using the Ionic Native Dialog plugin to prompt our user to enter their point of interest, let's use the `AlertController` component. Again, we need to import it from the proper library:

```
import { NavController, NavParams, AlertController } from 'ionic-angular';
```

One of the difficulties in using the Ionic Native Alert is the degree to which you can extend it. The alert also requires you to test your application either in a simulator or on-device. By using the standard Ionic Alert component, we can keep developing directly in our browser. However, unlike the Ionic Native dialog, there is quite a bit more JavaScript that you need to write. We will need to update our constructor to include the `AlertController`:

```
constructor(public navCtrl: NavController,
            public navParams: NavParams,
            public locationsService: LocationsService,
            public geocodeService: GeocodeService,
            public alertCtrl: AlertController) {
```

Here is the completed `addLocation` method with the Alert component used:

```
addLocation() {
  let prompt = this.alertCtrl.create({
    title: 'Add a City',
    message: "Enter the city's name",
    inputs: [
      {
        name: 'title',
        placeholder: 'City name'
      },
    ],
    buttons: [
      {
        text: 'Cancel',
        handler: data => {
```

```
        console.log('Cancel clicked');
      }
    },
    {
      text: 'Add',
      handler: data => {
        console.log('Saved clicked');
      }
    }
  ]
});

prompt.present();
}
```

The key line of code not to forget is telling the `AlertController` to present our alert with `prompt.present()`.

Now, we are not doing anything with any city that you might enter, so let's add that code. Replace this line:

```
console.log('Saved clicked');
```

with:

```
if (data.title != '') {
  this.geocodeService.getLatLong(data.title).then(res => {
    let newLoc = { title: '', component: WeatherPage, icon: 'pin', ↵
                   loc: { lat: 0, lon: 0 } }
    newLoc.title = res.name;
    newLoc.loc.lat = res.location.latitude;
    newLoc.loc.lon = res.location.longitude;

    this.locationsService.addLocation(newLoc);
  });
}
```

We will also need to import our `Weather` component as well:

```
import { WeatherPage } from '../weather/weather';
```

So now we can take city name, parse it into a latitude and longitude value, and add it to our list of locations.

There are a couple of open issues I do want to point out with this code block. The first issue is that we are not handling the case of when the geocoding service fails to find a location. If you are up for that programming challenge, you need to add code that rejects the Promise. The second issue is handling when the geocoding service returns more than one answer. For example, if I enter Paris, do I want Paris, France or Paris, Texas? For this solution, you might want to look at the flexibility of the `Alert` component to have radio buttons in a dialog.

Dynamically Updating the Side Menu

If you add a new location to your list and then use the side menu to view that location's weather, you will see that it is not listed. That is because that list is still referencing the local version and not using the array in `LocationsService`. We will open the *app.component.ts* file and refactor it to enable this.

First, we need to import the service:

```
import { LocationsService } from '../providers/locations-service';
```

Next, we need to include in our constructor:

```
constructor(
  public platform: Platform, public locationsService: LocationsService
) {
  this.initializeApp();
  this.getMyLocations();
}
```

The `getMyLocations` function will get the data from the `LocationsService` provider and then populate the `pages` array:

```
getMyLocations(){
  this.locationsService.getLocations().then(res => {
    this.pages = [
      { title: 'Edit Locations', component: LocationsPage, icon: 'create' },
      { title: 'Current Location', component: WeatherPage, icon: 'pin' }
    ];
    for (let newLoc of res) {
      this.pages.push(newLoc);
    }
  });
}
```

Save all the files and run `$ ionic serve` again. The side menu should still show our initial list of places. If we add a new location, the Edit Locations screen is properly updated. However, the side menu is not showing our new location. Even though the side menu is getting its data from our shared provider, it does not know that the data has changed. To solve this issue, we need to explore two different options: Ionic Events and Observables. You might want to save a version of the progress so far, since each solution is a bit different.

Ionic Events

The first solution is to use Ionic `Events` to communicate the change in the dataset. According to the documentation:

> Events is a publish-subscribe style event system for sending and responding to application-level events across your app.

Sounds pretty close to what we need to do. In the *locations.ts* file, we will need to import the Events component from ionic-angular:

```
import {NavController, NavParams, AlertController, Events} from 'ionic-angular';
```

Within the constructor we need to have a reference to the Events module:

```
constructor(public navCtrl: NavController,
            public navParams: NavParams,
            public locationsService: LocationsService,
            public geocodeService: GeocodeService,
            public alertCtrl: AlertController,
            public events: Events) {
```

Now, in both the deleteLocation and addLocation functions, we just need to add this code to publish the event:

```
this.events.publish('locations:updated', {});
```

So the deleteLocation becomes:

```
deleteLocation(loc) {
  this.locations.removeLocation(loc);
  this.events.publish('locations:updated', {});
}
```

For the addLocation function, it is added within the 'Add' handler callback:

```
handler: data => {
  if (data.title != '') {
    this.geocode.getLatLong(data.title).then(res => {
      let newLoc = { title: '', component: WeatherPage, icon: 'pin', ↵
                    loc: { lat: 0, lon: 0 } }
      newLoc.title = res.name;
      newLoc.loc.lat = res.location.latitude;
      newLoc.loc.lon = res.location.longitude;

      this.locations.addLocation(newLoc);
      this.events.publish('locations:updated', {});
    });
  }
}
```

The parameters are the event name—in this case, locations:updated, and any data that needs to be shared. For this example, there is no additional data we need to send to the subscriber.

The subscriber function will be added to the *app.component.ts* file. First, we need to update our imports:

```
import { Nav, Platform, Events } from 'ionic-angular';
```

and pass it into our constructor:

```
constructor(public platform: Platform,
            public locationsService: LocationsService,
            public events: Events) {
```

Within the constructor itself, we will add this code:

```
this.initializeApp();
this.getMyLocations();
events.subscribe('locations:updated', (data) => {
  this.getMyLocations();
});
```

This code will listen for a `locations:updated` event. Then it will call the `getMyLoca
tions` function. In doing so, our array will be refreshed, and the side menu will be
kept up to date.

Using Ionic `Events` may not be the best solution to this problem, but it is worth
knowing how to communicate events across an application.

Observables

You might be wondering if there was some other way for the data updates to propagate through our app without the need to manually send events. In fact, there is a solution available to us. One of the elements inside the RxJS library is Observables.
From the documentation:

> The Observer and Observable interfaces provide a generalized mechanism for push-
> based notification, also known as the observer design pattern. The Observable object
> represents the object that sends notifications (the provider); the Observer object repre-
> sents the class that receives them (the observer).

In other words, the event notification system that we wrote with Ionic `Events` can be
replaced. In our simple example using Ionic `Events`, we did not have to write a lot of
code for our system to work. Now imagine a much more complex app and the messaging infrastructure that could quickly become a Gordian knot.

Now, to say that RxJS is a powerful and complex library is an understatement. But
here are the basics of what we need to do within our app. First, we need to create an
RxJS Subject, specifically a Behavior Subject. This will hold our data that we wish to
monitor for changes. Next, we need to create the actual Observable that will watch
our subject for changes. If it sees a change, it will broadcast the new set of data. The
third and final part are the subscribers to our `Observable`. Once they are bound
together, our data will always be the latest.

We will start our refactoring in the *locations-service.ts* file. This is where the majority
of the changes will occur as we shift our app from using Ionic `Events` to `Observa
bles`.

As always, we need to import the needed modules:

```
import { Observable, BehaviorSubject } from 'rxjs/Rx';
```

Now, there are several types of Subject in the RxJS library. The `BehaviorSubject` is the best type for our needs, as it will send an update as soon as it gets data. Other types of Subjects require an additional method call to broadcast an update.

Next, we need to define the actual `BehaviorSubject` and `Observable` within the class:

```
locations: Array<WeatherLocation>;
locationsSubject: BehaviorSubject<Array<WeatherLocation>> =
new BehaviorSubject([]);
locations$: Observable<Array<WeatherLocation>> =
this.locationsSubject.asObservable();
```

Variable Naming

The inclusion of the $ after the variable name is a naming conven-
tion for `Observable` data types. To learn more about Angular best
practices, see John Papa's Style Guide (*http://bit.ly/2lva17N*).

We have only associated the `locations$` with the `locationsSubject` by setting it to `this.locationsSubject.asObservable()`. The locationsSubject knows nothing about our data in the `locations` array. To solve this issue, simply pass in our locations array as the parameter to the locationsSubject's next method:

```
this.locationsSubject.next(this.locations);
```

Upon doing this, our `Observable` will emit an update event, and all the references will be changed. Rather than repeating this call whenever our `locations` array changes, let's wrap it in a `refresh` function:

```
refresh() {
  this.locationsSubject.next(this.locations);
}
```

Then in the `constructor`, `addLocation`, and `removeLocation` methods, we can call this method after we have done whatever changes we needed to make to the `loca tions` array. Here is the completed code:

```
import { Injectable } from '@angular/core';
import { WeatherLocation } from '../interfaces/weather-location';
import { Weather } from '../pages/weather/weather';
import { Observable, BehaviorSubject } from 'rxjs/Rx';

@Injectable()

export class LocationsService {
  locations: Array<WeatherLocation>;
  locationsSubject: BehaviorSubject<Array<WeatherLocation>> =
  new BehaviorSubject([]);
  locations$: Observable<Array<WeatherLocation>> =
```

```
      this.locationsSubject.asObservable();

  constructor() {
    this.locations = [
      { title: 'Cape Canaveral, FL', component: Weather, icon: 'pin', ↵
        loc: { lat: 28.3922, lon: -80.6077 } },
      { title: 'San Francisco, CA', component: Weather, icon: 'pin', ↵
        loc: { lat: 37.7749, lon: -122.4194 } },
      { title: 'Vancouver, BC', component: Weather, icon: 'pin', ↵
        loc: { lat: 49.2827, lon: -123.1207 } },
      { title: 'Madison, WI', component: Weather, icon: 'pin', ↵
        loc: { lat: 43.0742365, lon: -89.381011899 } }
    ];
    this.refresh();
  }

  getLocations() {
    return Promise.resolve(this.locations);
  }

  removeLocation(loc) {
    let index = this.locations.indexOf(loc)
    if (index != -1) {
      this.locations.splice(index, 1);
      this.refresh();
    }
  }

  addLocation(loc) {
    this.locations.push(loc);
    this.refresh();
  }

  refresh() {
    this.locationsSubject.next(this.locations);
  }
}
```

With the service converted to using an Observable, we need to create the data subscribers to it. In *locations.ts* we now need to replace:

```
locationsService.getLocations().then(res => {
  this.locs = res;
});
```

with:

```
locationsService.locations$.subscribe( ( locs: Array<WeatherLocation> ) => {
  this.locs = locs;
});
```

Now our locs array will be automatically updated whenever the data changes in our service. Go ahead and remove the two this.events.publish calls.

A similar change is needed the *app.component.ts* file. First, let's remove the event listener:

```
events.subscribe('locations:updated', (data) => {
  this.getMyLocations();
});
```

Next, we need to include the `WeatherLocation` interface in the imports:

```
import { WeatherLocation } from '../interfaces/weather-location';
```

Finally, we can replace the `getMyLocations` function:

```
getMyLocations(){
  this.locationsService.getLocations().then(res => {
    this.pages = [
      { title: 'Edit Locations', component: LocationsPage, icon: 'create' },
      { title: 'Current Location', component: WeatherPage, icon: 'pin' }
    ];
    for (let newLoc of res) {
      this.pages.push(newLoc);
    }
  });
}
```

with:

```
getMyLocations(){
  this.locationsService.locations$.subscribe( ( locs: Array<WeatherLocation> ) =>
  {
    this.pages = [
      { title: 'Edit Locations', component: LocationsPage, icon: 'create' },
      { title: 'Current Location', component: WeatherPage, icon: 'pin' }
    ];
    for (let newLoc of locs) {
      this.pages.push(newLoc);
    }
  } );
}
```

With that, our weather app is now using RxJS Observables. Observables are a power solution when working with dynamic data. You would be well served to spend some time exploring their capabilities. Let's now turn our attention to making our app a bit more visually pleasing.

Styling the App

With our app now functioning rather well, we can turn our attention to some visual styling. Included with the source code is a nice photograph of a partially cloudy sky. Let's use this as our background image. Since our Ionic apps are based on HTML and CSS, we can leverage our existing CSS skills to style our apps. The only challenge in working with Ionic is uncovering the actual HTML structure that our CSS needs to properly target.

With the improved selector system within Ionic, targeting a specific HTML element is much easier. Let's include a nice sky image to serve as our background for the Weather page. Open the *weather.scss* and add the following CSS:

```
page-weather {
  ion-content{
    background: url(../assets/imgs/bg.jpg) no-repeat center center fixed;
    -webkit-background-size: cover;
    background-size: cover;
  }
}
```

Writing Sass

The CSS that we are adding should be nested within the page-weather {}.

Now, let's increase our base font size as well to make the text more readable:

```
ion-content{
  background: url(../assets/imgs/bg.jpg) no-repeat center center fixed;
  -webkit-background-size: cover;
  background-size: cover;
  font-size: 24px;
}
```

However, the default black text is not really working against the sky and clouds. So we can adjust the ion-col and its two children. We will change the color to white, center the text, and apply a drop shadow that has a little transparency:

```
ion-col, ion-col h1, ion-col p {
  color: #fff;
  text-align: center;
  text-shadow: 3px 3px 3px rgba(0,0, 0, 0.4);
}
```

Now, adjust the current weather information's text:

```
h1 {
  font-size: 72px;
}

p {
  font-size: 36px;
  margin-top: 0;
}
```

But, what about the header? It is looking a bit drab and out of place. Let's add a new class, opaque, to the `<ion-header>` tag in the *weather.html* file.

In the *weather.scss* file we can apply a series of classes to give our header a more modern look. The first class we add will use the new `backdrop-filter` method:

```
.opaque {
  -webkit-backdrop-filter: saturate(180%) blur(20px);
  backdrop-filter: saturate(180%) blur(20px);
}
```

Unfortunately, backdrop-filter is only supported in Safari at this time. This means we need to also create a fallback solution:

```
.opaque .toolbar-background {
  background-color: rgba(#f8f8f8, 0.55);
}
```

With this pair of CSS classes, we have a much more current design style in place.

But there are still more elements to style on this screen, namely the `Refresher` component. This one is a bit more complex than components we have styled before. Namely, it has a series of states that each need to be styled.

Let's start with the two text elements; the pulling text and the refreshing text. Unfortunately, the current documentation does not list out the structure or style method. But with a little inspection with the Chrome Dev Tools, these elements did already have CSS classes applied to them. So we can just add the following:

```
.refresher-pulling-text, .refresher-refreshing-text {
    color:#fff;
}
```

The arrow icon is also easily styled using:

```
.refresher-pulling-icon {
    color:#fff;
}
```

But what about the spinner? The dark circles aren't really standing out against our background. This element is a little tricky to style as well. The spinner is actually an SVG element. This means we cannot change it just by changing the CSS of the `<ion-spinner>`, but instead we need to modify the values within the SVG. One thing to note is that some of the CSS properties on an SVG element have different names. For example, SVG uses the term *stroke* instead of *border*, and *fill* instead of *background-color*.

If you are using the circles option for your `refreshingSpinner` attribute, then the styling is:

```
.refresher-refreshing .spinner-circles circle{
    fill:#fff;
}
```

But, say you decided to use crescent as your spinner, then the styling would be:

```
.refresher-refreshing .spinner-crescent circle{
    stroke:#fff;
}
```

There is one last item that we should change. You probably did not see that while the Refresher is visible, there was a solid 1-pixel white line between the Refresher and the content. With our full background image, this doesn't quite work for this design. Again, with some inspection with Chrome Dev Tools, the CSS was found where this attribute was set. So, we can now override it with:

```
.has-refresher > .scroll-content {
    border-width: 0;
}
```

Here is the full *weather.scss* code:

```
page-weather {
  ion-content{
    background: url(../assets/imgs/bg.jpg) no-repeat center center fixed;
    -webkit-background-size: cover;
    background-size: cover;
    font-size: 24px;
  }

  ion-col, ion-col h1, ion-col p {
    color: #fff;
    text-align: center;
    text-shadow: 3px 3px 3px rgba(0,0, 0, 0.4);
  }

  h1 {
    font-size: 72px;
  }

  p {
    font-size: 36px;
    margin-top: 0;
  }

  .opaque {
    -webkit-backdrop-filter: saturate(180%) blur(20px);
    backdrop-filter: saturate(180%) blur(20px);
  }

  .opaque .toolbar-background {
    background-color: rgba(#f8f8f8, 0.55);
  }
```

```
.refresher-pulling-text, .refresher-refreshing-text  {
  color:#fff;
}

.refresher-pulling-icon {
  color:#fff;
}

.refresher-refreshing .spinner-circles circle{
  fill:#fff;
}

.has-refresher > .scroll-content {
  border-top-width: 0;
}
}
```

See the style weather app in Figure 9-6.

Figure 9-6. Our styled Ionic weather app

With that our main weather page is looking rather nice. But we can add one more touch to the design. How about a nice icon as well?

Add a Weather Icon

The Dark Sky data set actually defines an icon value, and the Ionicons also support several weather icons as wells. Table 9-1 maps each icon.

Table 9-1. Dark Sky data set mapped out

Dark Sky name	Ionicon name
clear-day	sunny
clear-night	moon
rain	rainy
snow	snow
sleet	snow
wind	cloudy
fog	cloudy
cloudy	cloudy
partly-cloudy-day	partly-sunny
partly-cloudy-night	cloudy-night

We don't have a complete one-to-one mapping, but it is close enough. To resolve the mapping between the Dark Sky name and the Ionicon name, we will create a custom `Pipe` function. If you recall, `Pipes` are functions that transform data in a template.

From our terminal, we can use the `ionic generate` command to scaffold our pipe for us:

```
$ ionic generate pipe weathericon
```

This will create a new directory named *pipes*, and a new file named *weathericon.ts*. Here is the stock code that Ionic will generate for us:

```
import { Injectable, Pipe } from '@angular/core';

/*
  Generated class for the Weathericon pipe.

  See https://angular.io/docs/ts/latest/guide/pipes.html for more info on
  Angular 2 Pipes.
*/
@Pipe({
  name: 'weathericon'
})
@Injectable()
export class Weathericon {
  /*
    Takes a value and makes it lowercase.
  */
  transform(value, args) {
```

```
    value = value + ''; // make sure it's a string
    return value.toLowerCase();
  }
}
```

Let's replace the code within the transform function. The goal of this function will be to take the Dark Sky icon string and find the corresponding Ionicon name. Here is the revised Pipe:

```
import { Injectable, Pipe } from '@angular/core';

@Pipe({
  name: 'weathericon'
})
@Injectable()
export class Weathericon {

  transform(value: string, args: any[]) {
    let newIcon:string ='sunny';
    let forecastNames:Array<string> = ["clear-day", "clear-night", "rain", ↵
"snow", "sleet", "wind", "fog", "cloudy", "partly-cloudy-day",↵
"partly-cloudy-night"];
    let ioniconNames:Array<string> = ["sunny", "moon", "rainy", "snow",↵
"snow", "cloudy", "cloudy", "cloudy", "partly-sunny", "cloudy-night"];
    let iconIndex:number = forecastNames.indexOf(value);
    if (iconIndex !== -1) {
      newIcon = ioniconNames[iconIndex];
    }

    return newIcon;
  }
}
```

In our *app.module.ts* file, we will need to import our pipe using:

```
import { Weathericon } from '../pipes/weatherIcon';
```

and then include Weathericon in the declarations array.

Finally, the last change is to markup in the *weather.html* file, which will become:

```
<ion-col width-100>
  <h1> {{currentData.temperature | number:'.0-0'}}&deg;</h1>
  <p><ion-icon name="{{currentData.icon | weathericon}}"></ion-icon>↵
{{currentData.summary}}</p>
</ion-col>
```

Figure 9-7 shows the Ionic weather app after applying the weather Ionicon.

Figure 9-7. Ionic weather app with a weather Ionicons applied

That really does finish off the look of this screen. Feel free to continue to explore styling the side menu and the locations page on your own.

Next Steps

Our weather app still has some things that can be improved upon. Most notably, our custom cities are not saved. For something as simple as a list of cities, using Firebase might be overkill. Some options you might consider would be either local storage or using the Cordova File plugin to read and write a simple datafile. The choice is up to you.

Another challenge you might consider would be to introduce dynamic backgrounds. You could use a Flickr API to pull an image based on the location or on the weather type.

One more challenge you could take on is to support changing the temperature units.

Summary

With this application, we explored how the sidemenu template functions. You were introduced to using Pipes to transform data within a template. We fetched data from an external source, and learned how to use the proxy system in Ionic to address any CORS issues. Finally we looked at both Ionic Events and Observables as methods to update our UI dynamically.

CHAPTER 10

Debugging and Testing Your Ionic Application

There will come a time when you need to debug your Ionic application. In this chapter, we will look at various solutions and tools you can use to help you resolve possible issues that may arise. Since Ionic is built atop a collection of technologies, this means that debugging your application may not always be straightforward. This can be a challenge for some developers who are used to having a complete ecosystem to work within. Let's learn how to use some of the debugging tools.

Debugging your Ionic application can be broken down into three distinct phases: browser level, emulator debugging, and on-device debugging. Each one of the phases offers different levels of insight into your application. Since Ionic is built atop web technologies, often the best place to start debugging is with our browser. But even before turning to those solutions, there are some other first steps we can take.

With Ionic 2 being developed in TypeScript, this is actually our first line of defense in writing a working application. If your IDE is complaining about a variable or a function, that is usually a good sign that something is amiss. There are times when a reference is incorrectly updated when refactoring or a path to a module is off by a sub folder. Spotting these simple mistakes can save a lot of questioning on why your application is having issues.

Now, your IDE won't be perfect in spotting everything while you are editing your code. The next element you can use in resolving issues is the compiler output itself. As you might have noticed, when compiling your Ionic 2 application, a lot of messages are written to your console's window. If you are like most, this is probably just a small window, tucked in the corner of your screen. However, more than once have we seen error messages get written to this window, only to have them quickly scroll out of view.

If your application isn't launching for some reason, the first place to start is to look at the build output to your console. You may find you missed a comma in an object or some equally hard to spot typo in your code. One recommendation we have is to have your console window actually show more than a few lines of output. This gives you the ability to see the various build events, and if an issue occurred.

Coming back to the fact that we are not working with complete IDE (like Xcode or Android Studio), some of the build debugging tools are not there to assist us. The most common one that we have found is that it does not recognize that there may be unsaved files in your project when you attempt to build your application. Often when working on a particular screen, you may have its HTML file open to adjust some markup, the SCSS open to modify the visual look, and the TypeScript file open as you edit the component's code. It is easy to forget to save one or more of the files before you attempt your next build. Then as you test your application, you are scratching your head wondering why something is not working correctly. One of the simplest steps you can take as you start to debug your application is to ensure that all the files are saved.

A lot of your development will be in your local browser and using $ `ionic serve` to run your application. Now, one of the features of `ionic serve` is that it will watch your source files and trigger a rebuild when it sees that one of the files has been updated. This is very useful most of the time, but the Ionic build process takes a moment or two to run. There are times when the build scripts are running, and something causes them to run again before they finish their first build of cycle. This can result in a "white screen of death," as it commonly known. In reality, the *main.js* file was incorrectly built or is missing altogether. Our recommendation when you encounter this issue is to make sure all your files are saved and run the build sequence again. In fact, we will stop our instance of $ `ionic serve`, and start fresh.

Once you have your application up in Chrome, Chrome's standard Developer Tools (DevTools) will become your primary method of debugging your application. You might recall a bit of advice that we had about the order of development: try to focus on everything that you can do *not* to have to test or run on your mobile until you have to. The ability to quickly leverage Chrome DevTools to work with your application can save you hours. If you are coming from a traditional web development background, then these tools should need no introduction. But for those who are not familiar with them, we recommend reading up on them on Google's developer site (*https://developer.chrome.com/devtools*).

To bring up the DevTools, you can use the Chrome menu, found on the top right of the browser window, then select Tools→Developer Tools. Or you can simply right-click or Ctrl-click on a Mac, and select Inspect Element.

There are several useful shortcuts for opening the DevTools:

- Use Ctrl+Shift+I (or Cmd+Opt+I on Mac) to open the DevTools.
- Use Ctrl+Shift+J (or Cmd+Opt+J on Mac) to open the DevTools and bring focus to the Console.
- Use Ctrl+Shift+C (or Cmd+Shift+C on Mac) to open the DevTools in Inspect Element mode, or toggle Inspect Element mode if the DevTools are already open.

With these tools, we have a variety of options we can use to debug our Ionic application. If it is an issue related to the visual display of an element, we can navigate the rendered DOM to locate the element, then use the CSS inspector to uncover the cascade of styles that are being applied to that element. We often use this technique in understanding the base styling of an element, so we can then apply the smallest amount of changes to our Sass file to achieve the desired look.

But, more often than not, we are actually leveraging the JavaScript console and the accompanying debugger. Now the Ionic build system will combine all our source code into one file; but by leveraging the source map, we are able to reference the original sources for our code.

There are a few features in DevTools that are extremely useful for mobile developers (see Figure 10-1).

Figure 10-1. Chrome's device preview toggle

Located in the upper left is the Device Toolbar, which will change your browser's window to allow you to see how your Ionic application would appear on a mobile screen (Figure 10-2).

Figure 10-2. The Ionic weather app running with Chrome's device mode enabled

This toolbar allows you to select a variety of popular mobile devices: Nexus 5x, Galaxy 5, iPhone 6, as well as the ability to define a custom device. For some devices, Chrome will automatically overlay the screen chrome (like a status bar or soft keys). You can also rotate the screen from portrait to landscape to see how the elements will respond.

> **iOS Mode**
>
> Even though iOS screen sizes are listed, you will need to append ?
> `platform-mode=ios` to the end of the URL in order for your appli-
> cation to trigger its iOS display rules. Alternatively, you can use
> `ionic serve --platform=ios` to append that flag automatically.

Another useful capability in DevTools is the ability to simulate a variety of network conditions and speeds. To do this, select the Network tab. There you can adjust the network's apparent speed. This is quite useful to make sure your application properly handles both the offline and online cases.

We have found that we are able to resolve 70%-80% of our issues just by working within DevTools and our browser.

Dealing with CORS Issues

As you start expanding out your application, you will likely begin to work with a range of services and their APIs calls. These remote requests are usually a source of frustration, as they often require some level of authorization. One of the first levels of security with remote APIs is Cross-Origin Resource Sharing (CORS). This is a mechanism that gives web servers cross-domain access controls, which enable secure cross-domain data transfers. Modern browsers (like our Ionic App) use CORS in an API container, such as `XMLHttpRequest` or `Fetch`, to mitigate risks of cross-origin HTTP requests. Make sure you review the security and access information of the APIs that your application might use.

Because we are testing our application locally in a browser, these external requests will now be blocked. This is not an issue when testing in an emulator or on an actual device, but having to run in both an emulator and on-device can lengthen your testing cycle. There are two options to enable local development. You can set up a proxy like we did for the IonicWeather application. Or a faster option is to simply launch Chrome with its CORS disabled. Now this is something you should only be doing while you are testing your application. We are going to launch an instance of Chrome with CORS disabled via the command line. For macOS users, the command will be:

```
open -n -a /Applications/Google\ Chrome.app --args --user-data-dir= ↵
"/tmp/chrome_dev_session" --disable-web-security
```

The `-a` flag opens the specified application. The `-n` flag will open a new instance of the application, even if one is already running. The two arguments that occur after the `--args` flag disable CORS and define a directory for user data.

For Windows users, the command is:

```
chrome.exe --user-data-dir="C:/Chrome dev session" --disable-web-security
```

Now when you use $ `ionic serve`, this version of Chrome that is running will allow your HTTP requests through.

Debugging through an iOS or Android Simulator

How do we tackle debugging issues that exclude using DevTools and our local browser? That is when we can turn to our device emulator. Although not a full substitute for a real device, it will allow a close approximation of our mobile environment. In order to run our Ionic application in this mode we need to use the $ `ionic emulate <platform>` command:

```
ionic emulate ios --consolelogs --serverlogs

ionic emulate android --consolelogs --serverlogs
```

or the shorthand version:

```
ionic run ios -c -s

ionic run android -c -s
```

livereload Flag

Ionic CLI used to support live reload through the `--livereload` or `--l` flag. However, some low-level changes in the security protocol caused this feature to stop working. The Ionic team is actively working on finding a solution.

Although we are now running within an emulator, we still have some other powerful debugging tools available to us. For macOS users, Safari will now become our tool of choice for finding and eliminating bugs. The first step is to enable the Develop menu in Safari. Go to Safari→Preferences→Advanced, then enable Show Develop menu in menu bar.

From this new Develop menu, we can now select our application running in the iOS simulator and debug it. Safari's developer tools are very similar to Chrome Dev Tools —they enable inspection of the page's DOM, the source files, and the JavaScript console.

Android

Chrome also offers the same type of functionality. In the address bar, type `chrome://inspect`. This will display a list of devices that Chrome will be able to remotely debug. Once you have your application successfully running in the emulator it will be listed here. Now you can use the same Chrome DevTools to work with your application running within the Android emulator.

Debugging On-Device

Just as the emulators are a step up from browser-based testing, the final level of testing should take place on an actual device. To do this, we need to build our Ionic application for installation on actual mobile devices. In order to run our Ionic application in this mode we need to use the $ ionic run <platform> command:

```
ionic run ios

ionic run android
```

This will produce either an IPA file (for iOS) or an APK file (for Android) that can be loaded and run on your device. Let's look at each platform independently.

Android

Before we load our application on the device, let's enable on-device debugging for Android. This is done within the Developer Options setting, which is not enabled by default. To reveal this setting, open the Settings, then the About Phone sections. Next, tap seven times on the Build Number section. If you encounter an issue in locating this option, the specific steps for your device should be found via your favorite search engine. Once this option is unlocked, you can then enable Allow USB debugging.

There is one restriction: to use Chrome's Remote Debugging, the device must be running Android 4.4 (KitKat) or later (aka API level 19). You will also need to be running Chrome 30 or later on your desktop.

Loading your application on your Android device can be done in multiple ways: you can upload the APK to a web server and download it, copy it to a service like Dropbox and install it from there, or even email the APK. Once the APK has been downloaded to your device, the Android installer should run, informing you of the permissions your application needs and then installing the app.

Just like debugging your Ionic application in the Android emulator, you follow the same steps for on-device debugging. Simply navigate to *chrome://inspect* in Chrome. With your Android device plugged into your computer and the Ionic application running, you should see your application listed. Selecting your application will then bring up the familiar Chrome Developer Tools.

If you can see your device in the inspect devices section but you can't see the Cordova Web View, you may need to add android:debuggable="true" in the <application> node of your *AndroidManifest.xml*.

Now, we are able to fully interact with our application running in its native environment. For example, if your application used the device's Camera, that functionality would not have been available in either the browser or in the emulator.

---

iOS

Debugging your Ionic application on iOS follows a very similar path to Android debugging.

Just as a reminder, you will still need to sign this IPA with your development certificate and make sure your application ID, found within the *config.xml* file, matches what is listed in the development certificate. If they do not match, your IPA will not be properly signed and will not run on your iOS device.

If you encounter errors using the Ionic CLI to generate your IPA, you may need to open the actual Xcode project file and manually set the signing profile. Once this is set, the Ionic CLI should function normally.

With the IPA now built and installed on our iOS devices, connect your iOS device to your computer, then launch Safari on the desktop. Next, launch your Ionic application on your iOS device. From the Develop menu, you should see your iOS device listed. You may need to wait a moment while the WebView is located. Once it is selected, the same Developer Tools that you used with the simulator are available to you.

Debugging Ionic Initialization

There are times when you are testing your Ionic application on either the emulator or live device and an issue occurs during the app's initialization. Consequently, your app needs to be running before the remote debugger can locate and connect to it. Unfortunately, any console messages or actual errors will not be captured. With your application connected to a remote debugging session, switch to the console tab. Here we can force the WebView to reload itself, allowing us to view any issues that we missed. You can use the Reload button in the Dev Toolbar or simply enter this command into the console input field:

```
window.location.reload();
```

Either will force the WebView to reload itself, and since your remote debugging is already connected, you will be able to see what the issue might be.

Additional Tools

Beyond these debugging solutions, there are several other options that you should be aware of that can assist your Ionic development:

Cordova Tools Extension for Visual Studio Code
Available for Visual Studio Code, the Cordova Tools Extension (*http://bit.ly/ 2l8D5Gn*) allows for code-hinting, debugging and integrated commands for Apache Cordova (PhoneGap). As an added bonus, it also has support for the

Ionic Framework (albeit version 1). We have found this extension invaluable during our Ionic development workflow.

Tools for Apache Cordova (TACO)

If you use Visual Studio as your IDE for Ionic development, then you should install Tools for Apache Cordova, or "TACO" for short. This extension provides IntelliSense, debugging, and build support for Apache Cordova and Ionic projects; and unlike the Cordova Tools Extension, TACO does have beta support for Ionic 2. Visual Studio can also debug your code running on an iOS, Android, or Windows device, an emulator or simulator, or a browser-based debug target like Apache Ripple.

An additional capability of TACO (*https://taco.visualstudio.com*) is its ability to build for Mac OS remotely via services like MacInCloud.

GapDebug

Genuitec's GapDebug (*https://www.genuitec.com/products/gapdebug/*) is another debugging solution that has proven useful in our workflow. Available for both Windows and Mac platforms, this tool offers easy installation application files onto your device using drag-and-drop. It has integrated versions of the Safari Web Inspector for iOS debugging and Chrome Dev Tools for Android debugging. You are also able to debug both iOS and Android apps whether you are running Windows or macOS. Unfortunately, Genuitec recently annouced that they will be ending development of this product.

Ripple

Ripple (*http://ripple.incubator.apache.org*) is a desktop-based emulator for Cordova projects. Essentially, it lets you run a Cordova application in your desktop application and fake various Cordova features. For example, it lets you simulate the accelerometer to test shake events. It fakes the camera API by letting you select a picture from your hard drive. Ripple lets you focus on your custom code so you can spend less time worrying about Cordova plugins.

Augury

Augury (*https://augury.angular.io*), formerly known as Batarangle, is a Chrome Developer Tools extension that allows developers to visualize their Angular 2 application's component tree and the data associated with it. Support for this solution is still emerging as Ionic 2 matures.

Summary

As you can see, there is a wide range of solutions to debug your Ionic application across a wide range of testing environments. Depending on the stage of development, you should find the right set of tools to enable you to resolve any issues that might arise.

CHAPTER 11

Deploying Your Application

Now with your application fully tested, it is time to create the versions that can be submitted to the various app stores. Before we generate the release build of our app, we should remove any assets that should not be included in our production release.

For example, the Console plugin was added when we first generated our Ionic application, so let's remove it from our installed plugins. To do this, simply run:

```
$ ionic plugin remove cordova-plugin-console
```

We also need to manually delete the reference to this plugin in our *config.xml* file. Locate this line and delete it:

```
<plugin name="cordova-plugin-console" spec="~1.0.4"/>
```

Adjusting the config.xml File

Before generating your production build, you may also need to adjust the *config.xml* file with some additional settings. By default, the *config.xml* that is generated by Ionic is fairly bare bones. There are many additional settings you may wish to configure for your application, such as restricting the OS versions your app will run on. Other items within the *config.xml* that you may want to adjust can include the version number, restricting the domain access list, and replacing development API endpoints with production API endpoints.

For a summary of these settings, see Appendix B or the full documentation at the Cordova website (*http://bit.ly/2l8zSqd*).

App Icons and Splash Screens

If you have not already replaced the stock icons and splash screens that are included when you use the Ionic templates, now would be the time. Rather than export the myriad of sizes required by each platform, we can use the Ionic CLI to generate them for us.

First, delete the existing icons and splash screens that were included. We have found that the CLI will not overwrite existing files; instead, they'll fail silently. Next, include your base icon file within the resources folder. For the best results, this file should be 1,024×1,024 pixels in size. You should also not include any platform-specific effects, such as round corners or glossy overlays. Once you have your icon ready, name it *icon.png*. The CLI will accept Photoshop (PSD) files, but rather than worry about an incompatibility with a filter or some other technique you might use, we recommend sticking with a flattened PNG file as the source.

For the splash screen, you should have a file that is 2,208×2,208 pixels in size. Unlike icons, which are always square, splash screens are rectangular and can be oriented in both portrait and landscape mode. If your application is constrained to only run in a particular orientation, then you only need to supply the splash screens for that orientation. The Ionic team has provided a template (*http://bit.ly/2mXe6Fc*) with guidelines about the safe zones for your artwork. Save your file as *splash.png*, also within the resources directory.

From the command line, run $ ionic resources. This will upload the files to Ionic, generate the various icons and sizes, and then save them in the correct directories.

Building Your Android APK

To generate a release build for Android, we simply use the following CLI command:

```
$ ionic build android --release -prod
```

If you have built Ionic 1 apps in the past, you might notice there is now an additional flag, the -prod. This tells the Ionic Build script to use the *main.prod.ts* file when building the *main.js* file. For those familiar with Angular 2 development, this file makes the call to enableProdMode().

Once the CLI is done working (hopefully with no errors), we can find our unsigned APK file in *platforms/android/build/outputs/apk/android-release-unsigned.apk*. Now we need to sign the unsigned APK and run an alignment utility to optimize it and prepare it for the app store.

Generating the Signing Key

To generate the signing key, we need to use the `keytool` command that is installed with the JDK. Here is the basic command:

```
$ keytool -genkey -v -keystore my-release-key.keystore -alias alias_name
-keyalg RSA -keysize 2048 -validity 10000
```

The *alias_name* is your key alias. This is just a descriptive string that will identify your app. This can be letters, numbers, and underscores. Note that the key alias is case-sensitive. You can also change the *my-release-key.keystore* to something more descriptive.

The tool will prompt you to create a password for the keystore file and the key alias. It will then ask you a series of questions that will be used as part of the key generation process:

```
Enter keystore password:
Re-enter new password:
What is your first and last name?
  [Unknown]:  Chris Griffith
What is the name of your organizational unit?
  [Unknown]:  None
What is the name of your organization?
  [Unknown]:  AJ Software
What is the name of your City or Locality?
  [Unknown]:  San Diego
What is the name of your State or Province?
  [Unknown]:  CA
What is the two-letter country code for this unit?
  [Unknown]:  US
Is CN=Chris Griffith, OU=None, O=AJ Software, L=San Diego, ST=CA, C=US correct?
  [no]:  y
```

After you provide this information, you will see this in the terminal:

```
Generating 2,048 bit RSA key pair and self-signed certificate (SHA256withRSA)
with a validity of 90 for: CN=Chris Griffith, OU=None, O=AJ Software,
L=San Diego, ST=CA, C=US

Enter key password for <my_alias_name>
    (RETURN if same as keystore password):
```

Once this is done, you will have a *my-release-key.keystore* file in the directory you ran the command from.

Make sure your store this file in a safe location. Once you sign and submit your application with this keystore, all updates to that app must be signed with the same keystore. There is no method to regenerate a replacement keystore file.

Next, we actually sign our APK with our keystore. To do this, we will use the `jarsigner` tool that is also included with the JDK:

```
$ jarsigner -verbose -sigalg SHA1withRSA -digestalg SHA1
-keystore my-release-key.keystore android-release-unsigned.apk alias_name
```

This command will ask you for the password you used when you created the keystore, and then it will sign the application.

The final step is to run the zip align tool (in */path/to/Android/sdk/build-tools/VERSION/zipalign*) to optimize the APK:

```
$ zipalign -v 4 path/to/android-release-unsigned.apk MyApp.apk
```

With that, we will have our release-ready APK named *MyApp.apk* ready for submission to the Google Play Store.

Submitting to the Google Play Store

We will now cover the basic steps needed to actually submit your app to the Google Play Store. First, you will need to create a Google Developer account (*https://play.google.com/apps/publish/*). This account requires a one-time fee of $25.

Once your developer account is active, you can sign in to the portal and begin the publishing process; it is fairly straightforward. However, the process is much easier if you have gathered all the supporting assets the actual Play Store listing needs, such as screenshots and marketing text (see Figure 11-1).

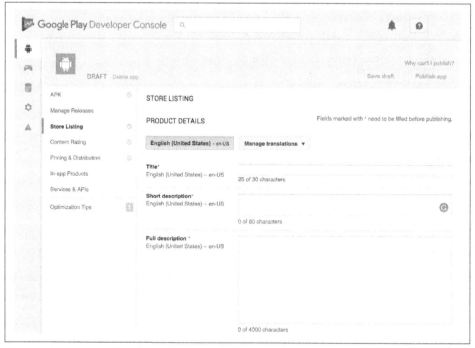

Figure 11-1. Google Play Store App submission screen

After all the required elements are submitted, your application should be available for purchase within a few hours, if not sooner.

Building Your iOS App

Although it is possible to build development versions of your iOS application without enrolling in the Apple Developer Program (*https://developer.apple.com/programs/*), if you wish to publish to the Apple App Store, you will need to pay the $99 yearly fee. Once you have completed your enrollment, we will need to next configure Xcode to use this account. Within Xcode, go to Preferences→Accounts, then fill in your Apple iOS developer account information.

Request a Distribution Certificate

With Xcode and your developer account linked, go to Preferences→Accounts, select your Apple ID, and then click the View Details button. You should see a pop up similar to the one in Figure 11-2.

Figure 11-2. Xcode pop up after pressing the View Details button

Click the Create button next to the iOS Distribution option, then choose Done to close the account details page.

Create a Distribution Provisioning Profile

The next step is to create a distribution provisioning profile that lets you submit your app to the App Store. This step is done on the Member Center page (*https://devel oper.apple.com/membercenter/index.action*). On that page, choose the Certificates, Identifiers & Profiles link. Then find the Provisioning Profiles panel (Figure 11-3) and select the Distribution option.

Figure 11-3. Provisioning Profiles panel

On this page, click the [+] button to begin the process of generating a distribution profile (see Figure 11-4).

Figure 11-4. Click the [+] button on the Provisioning Profiles panel

You will then be asked what kind of provisioning profile you need to generate. Hopefully, you recognize this screen from when you created your development profile. Instead of choosing iOS App Development, select the App Store option, then click the Continue button (Figure 11-5).

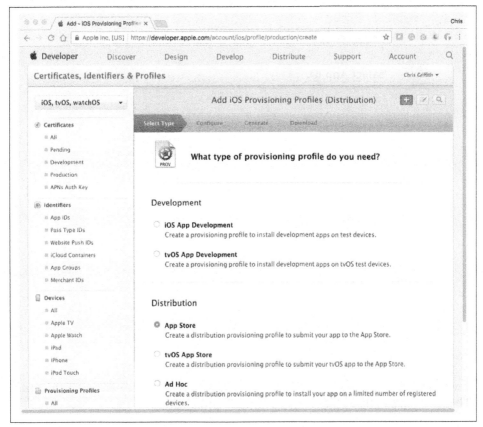

Figure 11-5. The provisioning options screen

On the Select App ID screen (Figure 11-6), we need to choose the App ID of your application. You should have already generated an App ID when you created your development certificate. If not, cancel out of this process, and use the App IDs link in the Identifiers pane to generate one. Once you have selected your App ID, click the Continue button to proceed to the next step.

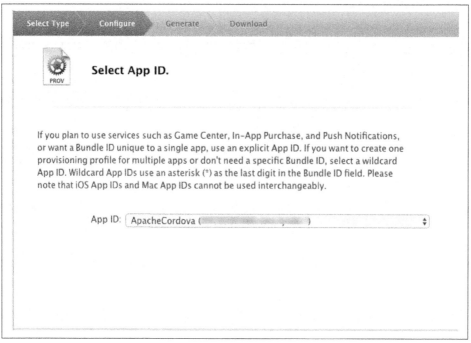

Figure 11-6. App ID selection screen

Now we need to select the distribution certificate that you created earlier in Xcode (Figure 11-7), and then choose the Continue button.

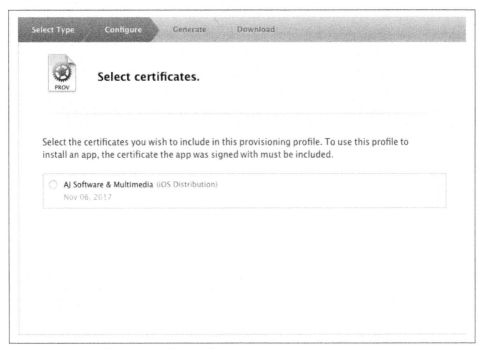

Figure 11-7. Distribution certificate selection screen

On the next screen (see Figure 11-8), you will need to name this profile, and then choose the Continue button.

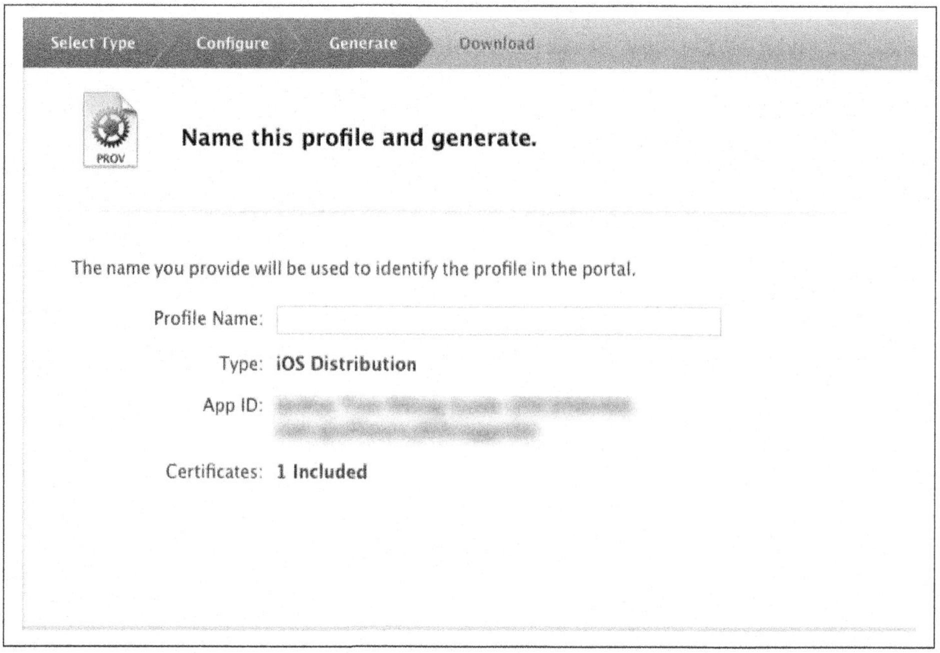

Figure 11-8. Profile generation screen

The distribution certificate will be generated and it can be downloaded to your computer by clicking the Download button (Figure 11-9).

Figure 11-9. Provisioning downloading screen

Once you have downloaded the provisioning profile, simply double-click it to install it.

Creating the App Listing

Apple uses iTunes Connect (*https://itunesconnect.apple.com*) to manage app submissions. After you sign in, you should see a screen similar to the one in Figure 11-10.

Figure 11-10. iTunes Connect portal

Choose the My Apps button, then select the [+] icon in the upper left. This will bring up the dialog in Figure 11-11.

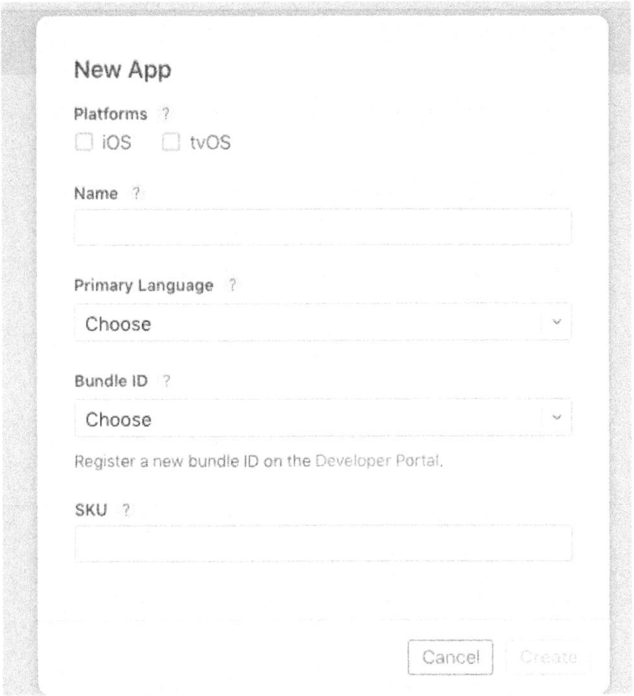

Figure 11-11. New app dialog

Select the iOS platform, and then fill in the rest of the information. Once you have completed this form, click the Create button.

The App Information screen will now be shown (Figure 11-12). Although we can set some of the information, you will be returning to this screen later in the process. The reason for creating your placeholder app is that the Application Loader tool needs it to exist before it can upload your app.

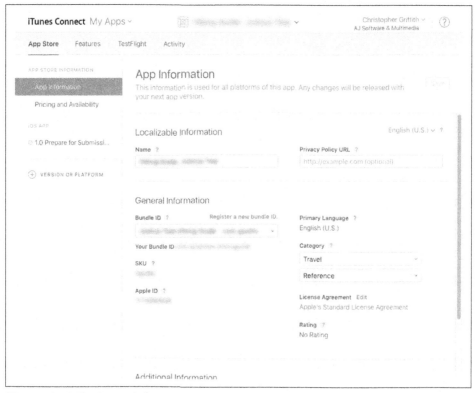

Figure 11-12. Basic app information screen

Building the App for Production

With our app store stub created, we can turn back to the process of completing the distribution build. Return to your command prompt and run `$ ionic build ios --release -prod`. After a few moments and a lot of output to the terminal, you should see `BUILD SUCCEEDED` output to the console. If not, scroll back through the output to identify the error.

Creating an Archive of the Application

To submit our application to iTunes Connect, we need to create an archive of the application. Return to Xcode and open your application's Xcode project. This file can be found in the *platforms/ios* directory.

On the project information screen, check that the bundle ID is correct, as well as the version and build numbers. The team option should be set to your Apple developer account. If you want to restrict which devices your app will run on, you can set that here as well.

Now select Product→Scheme→Edit Scheme to open the scheme editor. Then select Archive from the list. Make sure that Build Configuration is set to Release.

To create the actual archive, we need to make sure that we are targeting the Generic iOS Device from the device list in the toolbar. Then, select Product→Archive, and the Archive organizer will appear and display the new archive (Figure 11-13).

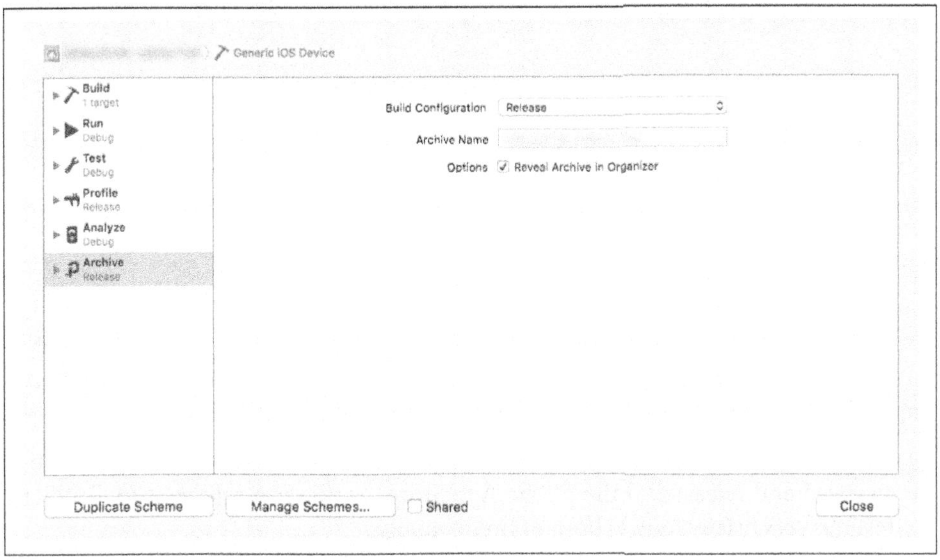

Figure 11-13. Product archive screen

Our application is now ready to be uploaded to iTunes Connect. Click the Upload to App Store button (Figure 11-14). Xcode will now sign our application, revalidate it, and upload to iTunes Connect. Once that process is complete, you should see the message in Figure 11-15.

Figure 11-14. App Store Archive Upload panel

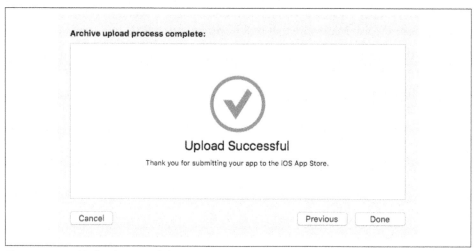

Figure 11-15. Upload successful message

After a few moments, you should receive a confirmation email. We can return to our app listing on iTunes Connect portal and finish the submission process.

At this point you have two options with your submission: you can release your app to be reviewed and released to the public App Store, or you can release it to TestFlight for testing. Let's briefly look at both of these options.

Using TestFlight Beta Testing

TestFlight Beta Testing is an Apple product that allows you to invite users to test your iOS apps before you release them into the App Store. With your iOS app uploaded to the iTunes Connect portal, simply select the TestFlight tab to begin the process. You will need to provide some basic information: an email for feedback, a marketing URL, and a privacy policy.

Next, you will need to answer a series of questions about encryption. Then your app will undergo a short review by Apple. Once it has been approved, you will be notified by email, and you can distribute it to both internal and external testers. Your testers will need to install the TestFlight app to access your app (Figure 11-16).

Figure 11-16. TestFlight app screens

Once you are ready to release the app for testing, your testers will receive an email with a link that will launch the TestFlight app on their iOS device and install the app. They then can use the app like any other app. One thing to note: these apps have an expiration date of 60 days once they are released, so this is not a long-term distribution solution. You are also limited to 2,000 testers at one time. When you are done with your testing, you can then move onto releasing the app to the public App Store.

Releasing to the App Store

With our iOS app uploaded and validated, we can complete the final steps to submit it to review by Apple. From the iTunes Connect portal, select the app you wish to release. Update or complete any app information you need to, and define the price of your app. Note that if you release your app for free, you can never charge for it.

Then click the Prepare for Submission link. This will bring up a long form where you can define the screenshots, store description, keywords, and app rating (Figure 11-17).

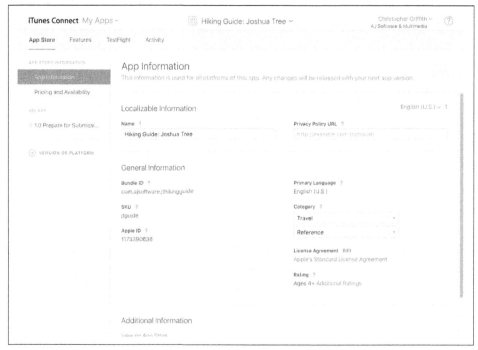

Figure 11-17. iTunes Connect app details screen

Once you have completed editing all these items, you can submit your app to be reviewed again by Apple. This process can take a few days or longer, depending on the backlog of reviews. Now you can turn to the hard work of promoting your new application!

Summary

You now know how to properly compile and submit your apps to both the Apple App Store and the Google Play Store. If you plan to release to the Windows Store, the Microsoft TACO team has a great resource (*http://bit.ly/2lTgrPl*) to guide you through that process.

CHAPTER 12

Exploring the Ionic Cloud

Ionic is more than just a framework to build mobile applications; it is also a collection of cloud-based services. These services include the ability to compile your application remotely, update deployed applications without resubmitting, and generating the user interface through a visual builder. The focus of the Ionic Cloud is to directly support the actual development of your mobile application. Unlike the Ionic Framework, which is open-sourced, these services require a monthly fee. But don't worry: most of them have a development version, so you can explore them at no charge—with some usage limitations.

 Initially, the Ionic Cloud also contained some additional services like, user authentication, push notifications, analytics, and database support. These services have been or being shut down.

Setting Up Ionic Cloud

Before we can begin using any of the Ionic Cloud services, we will need to create a free Cloud account (*https://apps.ionic.io/signup*).

Next, we need to install the Ionic Cloud client in the app. Make sure your active directory is the at the root level of your application. Then run this command to install the client:

```
$ npm install @ionic/cloud-angular --save
```

Generating Your Ionic App ID

Before we can configure our app to use the Ionic Cloud, we need to have an Ionic App ID. This a different ID from the app ID found within the *config.xml* file. Still within your project directory, run this command:

```
$ ionic io init
```

This command will automatically generate your Ionic App ID and save it in your *ionic.config.json* file. You may need to provide your Ionic.io username and password to proceed. Once it has updated the *ionic.config.json* file, go ahead and open this file; we are going to need this value in the next step.

In addition to updating our local app, that command also created an entry in your Ionic Cloud Dashboard (Figure 12-1).

Figure 12-1. The Ionic Cloud Dashboard

To access this Ionic Cloud Dashboard, simply navigate to Ionic.io and log in.

Configuring Your Application

With our app now registered with the Ionic Cloud, we need to update our app's bootstraping process. Open your *app.module.ts* file in your editor.

We first need to import the Ionic Cloud module:

```
import { CloudSettings, CloudModule } from '@ionic/cloud-angular';
```

Next, define a constant that will define our Ionic Cloud setting. Replace the APP_ID in the code sample with the value you found in the *ionic.config.json*:

```
const cloudSettings: CloudSettings = {
  'core': {
    'app_id': 'APP_ID'
  }
};
```

Within the @NgModule, we need to include our CloudModule in the imports array:

```
@NgModule({
  declarations: [ ... ],
  imports: [
    IonicModule.forRoot(MyApp),
    CloudModule.forRoot(cloudSettings)
  ],
  bootstrap: [IonicApp],
  entryComponents: [ ... ],
  providers: [ ... ]
})
```

Our application is now ready to utilize the Ionic Cloud services.

Ionic Deploy

One service offered in the Ionic Cloud is Ionic Deploy. Since the core of our application is not really compiled into the native app's codebase, it is possible to swap out our HTML, JS, and CSS without needing to recompile the application. If you have used either the Ionic View app or the PhoneGap Developer App, this is core technology that powers both of those applications.

Here's what you can do by enabling live deployment of your application:

- Bypass app store approvals
- Update your app on demand
- Push new features and bug fixes to your users effortlessly
- Perform A/B user testing

When working with Ionic Deploy, you will need to know some specific terminology (*http://docs.ionic.io/services/deploy/#terminology*):

Snapshot
    The bundled version of your app's code. This is the package that will be sent to the user's device.

Live Deployment
    This refers to when the active snapshot is download and running on a device.

Channel
    Snapshots are released to specific deploy channels. Channels allow you to deploy different snapshots of your app to different devices.

Binary Update
    When you need to update the native portion of your application, usually if a plugin or a Cordova update is needed.

Setting Up Ionic Deploy

To demonstrate this service, we are going to create a new Ionic project based on the blank template. From the command line, run the following:

```
$ ionic start IonicDeploy blank --v2
```

You will need to install the initial Ionic Cloud component and initialize your app to use the Ionic Cloud.

In addition, you will need to install the Ionic Deploy plugin. This plugin will handle the actual updating of your app on both Android and iOS devices. With your application's project directory active in your terminal, run this command:

```
$ ionic plugin add ionic-plugin-deploy --save
```

With the plugin installed, we can create the system to check for new deployments, download and extract them, and then enable them.

Testing Ionic Deploy

The Ionic Deploy functionality can only run in an emulator or on an actual device. You will not be able to service within a browser.

Enabling Ionic Deploy

Open the *home.ts* file and first add the `Deploy` module to the imports:

```
import { Deploy } from '@ionic/cloud-angular';
```

Then include it within the `constructor`:

```
constructor(public navCtrl: NavController, public deploy:Deploy) {

}
```

Before we continue, we need to explore the concept of deploy channels. By setting different channels, you can manage various snapshots of your app to different devices. By default, there are three channels available: production, staging, and dev. You can create more channels if you need to (Figure 12-2).

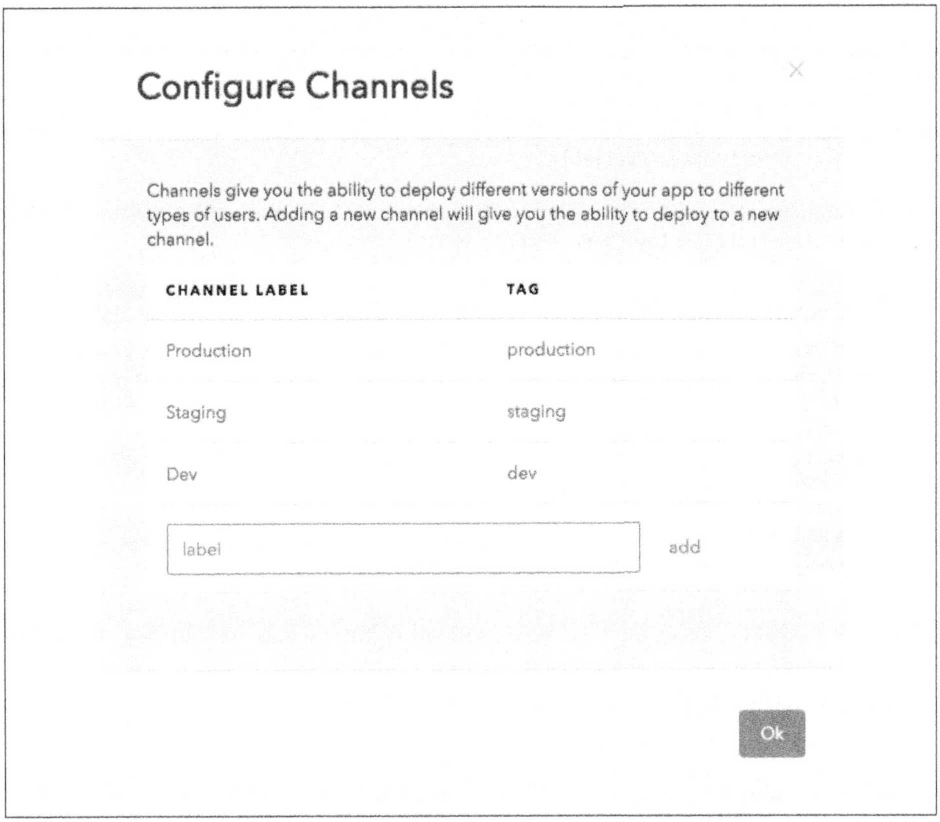

Figure 12-2. Channel configuration dialog

Within our constructor, let's set our deploy channel to "dev".

```
this.deploy.channel = 'dev';
```

This will tell Ionic Deploy to only refer to that channel when looking for any snapshots. If you do not define a channel, then it will default to production.

The app will need to conduct the following steps to implement live deployments:

1. Check if a new snapshot has been deployed.
2. Apply the snapshot.
3. Reload the app.

Checking for a new snapshot

To see if a new snapshot is available from the Ionic Cloud, we simply call `deploy.check()`. Since this is a network call, we will wrap it within a Promise:

```
this.deploy.check().then((snapshotAvailable: boolean) => {
  // When snapshotAvailable is true, you can apply the snapshot
  if (snapshotAvailable) {
    alert('Update is Available');
  } else {
    alert("No Updates Available");
  }
}).catch ((ex) => {
  console.error('Deploy Check Error', ex);
});
```

When check() is called, it returns a boolean if there is a snapshot available to be downloaded. Note that we will use alerts to monitor the flow through the process.

If there is a snapshot available, we can begin the download by calling download(). This call should also be wrapped within a Promise:

```
this.deploy.download().then(() => {
  alert('Downloading new snapshot');
}).catch((ex) => {
  console.error('Deploy Download Error', ex);
});
```

Once the snapshot has completed its download to the device, we can have the snapshot extracted:

```
this.deploy.extract().then(() => {
  alert('Extracting snapshot');
}).catch((ex) => {
  console.error('Deploy Extract Error', ex);
});
```

After the extract() method's Promise resolves, you can then trigger an immediate app restart using the load() method. Otherwise, the new snapshot will be run the next time the app is run. For this sample, we will trigger the automatic restart, although we would highly recommend that you give the user the opportunity to control the restart:

```
this.deploy.extract().then(() => {
  alert('Extracting snapshot');
  this.deploy.load();
}).catch((ex) => {
  console.error('Deploy Extract Error', ex);
});
```

Here is the complete code block:

```
this.deploy.check().then((snapshotAvailable: boolean) => {
  // When snapshotAvailable is true, you can apply the snapshot
  if (snapshotAvailable) {
    alert('Update is Available');
    this.deploy.download().then(() => {
      alert('Downloading new snapshot');
```

```
        this.deploy.extract().then(() => {
            alert('Extracting snapshot');
            this.deploy.load();
        }).catch((ex) => {
          console.error('Deploy Extract Error', ex);
        });
        // return this.deploy.extract();
      }).catch((ex) => {
        console.error('Deploy Download Error', ex);
      });
    } else {
      alert("No Updates Available");
    }
  }).catch ((ex) => {
    console.error('Deploy Check Error', ex);
  });
```

With our live deployment code in place, save this file and then let's create our first snapshot.

Creating a snapshot

When creating a snapshot, the contents of the *www* directory are uploaded to the Ionic servers. This means we need to generate a build into this directory before we call $ `ionic upload`. The easiest method is to simply run $ `ionic serve`. Don't be concerned that our deploy checking code will not function in our browser; we just need a current build.

To create a snapshot, we need to upload our app's code to the Ionic Cloud via the CLI. The base command is:

```
$ ionic upload
```

However, you can additionally include a short description of the snapshot, as well as the channel you want the snapshot deployed to. Run this command to create our first snapshot:

```
$ ionic upload --note "Initial Deploy" --deploy dev
```

Now if you run your application in an emulator, you might be surprised to see that our app will actually go through the update process. Since no snapshot has been downloaded, Ionic Deploy will check the local registry, and inform the system that there is an update available. Go ahead and let the process proceed. Once the initial snapshot is downloaded, extracted, and applied, our app will reboot. Now when our code checks the snapshot version, it will match and our update logic will exit. Let's make a small change to our app so we can see a real update in action.

Open *home.html* and change the title of the page to Ionic Deploy Test. Since the first line of the text is from *The Merry Wives of Windsor*, let's swap it out as well.

Save our file and make sure you run your application once with $ ionic serve. Then create a new snapshot by running:

```
$ ionic upload --note "Second Deploy" --deploy dev
```

Now if you emulate or build your app again, it will create a new version, and you will not see the live deployment functioning. Simply run the app in either your emulator or on an actual device. Our update alerts will appear again, and then we will see our new content (Figure 12-3).

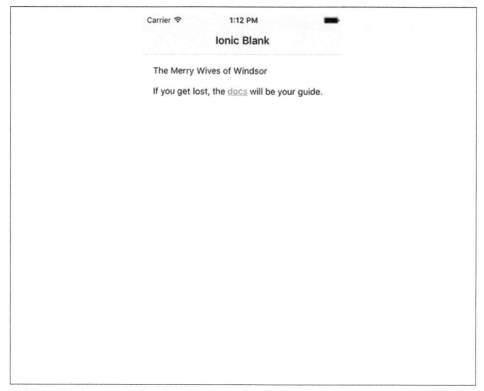

Figure 12-3. Our app updated via Ionic Deploy

If we bring up our Ionic Cloud dashboard, we can see our snapshots (Figure 12-4).

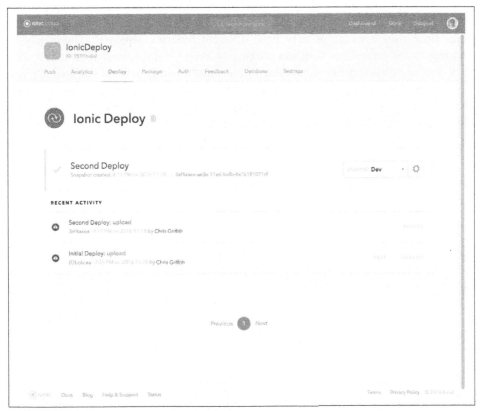

Figure 12-4. Ionic Deploy dashboard

From this page, we can manage our deployments in our various channels. If we need to channel an active snapshot, we can do this as well. At the time of writing, there is no method to delete a snapshot from the Ionic Cloud. Proper descriptions will be critical in identifying your snapshots. You may also want to test out your application's live deployment logic in a sample app, not your production app.

Setting snapshot metadata

You can also include custom metadata with your snapshot. This metadata is added through the dashboard as key/value pairs, For example, you could include release notes as a metadata item.

To retrieve this information from the Ionic Cloud, use the getMetadata() method:

```
this.deploy.getMetadata().then((metadata) => {
  // use metadata
});
```

Using binary versioning

Over time your application may have different binaries deployed. There may be changes in the versions of Cordova plugins, or even Cordova itself in your app. This may cause an incompatibility between a new snapshot and the older released application. To prevent this, you can use Ionic Cloud's binary versioning feature. Binary versioning lets you halt live deployments on devices that would otherwise break the app. Binary versioning requires that you use a semantic version for your build version (which is set in your *config.xml* file).

Semantic Versioning Scheme

The semantic versioning format comprises three parts: major.minor.patch. When we compare versions, we adhere to version precedence. Example: 1.0.0→2.0.0→2.1.0→2.1.1.

There are three mechanisms you can use for both iOS and Android:

Minimum
Perform the deploy if the installed version is equal or higher.

Maximum
Perform the deploy if the installed version is equal or lower.

Equivalent
If the installed version is equivalent, do not perform the deploy. Remember to set this value when you publish to the app stores to prevent unnecessary live deployments.

With a little planning, you can introduce a powerful and rapid live deployment solution for your application.

Security Profiles

When using the Ionic Packaging service, the Ionic Cloud will need various signing certificates and keys in order to function. Security Profiles is a service that allows you to securely store these credentials and use them with those other services. So before we explore the Ionic Package service, let's create our profile.

The following are the certificates and keys you will need based on the service and the platform:

Cloud Builds
- Android: Keystore
- iOS: Certificate & Provisioning Profile (dev/prod)

Push Notifications
- Android: FCM Project & API Key
- iOS: Certificate & Provisioning Profile & Push Certificate (dev/prod)

 You will need both a signing certificate and push notification certificate from Apple for each release mode (development or production).

Security profiles do not allow you to pick which certificate to use, so you will need to create two profiles: one for your development phase, and one for production.

Creating a Profile

Sign in to the Ionic.io website and select the app you want to create your profile(s) for. Since signing certificates and keys are directly tied to a particular app ID, so are security profiles. With an app selected, navigate to the Settings page and select Certificates, as shown in Figure 12-5.

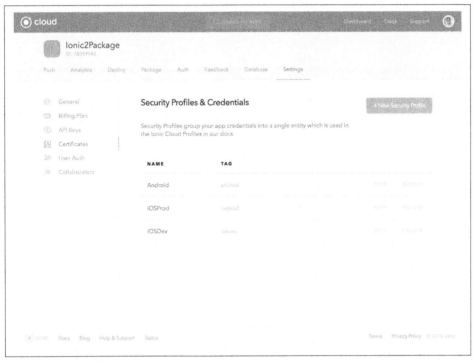

Figure 12-5. Security Profile & Credentials dashboard

Click the New Security Profile button to bring up the New Security Profile dialog. Give your profile a name. The Ionic Cloud will generate a tag based on the profile name. This tag needs to be something command-line safe, meaning spaces will be replaced with underscores, and everything will be converted to lowercase. Referencing a security profile is done via its tag, not its profile name. Note that you can't change this name at a later time. So feel free to provide a slightly more descriptive name. A single Security Profile can support both iOS and Android information (Figure 12-6).

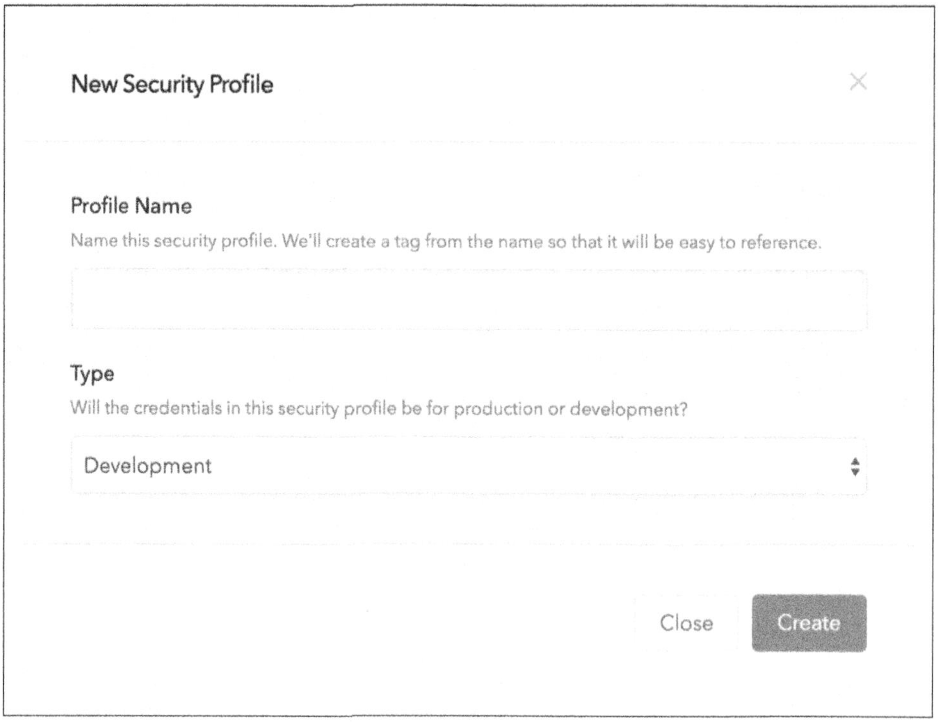

Figure 12-6. New Security Profile dialog

iOS Setup

You will need to generate your App Development/App Store Certificate and your Provisioning Profile and uploaded them to your Security profile. These files are generated through the Apple Developer Center website and either the Keychain Access tool (on macOS) or OpenSLL (on Windows). Rather than recreate these steps, follow the instructions (*http://docs.ionic.io/services/profiles/#ios-setup*) to generate the *.p12* and *.mobileprovision* files.

If you attempt to create an iOS App Development certificate and find that option disabled, it is because each team can have only one active distribution certificate. Locate the existing certificate and export it and continue the process as outlined.

With these files downloaded, we can now upload them to our Security Profile.

Supporting iOS Push Notifications

In order to use push notification, an additional certificate is required, as well as some additional settings. Just like you need to create two signing certificates for development and production, the same is true for push notifications.

Again, follow the instructions (*http://docs.ionic.io/services/profiles/#ios-push-certificate*).

The main differences are you will need to define an explicit app ID instead of using a wildcard app ID, and you will need to make sure you enable push notifications in the options.

Xcode 8 and Higher

If you're using the latest version of Xcode, you will likely need to activate the Push Notifications capability before your app is able to receive notifications.

We will explore push notifications later in this chapter.

Android Setup

Android does not use a web portal to generate your signing key. Instead, it relies on the keytool command included in the Java JDK.

```
$ keytool -genkey -v -keystore MY-RELEASE-KEY.keystore -alias MY_ALIAS_NAME
-keyalg RSA -keysize 2048 -validity 10000
```

Replace *MY-RELEASE-KEY* and *MY_ALIAS_NAME* to be relevant to your app. The tool will ask you to enter a keystore password and a key password. You will need to remember the alias name that you supplied when generating this keystore.

Then, simply upload the *.keystore* file to your Security Profile (Figure 12-7).

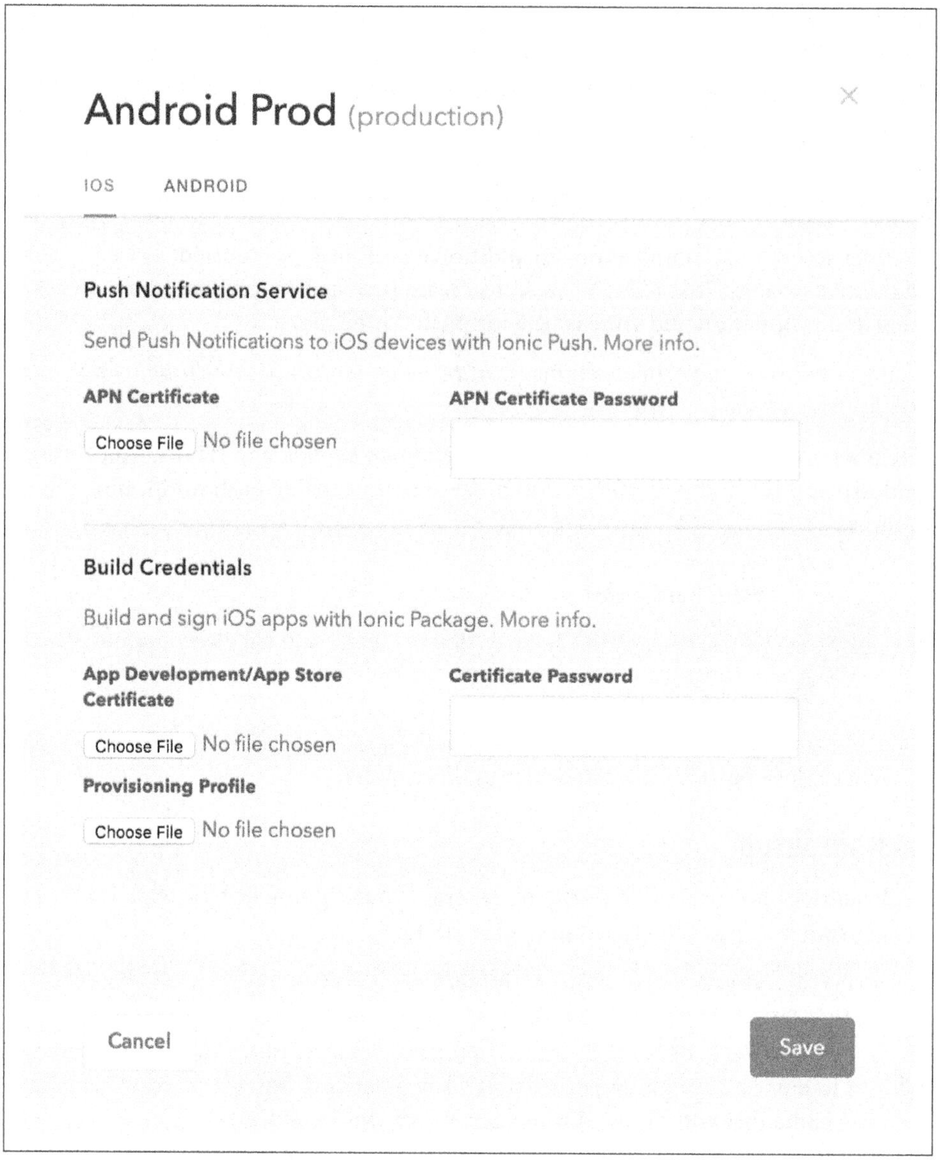

Android Prod (production)   ✕

IOS   ANDROID

Push Notification Service

Send Push Notifications to iOS devices with Ionic Push. More info.

APN Certificate   **APN Certificate Password**

Choose File   No file chosen

Build Credentials

Build and sign iOS apps with Ionic Package. More info.

App Development/App Store   **Certificate Password**
Certificate

Choose File   No file chosen

Provisioning Profile

Choose File   No file chosen

Cancel   Save

Figure 12-7. Android Security Profile dialog

Android Push Notifications

Like in iOS, some additional items are required in order to use push notifications. Google recently rebranded its cloud messaging service from Google Cloud Messaging (GCM) to Firebase Cloud Messaging (FCM).

To obtain your Google FCM server key, you will need to first create a new project on your Firebase console (*https://console.firebase.google.com*). Then enter a name for your project and select the region for your project. Once your project is generated, display the project settings by clicking the gear icon next to your project's name. Then select the Cloud Messaging tab. This screen will have your server key, which the Ionic Security Profile needs. Return back to your app in the Ionic dashboard, and select the profile you wish to attach this server key to (Figure 12-8).

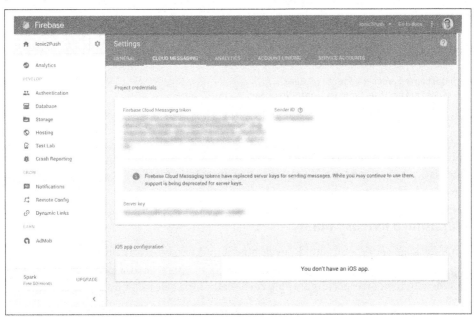

Figure 12-8. Firebase Cloud Messaging console

We will explore push notifications later in this chapter.

With our Security Profiles set up, we can now use them with the Ionic Package service.

Ionic Package

Ionic Package allows you to build native binaries of your application without the need for installing local SDKs. This can be very useful for Windows developers who want to build for iOS. This service is very similar to PhoneGap Build from Adobe.

This process is done via the Ionic CLI, with a similar syntax to the `ionic build` command. As a reminder, you will need a Security Profile attached this app. You can verify this by going to your app's profile on ionic.io.

A security profile is not needed for Android development builds.

The base package command is:

```
$ ionic package build PLATFORM_TAG --profile PROFILE_TAG
```

The PLATFORM_TAG can be either android or ios. The PROFILE_TAG is the generated Security Profile tag found in Settings→Certificates in the Dashboard. Here is a sample of the output to the terminal:

```
Uploading your project to Ionic...
Submitting your app to Ionic Package...
Your app has been successfully submitted to Ionic Package!
Build ID: 1
We are now packaging your app.
```

Your code is then uploaded to Ionic.io and queued for building. Your app will be automatically assigned an ID; after a few minutes, a build should be available to download or share.

Preparing a Release Build

Ionic Package service can build development and release-ready builds. To build your app for production, include --release flag (you must have a production Security profile with the corresponding Apple certificates for a release build):

```
$ ionic package build PLATFORM_TAG --profile PROFILE_TAG --release
```

Getting Build Information

Since your build request is now queued and it does take some time to perform, you can check the status of your builds by listing them:

```
$ ionic package list
```

This can be useful if you integrate this process into a generated build process. Here is a sample output:

```
id | status   | platform | mode
---+----------+----------+------
 1 | BUILDING | android  | debug

Showing 1 of your latest builds.
```

Getting Your Build Results

Once your build is complete, you can get its status by using this command:

```
$ ionic package info BUILD_ID
```

Here is what a successful build message will look like:

```
id        | 1
status    | SUCCESS
platform  | android
mode      | debug
started   | Nov 19th, 2016 14:43:08
completed | Nov 19th, 2016 14:43:29
```

Downloading Your Build

Once your app has been successfully built, download the *.ipa* or *.apk*. These files will download to the app's project folder:

```
$ ionic package download BUILD_ID

Downloading... [==============================] 100%  0.0s
Wrote: /Users/chrisgriffith/Desktop/Ionic Book Apps/
        Ionic2Package/Ionic2Package.apk
Done!
```

You can now install your app on any authorized device.

Updating Your Cordova Plugins

To ensure that Ionic Package's (*http://docs.ionic.io/services/package/*) build servers know which Cordova plugins your app needs, you should reinstall them into the project with the --save flag added:

```
$ ionic plugin add PLUGIN_NAME --save
```

To get a listing of the plugins used in your application, run:

```
$ ionic plugin ls
```

Ionic View

Ionic View makes it easy to share your app with clients and testers without using TestFlight Beta Testing or Beta Testing through Google Play. Just upload your app and share it. The free mobile app is available for iOS and Android. This application will act as a native shell for your application to run within. The advantage of this option is that you do not need to compile your application before running it on an actual device.

Ionic View leverages the capabilities of Ionic Deploy to make this possible. Since it hosts your application within another shell, only a subset of Cordova plugins are available to be used.

Supported Plugins

Here is the current list of plugins that Ionic View supports:

- ActionSheet (2.2.2)
- BarcodeScanner (5.0.0)
- BLE (1.1.1)
- Bluetooth Serial (0.4.5)
- Calendar (4.5.0)
- Camera (2.2.0)
- Capture (1.3.0)
- Contacts (2.1.0)
- DatePicker (0.9.3)
- DBMeter (1.0.3)
- Device (1.1.2)
- Device Motion (1.2.1)
- Device Orientation (1.0.3)
- Dialogs (1.2.1)
- Email Composer (0.8.3)
- Geolocation (2.2.0)
- Globalization (1.0.3)
- ImagePicker (1.1.1)
- Keyboard (2.2.0)
- Media (2.3.0)
- Network Information (1.2.1)
- SocialSharing (5.1.1)
- SQLite (1.4.2)
- StatusBar (2.1.3)
- Toast (2.5.2)
- Touch ID (3.2.0)
- Vibration (2.1.1)

Check the Ionic website (*https://docs.ionic.io/tools/view/#supported-plugins*) for the latest information about which plugins are available for use by your app.

Uploading Your App

For Ionic View to run your app, you will need to upload it to Ionic.io with this command:

```
$ ionic upload
```

Your app will be uploaded to Ionic.io and the status will be displayed in the terminal:

```
Uploading app....
Saved app_id, writing to ionic.io.bundle.min.js...
Successfully uploaded (76059942)

Share your beautiful app with someone:
$ ionic share EMAIL

Saved api_key, writing to ionic.io.bundle.min.js...
```

Viewing Your App

Now simply launch the Ionic View mobile app, and it will automatically give you a list of apps that you have uploaded. You also have the ability to manually enter an app ID that's been shared with you.

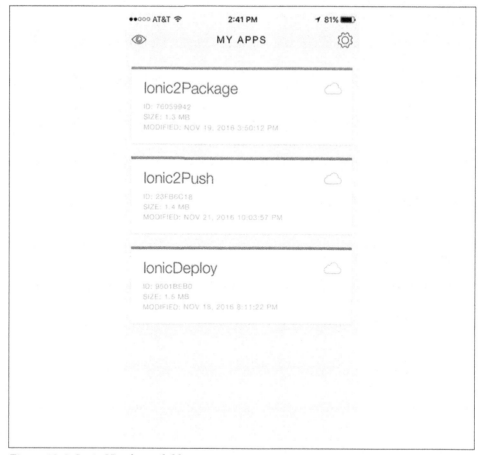

Figure 12-9. Ionic View's available apps

Tap one of the app cards to bring up a pop up with possible actions. You can view the app, clear its local files, sync the local files with the latest upload from the Ionic Cloud, or remove it from your account.

Ionic View is a powerful tool to quickly test and view your app on a physical device without the need to compile it or formally install it.

Ionic Creator

There is one last item from Ionic that does need a brief mention. In exploring the Ionic websites, you may have seen a reference to Ionic Creator (*http://ionic.io/prod ucts/creator*) (see Figure 12-10). Before Drifty (the team behind most of Ionic) developed the Ionic Framework, they developed a visual design tool for jQuery Mobile called Codiqa. Ionic Creator is its descendant (in spirit).

Figure 12-10. Ionic Creator

This web-based tool allows you to design and author Ionic 1 applications all within your browser. The Creator team has done a fantastic job evolving this tool. There is a companion mobile app (a custom version of the Ionic View app) that allows you to seamlessly view your designs on an actual device.

Ionic Creator Is for Ionic 1 Only

Unfortunately, at this time Ionic Creator only supports Ionic 1. The source files and code samples are not usable within an Ionic 2 project. The team has not announced when an Ionic 2–compatible version will be available.

The tool is a great method to learn the Ionic 1 framework for those who might be more visually inclined. Even if you are developing with Ionic 2, you can still leverage its design tools to generate mockups for review and prototyping.

Summary

The Ionic Services provide a lot of additional functionality beyond the core framework. Although it is a paid service, its tight integration with the framework might make it the right choice for your development needs.

CHAPTER 13

Progressive Web Apps

Since Ionic apps are built with web technologies, you might be wondering if they can be deployed as a traditional web app viewable via a standard browser. The simple answer is yes. That is what we have been doing while we were building and testing our application with $ ionic serve. You can certainly take the contents of the *www* directory and place them on your web server. The main caveat is that none of the Cordova plugins will function in this environment. The best way to think about publishing your application this way is to think of it as a completely new platform: the browser.

While we don't have the same capabilities that a native application might have, today's modern browsers do support several key features, such as geolocation, notifications, and offline storage.

One of the challenges in delivering your application in this manner is the overall file size of our Ionic application. The *main.js* file that is generated by the CLI (using $ ionic build --prod), starts just under 2 MB.

Reducing Future Build Sizes

The Ionic team is actively working with Angular to reduce the file size of the application further.

Then start factoring in all your visual assets and any other resources you might need very quickly, your app will probably run very slowly as all these items are each fetched across the network. Compound this if you are running over a cellular network or a weak WiFi connection.

However, there is a new idea that is gaining a lot of traction within the web app development community: *progressive web apps*. Originally proposed by Google in 2015, this solution takes advantage of the latest technologies to combine the best of web and mobile apps. While not every browser supports all the features of a complete progressive web app, there is enough support to consider it as an option.

But What, Exactly, Is a Progressive Web App?

According to Google Developers (*http://bit.ly/2mKBYZv*), a progressive web app uses modern web capabilities to deliver an app-like user experience.

Let's start with the first term in the name: progressive. By definition, a progressive web app must work on any device and have its functions enhanced in a progressive manner. That is, if the device is more capable, then the app can use that capability. If a feature is not supported, then the web app offers an alternative experience.

Progressive Web Apps are also both discoverable and linkable, meaning that both users and search engines can discover the content within the app. This lack of discoverability is one clear disadvantage of native apps. Since our app exists within the web, users should be able to link or bookmark their "place" within the application and return to it.

Since we are expanding beyond the confines of fixed screen sizes, these applications must also be responsive in their visual design. In reality, although screen sizes are fixed on mobile devices, the range of device screen size causes us to already have addressed this issue.

In terms of visual design, a progressive web app should look and feel like a native application. Again, this is an example of leveraging Ionic's components to achieve this with little effort.

We also need to break free from the browser itself and become something that the user can install on their device's home screen. Otherwise, it becomes too burdensome for users to use your application if they have to launch the browser, navigate to a URL or recall it from a bookmark.

The interactions are also considered "safe"—for a progressive web app to function, it must be served over an HTTPS connection.

Finally, it must work without a network connection. Again, once a native app is installed, it is available for use. Progressive web apps must offer the same level of functionality.

Now that you have a sense of the requirements for a progressive web app, let's look at what we need to do to make our Ionic application into a progressive web app.

The manifest.json File

If you recall when we were exploring the files and directories of our Ionic application, there were two files that we skipped over: the *manifest.json* and *service-worker.js* files.

First, let's make our web app more app-like in appearance. To do this, we can leverage the *manifest.json* file. This file follows the W3C specification for web apps (*https://w3c.github.io/manifest/*). Here is the default *manifest.json* file that is auto-generated for us:

```
{
  "name": "Ionic",
  "short_name": "Ionic",
  "start_url": "index.html",
  "display": "standalone",
  "icons": [{
    "src": "assets/imgs/logo.png",
    "sizes": "512x512",
    "type": "image/png"
  }],
  "background_color": "#4e8ef7",
  "theme_color": "#4e8ef7"
}
```

Let's look at these properties in more detail:

name
> This is the name that will be used for the application listing.

short-name
> This is the name that is usually displayed along with the home screen icon.

start_url
> The entry point to your applications, usually it is your index.html file.

display
> Defines how the browser should display the web application. The options are: fullscreen, standalone, minimal-ui, or browser. Here is what each option does:

> *fullscreen*
>> The web application is shown without any browser chrome and will take up the entire display area.

> *standalone*
>> The web application will be launched to look and feel more like a standalone native application. The browser chrome will not be displayed but, can include other system UI elements such as a status bar and/or system back button.

minimal-ui
> The web application will be shown with a minimal set of UI elements for controlling navigation (i.e., back, forward, reload, and perhaps some way of viewing the document's web address).

browser
> The web application will be shown in the standard browser chrome.

icons
> This array defines the various icons that will be used by the home screen, task switcher, and so on. It is an array of objects defines the icon url, size and file type. We recommend having 48, 96, 144, 192, and 256-pixel icons specified.

background_color
> This hex value defines the background color of the web application. In Chrome, this value also defines the background color of the splash screen.

theme_color
> On Android, this hex value is used define the color the status bar.

Not listed in the auto-generated version of the *manifest.json* file is the `orientation` property. This property will define the default orientation for the application. It can be either portrait or landscape.

This file is already referenced within our *index.html* in the head tag:

```
<link rel="manifest" href="manifest.json">
```

Service Workers

The engine of every progressive web app is actually the Service Worker API. This API introduces another layer between the code that runs within your application and the code that might run on a remote server. This code acts an intermediary between our client and server. Once the service worker is registered, it sits independently of any browser window or tab.

This API is currently supported in Chrome, Firefox, and Opera, and it is coming very soon to Edge. Apple's WebKit team has it marked "under consideration."

Service workers have the ability to intercept and rewrite all of your application's network requests. This gives you the ability to provide cached responses when there is no data connection available. Because of this ability, it will only function in secure contexts (i.e., HTTPS).

Within the default *index.html* file, the Ionic team has included a snippet of code to assist in registering your app's service worker. By default, this code is commented out:

```
<!-- un-comment this code to enable service worker
<script>
  if ('serviceWorker' in navigator) {
    navigator.serviceWorker.register('service-worker.js')
      .then(() => console.log('service worker installed'))
      .catch(err => console.log('Error', err));
  }
</script>-->
```

This snippet will simply register it if it is supported by the browser. The real code is within the *service-worker.js* file.

The auto-generated *service-worker.js* is nicely commented, and we won't rehash it here. Instead, let's look at this basic service worker sample, so you can understand what you can do with a service worker.

Let's replace the default *service-worker.js* with this. But, before you do, go ahead and save a copy of the original *service-worker.js* file. Here is the new code:

```
self.addEventListener('fetch', function(event) {
  if (event.request.url.indexOf('/img/my-logo.png') !== -1) {
    event.respondWith(
      fetch('/img/my-logo-flipped.png')
    );
  }
});
```

This sample will intercept any request for "/img/logo.png" and instead return the flipped version.

Remember, in order for this to function, it must be served on an HTTPS connection and by a supported browser.

By properly caching our assets, we can reduce our applications' start times dramatically. In fact, we should be able to launch faster than a native application!

Note that because a service worker is a special type of shared web worker, it runs in a separate thread to your main page's JavaScript. This means that it is shared by all web pages on the same path as the service worker. For example, a service worker located at */my-app/sw.js* would be able to affect */my-app/index.html* and *my-app/images/ header.jpg*, but not */index.html*.

Beyond intercepting our network requests, it can provide offline functionality, push notifications, background content updating, content caching, and a whole lot more.

Here is a sample of providing a custom text response if you are offline when trying to access the web app:

```
self.addEventListener('fetch', function(event) {
  event.respondWith(
    fetch(event.request).catch(function() {
      return new Response(
```

```
            'Welcome to the Upside Down.\n'+
            'Please look out for the Demogorgon.\n'+
            'We look forward to telling you about Hawkins National Laboratory
             as soon as you go online.'
        );
    })
  );
});
```

Reload your browser with this service worker installed, then reload your page, but this time offline. Instead of the default not-connected screen, we will be presented with this information instead. With a little work, you could provide a custom experience, including images and stylesheets.

Here is a sample of caching most of the default Ionic files and returning the cached version if the user is offline:

```
var CACHE_NAME = 'ionic-cache';
var CACHED_URLS = [
  '/assets/fonts/ionicons.eot',
  '/assets/fonts/ionicons.scss',
  '/assets/fonts/ionicons.svg',
  '/assets/fonts/ionicons.ttf',
  '/assets/fonts/ionicons.woff',
  '/assets/fonts/ionicons.woff2',
  '/build/main.css',
  '/build/main.js',
  '/build/polyfills.js',
  'index.html'
];

self.addEventListener('install', function(event) {
  event.waitUntil(
    caches.open(CACHE_NAME).then(function(cache) {
      return cache.addAll(CACHED_URLS);
    })
  );
});

self.addEventListener('fetch', function(event) {
  event.respondWith(
    fetch(event.request).catch(function() {
      return caches.match(event.request).then(function(response) {
        return response;
      });
    })
  );
});
```

Service workers have tremendous potential to improve the user experience of our applications. Besides providing a solution for our application to function in an offline mode, they can also be used when the user might have a poor network connection.

Consider how much of your application might be very static in nature and could always be served locally, rather than making a network request.

Push Notifications

Another new API that bridges the gap between native mobile applications and the web is the Push Notification API. This API also leverages the use of service workers in order to receive the notification when no browser is open. For more information about adding push notifications to your progressive web app, check out some tutorials from Google (*http://bit.ly/2mKVvZX*).

What's Next?

Progressive web app support will continue to grow with the Ionic Framework, so look for additional enhancements to be added over time. Ionic has a collection of progressive web app samples (*https://pwa.ionic.io*).

To learn more about progressive web apps in general, we suggest getting a copy of *Building Progressive Web Apps: Bringing the Power of Native to the Browser,* by Tal Ater (O'Reilly).

CHAPTER 14

Conclusion

Components You Should Know About

In this final chapter, we will touch upon a few components that we were not able to use within our sample applications and look at where to go next in your journey to learn the Ionic Framework.

Although we touched on a lot of the components in the Ionic Library, there are some additional ones that we wanted to highlight. For a more complete list, see Appendix C.

Slides

The first component to explore briefly is slides. This component allows you to have a carousel of items. These could be as simple as just images, or as complex as individual pages. The component is actually built in two parts: the container component <ion-slides> and each slide <ion-slide> that is nested within. Here is a very basic sample from the Ionic documentation:

```
<ion-slides pager>

  <ion-slide style="background-color: green">
    <h2>Slide 1</h2>
  </ion-slide>

  <ion-slide style="background-color: blue">
    <h2>Slide 2</h2>
  </ion-slide>

  <ion-slide style="background-color: red">
    <h2>Slide 3</h2>
  </ion-slide>
```

```
</ion-slides>
```

The inline styles are included for demonstration purposes only.

Table 14-1 lists the various settings you can apply to your `<ion-slides>` component.

Table 14-1. Various settings for <ion-slides>

Property	Type	Default	Description
autoplay	number	-	Delay between transitions (in ms). If this parameter is not passed, autoplay is disabled
direction	string	'horizontal'	Swipe direction: 'horizontal' or 'vertical'
initialSlide	number	0	Index number of initial slide
loop	boolean	false	Whether to continuously loop from the last slide to the first slide
pager	boolean	false	Show the pagination bullets
speed	number	300	Duration of transition between slides (in ms)

This component is actually a wrapper for the Swiper component built by iDangero.us. By default, the Ionic team has restricted some of the methods that are directly exposed by their component. If you need to access something that is supported within the iDangero.us source, you will need to use the `getSlider()` method for information on getting the Swiper instance and using its methods directly.

If you want to explore using this component with the sample apps, you could introduce it as a container for each city's weather or as an image gallery for each national park.

Date-Time

Working with dates and time are not only challenging in code (although *moment.js* certainly helps out in that department) but also from a user interface point of view. Although HTML5 did introduce the input type of datetime-local, the visual display of the use of this component would vary and be difficult to customize. So Ionic introduced `<ion-datetime>` as a way to solve this issue:

```
<ion-datetime displayFormat="h:mm A" pickerFormat="h mm A"
  [(ngModel)]="event.timeStarts"></ion-datetime>
```

You have control over both the display and picker formats of the date-time (there are many options (*http://bit.ly/2mKWMAo*)). These formats are defined by standard filters. In the preceding sample, the display format will show the hour as 1–12, followed by a colon, then the minutes with a leading zero. While the picker will display the hours as a range from 1–12, the minutes from 00 to 59, and a picker for AM or PM (see Figure 14-1).

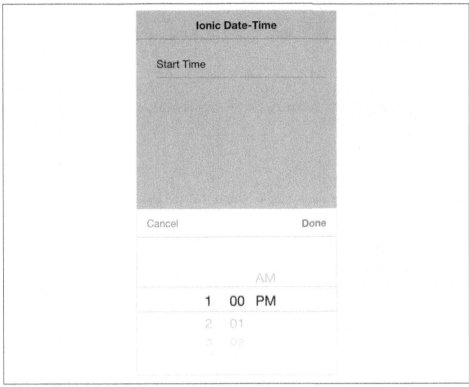

Figure 14-1. Ionic Date-Time picker component

You could introduce this component to set a due date for an item on the To Do application we wrote in Chapter 7.

Popover

You may often want to either present some additional information to the user about an item or expose additional controls, but not want to clutter your app's interface. This is where the Popover component can come in handy. Some common examples of this component in action are changing the sort order of a list or filtering some data. Unlike components that are within the HTML template, this component is dynamically added, much like the Ionic Alert component:

```
import { Component } from '@angular/core';
import { PopoverController } from 'ionic-angular';
import { MyPopOverPage } from './my-pop-over';

@Component({
  selector: 'page-home',
  templateUrl: 'home.html'
})
```

```
export class HomePage {

  constructor(public popoverCtrl: PopoverController) {

  }

  presentPopover(ev) {
    let popover = this.popoverCtrl.create(MyPopOverPage);
    popover.present({
      ev: ev
    });
  }
}
```

In our HTML, we can have a simple button that we will call the presentPopover function:

```
<button ion-button (click)="presentPopover($event)">
  <ion-icon name="more"></ion-icon>
</button>
```

The actual popover component is (see Figure 14-2):

```
import { Component } from '@angular/core';
import { ViewController } from 'ionic-angular';

@Component({
  template: `
    <ion-list>
      <ion-list-header>Units</ion-list-header>
      <button ion-item (click)="close()">Celsius</button>
      <button ion-item (click)="close()">Fahrenheit</button>
    </ion-list>
  `
})
export class MyPopOverPage {

  constructor(public viewCtrl: ViewController) {}

  close() {
    this.viewCtrl.dismiss();
  }

}
```

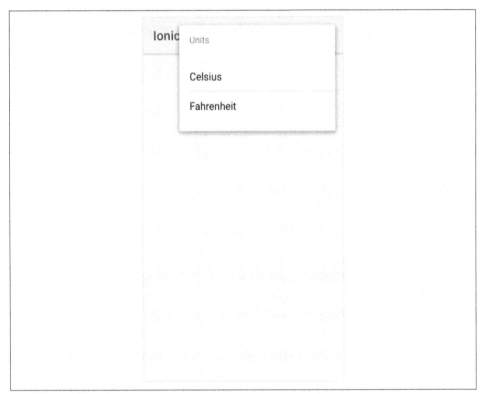

Figure 14-2. Ionic Popover component

One last thing you need to do is to update the *app.module.ts* file with your Popover component. If you forget to do this, your component will not work.

If you wanted to sort your list items, like in the Ionic2Do app, you could use this component to display the sort options to your user. Another example would be making our temperature unit choice via this component.

Reorder List

Another component that we want to highlight is ItemReorder. Built into the standard Ion List component is the ability to allow the user to reorder the list. To enable this function, simply add the attribute reorder to the `<ion-list>` and set its value to `true`. This will expose the reorder controls on the list items.

Ionic will handle the array reordering for you. But if you need to handle the reordering for some reason, you can bind the `ionItemReorder` event to a custom function:

```
<ion-list reorder="true" (ionItemReorder)="reorderItems($event)">
    <ion-item *ngFor="let item of items">{{ item }}</ion-item>
</ion-list>
```

When this event is emitted, it provides the initial index (from) and the new index value (to) for the item that was just reordered. Here the reorderItems function will write to the console the reorder indexes, do the actual reorder, then write the new array to the console:

```
reorderItems(indexes) {
  console.log(indexes);  //{from: 0, to: 4}
  this.items = reorderArray(this.items, indexes);
  console.log(this.items);   //the reordeed array.
}
```

Ionic has included a helper function called reorderArray to make life a bit easier than storing indexes and splicing arrays.

DeepLinker

This is one of the newest components/features to Ionic 2. With Ionic 1, navigation was handled through the use of URLs. Although this posed some challenges with complex apps, it did provide a method to expose deeper sections of your application. With Ionic 2 shifting to a new navigation system, we no longer had a method to easily navigate to a particular screen. This proved to be problematic for a lot of app designers. To solve this issue, Ionic introduced its DeepLinker system.

To utilize this feature, we will need to update the *app.module.ts* file. When we call the IonicModule.forRoot method, simply pass an object that contains an array of links as the third parameter:

```
imports: [
  IonicModule.forRoot(MyApp, {}, {
    links: [
      { component: HomePage, name: 'Home', segment: 'home' },
      { component: DetailPage, name: 'Detail', segment: 'detail/:userId' }
    ]
  })
]
```

If we need to pass some data to the page we are navigating to, we can use the :param syntax to do so.

This feature will allow us to launch our app on a specific screen, or if we have deployed our app as a progressive web app, to bookmark it.

Storage

The last feature we want to touch on is Ionic's built-in storage system. We spent some time exploring Firebase as a cloud storage system, but that might be overkill when you need to save some simple data (like a user's list of cities they wanted weather for).

Ionic Storage allows you to save key/value pairs and JSON data with little effort. One of the challenges in working with local data storage is the wide range of solutions and their respective shortcomings. Ionic Storage uses a variety of different storage solutions, automatically selecting the proper one for the platform the app is running on.

For example, if you are running on the web, Ionic Storage will first attempt to use IndexedDB to save your data. If that browser does not support IndexedDB, it will try WebSQL to save your data. If that fails, it will use localstorage as its solution. If you deploy your app as a native application, you can install the SQLite plugin and leverage it.

Using Ionic Storage is fairly straightforward. First, if you plan to use SQLite for your native app, you will need to install the Cordova plugin:

```
ionic plugin add cordova-sqlite-storage --save
```

The package is already included in our node modules, so we only need to declare it in our providers array in our *app.module.ts* file:

```
import { Storage } from '@ionic/storage';

@NgModule({
  declarations: [
    // ...
  ],
  imports: [
    IonicModule.forRoot(MyApp)
  ],
  bootstrap: [IonicApp],
  entryComponents: [
    // ...
  ],
  providers: [
    Storage
  ]
})
export class AppModule {}
```

Ionic Storage can be used within our application:

```
import { Storage } from '@ionic/storage';

export class MyApp {
  constructor(storage: Storage) {

    // set a key/value
    storage.set('name', 'Chris');

    // Or to get a key/value pair
    storage.get('name').then((val) => {
      console.log('Your name is', val);
    })
```

```
    }
  }
```

Now that you see how simple using Ionic Storage is, why don't you upgrade our Ion-icWeather app to save the cities?

Next Steps

This book has been about providing a good foundation on Ionic, but there might be something that does not make sense to you or perhaps there was an update to the framework or some other part of the toolchain that breaks something. Where should you look for help?

For this, there are several resources you should turn to first. But before you post that question to a forum or Slack channel, take a moment and ask if you have worked through the issue. So often questions like "My screen does not update the data when I pull to refresh!" are posted. But there is so much information not included in the question. What version of Ionic are you using? What environment are you testing on? What have you tried to do to resolve it?

So for that question, we need to see where the issue truly lies. Is the pull to refresh being properly triggered? If it is being called, then was the next function being called? Continue along the code execution chain, checking along the way.

Eventually, this example issue may not have been about the pull to refresh component, but the data provider returning cached data. But you never wound have guessed that from the initial question.

Ionic Forums

One of the first places to look for help is on Ionic's own forums. This is a great resource to help resolve any issues you might encounter. It is staffed by various Ionic team members and knowledgeable community experts.

Ionic Worldwide Slack Channel

Another great resource for help is the Ionic Worldwide Slack channel (*http://ionic worldwide.herokuapp.com*). It is not as formal as the forums, so it can be useful when you need to ask a question or get an opinion on a solution.

GitHub

The Ionic Framework is open source, so if you do encounter a real issue, you can open an issue on the repo. Or even better, fix the issue and submit a pull request. When you think the issue might be within the framework itself, take the time to look at the GitHub repo (*https://github.com/driftyco/*) to see if it is a known issue, and hopefully a solution—or at least a workaround—will be posted.

Conclusion

This concludes our journey together through this book. We tried to cover many of the various parts of Ionic and its supporting technologies at a reasonable depth in an order that made sense. There is nowhere near enough space or time for this book to cover each and every part of the Ionic Framework, but this should give you a very strong base on which to rapidly build amazing, sleek, and performant hybrid mobile applications. Keep trying new things, and join us in the journey of making Ionic a great framework!

Migrating Ionic 1 to Ionic 2

If you have an existing Ionic 1 application, you might be wondering how to migrate your application. Unfortunately, there is no easy solution to do this. So much has evolved in both the Ionic Framework and Angular that it is just not practical. We were faced with the same challenges with several of our applications as well. Here are some guidelines that can help you rebuild your application, based on what we found worked.

Create a New Ionic 2 Application

The cleanest method to migrate your Ionic 1 app is actually to start fresh. With so many improvements and changes, it is just easier to build from scratch. Select the template that best matches your application's navigation structure and generate a new app using the CLI.

Create Your Page Structure

With your base application in place, the next step we recommend is to lay down the page structure. Think of this step as the framing of the new house, while the previous step was the pouring of the foundation. First, remove any pages that might have been generated by the CLI, then create stub pages for your application. The Ionic CLI makes this very easy with the $ ionic g page command. If you are building a tab-based application, remember the generate command can also assist with that.

Update the Theming

Ionic 1 could use SCSS, if you enabled it. Now this is how your CSS is generated in Ionic 2. The main *.scss* file in located in *src/theme/variables.scss*, and this is where any global changes to the styling should be applied. One of the other changes in Ionic 2 was each page now has its own *.scss* file that your can use to target specific styling changes you might need to make. Ionic 2 has exposed a lot more variables within the theming framework, so you might find the workaround that you had to do in Ionic 1 may no longer be needed.

Replacing Your Controllers and Views

One of the biggest challenges you might have is rewriting all your controllers and views. The Angular 1 `$scope` concept has been replaced with a modern class and component design. You will want to take some time to understand this new architecture before diving into converting your application. Once you have an understanding of it, most everyone agrees it is a cleaner and more intelligent approach. If you have a more traditional class-based programming background, you will find this refreshing. The additional use of TypeScript will also improve your code quality.

Our views—those HTML templates—will need some minor updating as well. Some components are the same as in Ionic 1, while others like cards and buttons have had a few modifications to them. One change to note is the inclusion of the `<ion-header>` and `<ion-navbar>` on every page. In Ionic 1, this was globally set and proved difficult to adapt to various designs.

Replace Your Factories/Services

In Ionic 1, shared data and functions were handled through the use of either factories or services. Now, this is handled as a standard ES6/TypeScript class that has the `@Injectable` decorator applied to it. With that decorator, Angular will allow this class to be used through dependency injection.

Convert the Application Initialization

The method of initializing our application has also changed in Ionic 2. No longer is there a concept of root run code; rather, this is replaced by a master component. In fact, in Ionic 2 our entire app is made of components. Now we just handle any initialization with our entry component.

Update the Routing

The page routing system in Ionic 1 was based on the UI-router module. While it was an improvement over the default router, it had difficulty with the navigation often found in mobile applications. In Ionic 2, the navigation system follows a more native push/pop style. That long code block that existed in your Ionic 1 app can be ignored. Your navigation system will now be handled screen by screen, instead of globally.

If you still need addressable URLs for your application, look at using the DeepLinking system to assist you. This can be easily defined in the *app.module.ts* file.

Switching to Ionic Native

If you used any Cordova plugins in your application, you probably used the ngCordova module to provide your code with an Angular style method of using them. The Ionic team has replaced this module with Ionic Native. This new library is now based on TypeScript and has support for Promises and Observables as well. The documentation will guide you through the conversion.

Conclusion

This is just the briefest of overviews on the key steps you will need to address when migrating an Ionic 1 application to Ionic 2. It is a challenge, but hopefully the benefits will outweigh the costs of doing so. We would recommend finishing this book and becoming comfortable with how Ionic 2 works before migrating your app.

Understanding the Config.xml File

Cordova uses a *config.xml* to control many of its build settings. When you scaffold your Ionic application, a basic *config.xml* file is generated for you. The *config.xml* file follows the W3C widget specification (*http://www.w3.org/TR/widgets/*). It allows developers to easily specify metadata about their applications. This appendix will explain the various elements in this file and how you can customize them for your application.

Essential Properties

The widget element is the root element of our *config.xml* file. It supports the following attributes:

ID

The unique identifier for your application. To ensure your ID conforms to all supported platforms, this *must* be reverse-domain name style (e.g., com.yourcom pany.yourapp). Unless you supply an app ID during the use of the Ionic CLI command, it will be com.ionicframework.[app name]+random number.

version

For best results, use a major/minor/patch style version, with three numbers, such as 0.0.1.

versionCode

(Optional) when building for Android, you can set the versionCode by specifying it in your *config.xml*.

CFBundleVersion

(Optional) when building for iOS, you can set the version for iOS.

packageVersion

(Optional) when building for Windows, you can set the version for Windows.

packageName

(Optional) when building for Windows, you can define the package name.

```
<widget id="com.ionicframework.ionic2do146695" version="0.0.1"↵
xmlns="http://www.w3.org/ns/widgets" ↵
xmlns:cdv="http://cordova.apache.org/ns/1.0">
```

Within the widget node, there are several other nodes that should be defined:

<name>

This is the display name of the application:

```
<name>Ionic2Do</name>
```

<description>

This is a general description of the application. It is a part of the specification, but it is not referenced in the app store:

```
<description>Standard To Do app using Ionic 2.</description>
```

<author>

The author of the application, either a company or individual (this is required for Windows 10 builds). This node has two attributes that can be set:

email

This is the email for the author

href

This is typically either the company home page or the app home page:

```
<author email="chrisgriffith@gmail.com" href="http://ajsoftware.com/">↵
Chris Griffith</author>
```

<content>

This node defines the initial *html* page that Cordova should load. It is not recommended that you change the src attribute from *index.html*:

```
<content src="index.html"/>
```

<access>, <allow-navigation>, and <allow-intent>

These nodes are used to define the set of external domains that the app will be allowed to communicate with. It is highly recommended that you read and understand the various settings in the Whitelist Guide (*http://bit.ly/2lcrhmx*).

```
<access origin="*"/>
<allow-intent href="http://*/*"/>
<allow-navigation href="http://example.com/*" />
<allow-intent href="https://*/*"/>
```

```
<allow-intent href="tel:*"/>
<allow-intent href="sms:*"/>
<allow-intent href="mailto:*"/>
<allow-intent href="geo:*"/>
```

<platform>

By setting the name attribute to either `ios`, `android`, or `winphone`, you can manage platform-specific settings such as permissions, icons, and splash screens:

```
<platform name="ios" />
<platform name="android" />
<platform name="winphone" />
```

Preferences

Cordova utilizes the `<preference>` tag to customize your application configuration. These can be applied globally to all the targeted platforms, or a specific platform. The options are set as pairs of name/value attributes.

Common General Preferences

```
<preference name="DisallowOverscroll" value="true"/>
<preference name="Fullscreen" value="true" />
<preference name="BackgroundColor" value="0xff0000ff"/>
<preference name="Orientation" value="portrait" />
```

DisallowOverscroll

Set to `true` if you don't want the interface to display any feedback when users scroll past the beginning or end of content. On iOS, overscroll gestures cause content to bounce back to its original position. On Android, they produce a more subtle glowing effect along the top or bottom edge of the content.

Fullscreen

Allows you to hide the status bar at the top of the screen.

BackgroundColor

Sets the app's background color. Supports a four-byte hex value, with the first byte representing the alpha channel, and standard RGB values for the following three bytes. (Android & Windows only)

Orientation

Allowed values: default, landscape, portrait

Allows you to lock orientation and prevent the interface from rotating in response to changes in orientation.

Common iOS Preferences

```
<preference name="BackupWebStorage" value="none"/>
<preference name="target-device" value="universal" />
<preference name="deployment-target" value="7.0" />
<preference name="SuppressesLongPressGesture" value="true" />
<preference name="Suppresses3DTouchGesture" value="true" />
```

BackupWebStorage
> Allowed values: none, local, cloud.
>
> Set to cloud to allow web storage data to backup via iCloud. Set to local to allow only local backups via iTunes sync. Set to none to prevent web storage backups.

target-device
> Allowed values: handset, tablet, universal
>
> This property maps directly to TARGETED*DEVICE*FAMILY in the Xcode project. Note that if you target universal (which is the default), you will need to supply screen shots for both iPhone and iPad or your app may be rejected.

deployment-target
> This sets the IPHONEOS*DEPLOYMENT*TARGET in the build, which ultimately tranlsates to the MinimumOSVersion in the *ipa*.

SuppressesLongPressGesture
> Set to `true` to avoid iOS9+ rendering a magnifying glass widget when the user longpresses the WebView.

Suppresses3DTouchGesture
> Set to `true` to avoid 3D Touch–capable iOS devices rendering a magnifying glass widget when the user applies force while longpressing the WebView.

Common Android Preferences

```
<preference name="android-minSdkVersion" value="16"/>
<preference name="android-maxSdkVersion" value="22"/>
<preference name="android-targetSdkVersion" value="20"/>
```

android-minSdkVersion
> Sets the `minSdkVersion` attribute of the `<uses-sdk>` tag in the project's *Android-Manifest.xml*.

android-maxSdkVersion
> Sets the `maxSdkVersion` attribute of the `<uses-sdk>` tag in the project's *Android-Manifest.xml*. It is not recommended to set this unless you know of an issue with a specific version of Android.

android-targetSdkVersion

Sets the `targetSdkVersion` attribute of the `<uses-sdk>` tag in the project's *AndroidManifest.xml*.

Common Windows Preferences

```
<preference name="windows-phone-target-version" value="8.1" />
<preference name="windows-target-version" value="8.1" />
<preference name="WindowsStoreIdentityName"
value="Cordova.Example.ApplicationDataSample" />
<preference name="WindowsStorePublisherName" value="AJ Software" />
```

windows-phone-target-version

Sets the version of Windows Phone for which the app will target. If none is specified, it will be set to the same version as windows-target-version (if found).

windows-target-version

Sets the version of Windows for which the app will target. If none is specified, it will be set to `"8.1"`.

WindowsStoreIdentityName

Identity name used for Windows store.

WindowsStorePublisherName

The publisher display name is the name under which your app will be listed in the Windows Store.

These are just some of the various preferences that you can control. For a complete list, see the Cordova website (*http://bit.ly/2lcIADN*).

Icons

The `<icon>` element is used to define the app icon. Each platform requires several icons at specific sizes. Often each collection of platform-specific icons is wrapped within a `<platform>` tag. Please notice that the value of the `"src"` attribute is relative to the project root directory and not to the *www* directory.

Android

```
<platform name="android">
  <!--
      ldpi    : 36x36 px
      mdpi    : 48x48 px
      hdpi    : 72x72 px
      xhdpi   : 96x96 px
      xxhdpi  : 144x144 px
      xxxhdpi : 192x192 px
  -->
```

```
    <icon src="res/android/ldpi.png" qualifier="ldpi" />
    <icon src="res/android/mdpi.png" qualifier="mdpi" />
    <icon src="res/android/hdpi.png" qualifier="hdpi" />
    <icon src="res/android/xhdpi.png" qualifier="xhdpi" />
    <icon src="res/android/xxhdpi.png" qualifier="xxhdpi" />
    <icon src="res/android/xxxhdpi.png" qualifier="xxxhdpi" />
  </platform>
```

iOS

```
  <platform name="ios">
    <!-- iOS 8.0+ -->
    <!-- iPhone 6 Plus  -->
    <icon src="res/ios/icon-60@3x.png" width="180" height="180" />
    <!-- iOS 7.0+ -->
    <!-- iPhone / iPod Touch  -->
    <icon src="res/ios/icon-60.png" width="60" height="60" />
    <icon src="res/ios/icon-60@2x.png" width="120" height="120" />
    <!-- iPad -->
    <icon src="res/ios/icon-76.png" width="76" height="76" />
    <icon src="res/ios/icon-76@2x.png" width="152" height="152" />
    <!-- iOS 6.1 -->
    <!-- Spotlight Icon -->
    <icon src="res/ios/icon-40.png" width="40" height="40" />
    <icon src="res/ios/icon-40@2x.png" width="80" height="80" />
    <!-- iPhone / iPod Touch -->
    <icon src="res/ios/icon.png" width="57" height="57" />
    <icon src="res/ios/icon@2x.png" width="114" height="114" />
    <!-- iPad -->
    <icon src="res/ios/icon-72.png" width="72" height="72" />
    <icon src="res/ios/icon-72@2x.png" width="144" height="144" />
    <!-- iPhone Spotlight and Settings Icon -->
    <icon src="res/ios/icon-small.png" width="29" height="29" />
    <icon src="res/ios/icon-small@2x.png" width="58" height="58" />
    <!-- iPad Spotlight and Settings Icon -->
    <icon src="res/ios/icon-50.png" width="50" height="50" />
    <icon src="res/ios/icon-50@2x.png" width="100" height="100" />
  </platform>
```

Windows

```
  <platform name="windows">
    <icon src="res/windows/storelogo.png" target="StoreLogo" />
    <icon src="res/windows/smalllogo.png" target="Square30x30Logo" />
    <icon src="res/Windows/Square44x44Logo.png" target="Square44x44Logo" />
    <icon src="res/Windows/Square70x70Logo.png" target="Square70x70Logo" />
    <icon src="res/Windows/Square71x71Logo.png" target="Square71x71Logo" />
    <icon src="res/Windows/Square150x150Logo.png" target="Square150x150Logo" />
    <icon src="res/Windows/Square310x310Logo.png" target="Square310x310Logo" />
    <icon src="res/Windows/Wide310x150Logo.png" target="Wide310x150Logo" />
  </platform>
```

Splashscreens

When your application launches, it can display an initial splashscreen to provide more instant feedback to the user while your application continues its start-up procedure. Like the <icon> elements, these are also usually wrapped with a <platform> tag. Please notice that the value of the "src" attribute is relative to the project root directory, not the *www* directory.

Android

```
<platform name="android">
  <splash src="res/screen/android/splash-land-hdpi.png" qualifier="land-hdpi"/>
  <splash src="res/screen/android/splash-land-ldpi.png" qualifier="land-ldpi"/>
  <splash src="res/screen/android/splash-land-mdpi.png" qualifier="land-mdpi"/>
  <splash src="res/screen/android/splash-land-xhdpi.png"
  qualifier="land-xhdpi"/>
  <splash src="res/screen/android/splash-land-xxhdpi.png"
  qualifier="land-xxhdpi"/>
  <splash src="res/screen/android/splash-land-xxxhdpi.png"
  qualifier="land-xxxhdpi"/>

  <splash src="res/screen/android/splash-port-hdpi.png" qualifier="port-hdpi"/>
  <splash src="res/screen/android/splash-port-ldpi.png" qualifier="port-ldpi"/>
  <splash src="res/screen/android/splash-port-mdpi.png" qualifier="port-mdpi"/>
  <splash src="res/screen/android/splash-port-xhdpi.png" qualifier="port-xhdpi"/>
  <splash src="res/screen/android/splash-port-xxhdpi.png"
  qualifier="port-xxhdpi"/>
  <splash src="res/screen/android/splash-port-xxxhdpi.png"
  qualifier="port-xxxhdpi"/>
</platform>
```

You do not need to supply splashscreens for orientations your application will not support.

iOS

```
<platform name="ios">
  <splash src="res/screen/ios/Default~iphone.png" width="320" height="480"/>
  <splash src="res/screen/ios/Default@2x~iphone.png" width="640" height="960"/>
  <splash src="res/screen/ios/Default-Portrait~ipad.png"
  width="768" height="1024"/>
  <splash src="res/screen/ios/Default-Portrait@2x~ipad.png"
  width="1536" height="2048"/>
  <splash src="res/screen/ios/Default-Landscape~ipad.png"
  width="1024" height="768"/>
  <splash src="res/screen/ios/Default-Landscape@2x~ipad.png"
```

```
    width="2048" height="1536"/>
  <splash src="res/screen/ios/Default-568h@2x~iphone.png"
  width="640" height="1136"/>
  <splash src="res/screen/ios/Default-667h.png" width="750" height="1334"/>
  <splash src="res/screen/ios/Default-736h.png" width="1242" height="2208"/>
  <splash src="res/screen/ios/Default-Landscape-736h.png"
  width="2208" height="1242"/>
</platform>
```

Windows

```
<platform name="windows">
  <splash src="res/screen/windows/splashscreen.png" width="620" height="300"/>
  <splash src="res/screen/windows/splashscreenphone.png"
  width="1152" height="1920"/>
</platform>
```

Plugins

Cordova's capabilities are extended through the use of plugins. By using the Ionic CLI to manage the installation of the Cordova plugins, it will update the *config.xml* file automatically for you. By default, the following plugins are automatically added to your project:

```
<plugin name="cordova-plugin-device" spec="~1.1.2"/>
<plugin name="cordova-plugin-console" spec="~1.0.3"/>
<plugin name="cordova-plugin-whitelist" spec="~1.2.2"/>
<plugin name="cordova-plugin-splashscreen" spec="~3.2.2"/>
<plugin name="cordova-plugin-statusbar" spec="~2.1.3"/>
<plugin name="ionic-plugin-keyboard" spec="~2.2.1"/>
```

name
> Plugins should be referenced by the plugin ID which is normally in a reverse domain format (e.g., com.phonegap.plugins.barcodescanner).

spec
> Optional, but we highly recommend locking your plugin version.

Some plugins may require additional parameters. See the specific documentation for each plugin for additional information.

Features

Used to target platform-specific plugins that may require initializing during the Web-View's initialization:

```
<feature name="StatusBar">
  <param name="ios-package" onload="true" value="CDVStatusBar"/>
</feature>
```

---

name
> Allowed values: android-package, ios-package, and osx-package.

onload
> Used to specify whether the corresponding plugin (as specified in the "value" attribute) is to be instantiated when the controller is initialized.

value
> Specifies the name of the package to be used to initialize the plugin code.

Reference

The complete documentation on the *config.xml* file can be found on the Cordova website (*http://bit.ly/2l8zSqd*).

Ionic Component Library

The Ionic applications are built atop a collection of components (*http://ionicframe work.com/docs/v2/components/*). These building blocks are essentially HTML and CSS, with just enough JavaScript to give them their functionality. This appendix briefly describes each component so you have a base familiarity with them.

Action Sheets

This component displays a set of options that is shown as an overlay from the bottom edge of the screen. This component is created directly via your code, not via any HTML.

Alerts

Although native dialogs are available through the use of the Dialogs plugin, you may need to display an alert that is either more complex (one that has radio buttons or checkboxes) or works without the need for the plugin. The component will simulate the native dialog for each platform. This component is created directly via your code and not via any HTML.

Badges

This component allows you annotate the counter of some item (unread notifications, for example). They can be given any color attribute.

Buttons

This will probably one of the most used components in your application. It supports a wide range of styles: Default, Outline, Clear, Round, Block, Full, Icon, and Floating. In addition, their coloring and sizing are easily controlled through the use of standard attributes.

Although they can be used independently, they also can be used within other Ionic components like Toolbars or Cards.

Cards

A popular UI component is the card component; it is a way to contain and organize information. This component is very flexible in it design capabilities, supporting headers, full-width images, button rows, and more.

Checkbox

This standard input type component holds a boolean value. The Ionic version of this HTML component will automatically adapt to the proper style for that platform.

DateTime

This is a new component in the Ionic Framework. It provides an easy method for users to input dates and times. Time and date formatting are customizable.

Gestures

The Ionic Framework has a gesture system built into it. This allows any component to respond to a collection of standard user gestures: tap, press, pan, swipe, rotate, and pinch.

Grid

Built atop the CSS Flexbox module, Ionic's grid system is comprised of three elements: grid, rows, and columns. Leveraging Flexbox's alignment system, grid content can be easily aligned vertically.

Icons

The framework ships with 700+ icons (and growing). This component supports both active and inactive states and will automatically adapt to the host platform's style.

Inputs

The Ionic version of this standard HTML component expands it to properly reflect the style and functionality of each mobile platform. It supports a variety of styles: Fixed Inline Labels, Floating Labels, Inline Labels, Inset Labels, Placeholder Labels, and Stacked Labels.

Lists

Next to the button, the List component is probably the component you will use most often in your application. This component will naturally display a scrolling list of content. Beyond the basic list, there are additional list styles that can be defined: Inset, No Lines, Multi Line, and Sliding.

The list headers and dividers are configurable. Icons and avatars are also easily supported, as are other Ionic controls like the Toggle component.

Loading

This overlay component displays a loading element. This spinner can be changed from a collection of styles. This component is created directly via your code and not via any HTML.

Menus

This is the component used to create the side menu component. The style and display method will adapt to the host platform. This component is complex since it involves navigation and interactions with additional elements within your application. If you are planning to use this in your application, take the time to fully read the API documentation.

Modals

The modal component is an alternate dialog type. It will slide onto the screen and display its content. This component is created directly via your code and not via any HTML.

Navigation

Ionic apps can use the `<ion-nav>` component to handle the flow of navigation through their application. It uses a standard push/pop model. Back buttons and screen titles will be updated based on the flow of the app.

Popover

The Popover component displays itself over the app's content. This component is often used to allow a quick change of a setting or filter. This component is created directly via your code and not via any HTML.

Radio

Just like the checkbox, a radio is an input component that holds a boolean value. Ionic radios are no different than HTML radio inputs. However, like other Ionic components, radios are styled differently on each platform.

Range

Also referred to as a Slider component, this Ionic component allows a user to select from a fixed range of values.

Searchbar

This component creates a platform-specific element that gives the user an input method to search. Typically, this component is paired with a list component.

Segment

This component, also referred to as a button-bar, displays a set of buttons inline.

Select

The `<ion-select>` component is similar to the standard HTML `<select>` element. Like the other enhanced controls, it will adapt to the platform it is running on.

Slides

The Slides component is designed as a mobile-friendly image carousel. Each slide is defined within a parent `<ion-slides>` element. It offers a variety of built-in functions such as autoplay, direction, looping, and paging.

Split Pane

This layout-level component allows you to define a two-column interface, with the menu-like pane and a main content pane. As the viewport's width reduces, the menu pane will collapse and act like a side menu. This component is useful for tablet or desktop application–sized interfaces.

Tabs

This layout-level component allows you to define a series of tabs, each with its own navigation stack. Tabs can be shown as text-only, icon-only, or both. They will adapt to the look and behavior of the mobile platform they are displayed on. This component is a mixture of HTML and TypeScript.

Toast

This component is used to display a brief message on top of the app's content. This component is created directly via your code and not via any HTML.

Toggle

The toggle is a simple two-state switch. It is the preferred user interface element for enabling and disabling a feature.

Toolbar

This component is a generic bar that can be used in several methods: header, sub-headers, or as a footer. It comes in three versions `<ion-header>`, `<ion-footer>`, and `<ion-toolbar>`. When wanting either a header or footer, it is recommended that you use `<ion-header>` or `<ion-footer>`, respectively. The component supports icons, buttons, segments, and searchbars as elements within it.

Index

About the Author

Chris Griffith is the User Experience Lead at a home automation and security company and is also an instructor at the University of California, San Diego Extension, teaching mobile application development. He is also an Adobe Community Professional specializing in PhoneGap/Cordova and Experience Design. Chris is regularly invited to speak at conferences such as Fluent, Adobe MAX, and ngConf. He has developed several mobile applications, a variety of code-hinters and ConfiGAP for PhoneGap Build. In addition, he has served as a technical reviewer for several publications and written for *uxmag.com*. In his spare time, Chris spends time with his family, sea kayaking, hiking, and drinking craft beer with friends. You can follow him on Twitter *@chrisgriffith* or at *chrisgriffith.wordpress.com*.

Colophon

The animal on the cover of *Mobile App Development with Ionic 2* is a Eurasian blackcap or blackcap warbler (*Sylvia atricapilla*).

The blackcap warbler gets its name from the neatly colored cap on its head—black on males and reddish-brown on females. The rest of its body is mainly gray—olive-gray on its upperparts and a pale gray underneath. Males have rich musical songs, or warblings, that end in loud, high-pitched crescendos. Simpler versions have been heard in more isolated habitats, such as the Alps. The blackcap is sometimes referred to as a "mock nightingale" because of its varied song.

This species of warbler breeds throughout Europe, western Asia, and northwest Africa. It prefers mature deciduous woodlands, and nests in a neat cup built in low brambles or scrubs. They typically lay from 4–6 eggs, which hatch after 11 days.

Its main threats are hunting in Mediterranean countries and natural threats such as predation and disease. Despite these hazards, the blackcap has been extending its range of habitat in the last few years.

Many of the animals on O'Reilly covers are endangered; all of them are important to the world. To learn more about how you can help, go to *animals.oreilly.com*.

The cover image is from *British Birds*. The cover fonts are URW Typewriter and Guardian Sans. The text font is Adobe Minion Pro; the heading font is Adobe Myriad Condensed; and the code font is Dalton Maag's Ubuntu Mono.

Learn from experts.
Find the answers you need.

Sign up for a **10-day free trial** to get **unlimited access** to all of the content on Safari, including Learning Paths, interactive tutorials, and curated playlists that draw from thousands of ebooks and training videos on a wide range of topics, including data, design, DevOps, management, business—and much more.

Start your free trial at:

oreilly.com/safari

(No credit card required.)

CPSIA information can be obtained
at www.ICGtesting.com
Printed in the USA
BVOW09s2307110417
480999BV00001B/1/P